The Quest for Development Success

The Quest for Development Success

Bridging Theoretical Reasoning with Economic Practice

Grzegorz W. Kolodko

LEXINGTON BOOKS
Lanham • Boulder • New York • London

Published by Lexington Books
An imprint of The Rowman & Littlefield Publishing Group, Inc.
4501 Forbes Boulevard, Suite 200, Lanham, Maryland 20706
www.rowman.com

6 Tinworth Street, London SE11 5AL, United Kingdom

British Library Cataloguing in Publication Information Available

Library of Congress Cataloging-in-Publication Data

Names: Kołodko, Grzegorz W., author.
Title: The quest for development success : bridging theoretical reasoning with economic practice / Grzegorz W. Kolodko.
Description: Lanham : Lexington Books, [2021] | Includes bibliographical references and index.
Identifiers: LCCN 2021002293 (print) | LCCN 2021002294 (ebook) | ISBN 9781793642554 (cloth) | ISBN 9781793642561 (epub)
Subjects: LCSH: Economic history—1990- | Economic development. | Economic policy. | Economic forecasting.
Classification: LCC HC59.15 .K656 2021 (print) | LCC HC59.15 (ebook) | DDC 330—dc23
LC record available at https://lccn.loc.gov/2021002293
LC ebook record available at https://lccn.loc.gov/2021002294

For Emma and all her peers, with the hope that they will live in a better world

Contents

List of Figures and Tables

FIGURES

TABLES

Acknowledgments

This book would not have been possible without the help of Irina K. Bezumnova during editing the volume. Thanks to her work, this book is a bit less flawed, and for all other imperfections you have to blame the author. She also prepared the indexes.

I am also grateful to Dr. Grzegorz Malinowski for many valuable comments given at various stages of work. I likewise thank Sergei Druchin for his help in preparing the graphic materials contained in the book.

Introduction

A Few Thoughts on Useful Economics

When looking for answers how to move and not get lost into the maze of contradictions of ideas and interests surrounding us—because, let us remember, these contradictions are always about these two "i," interests and ideas—one cannot avoid preaching controversial views. I hope these presented on the pages of this book are not wrong. Yet, it would be impossible to touch on so various issues and avoid debatable views. The purpose of this volume is to contribute to the controversial policy disputes on how to integrate lessons of three or four decades of economic change in the world—in Europe and America, in Asia and Africa—into thinking about macroeconomic policies and conducting them for a better future.

An action causes a reaction. The defeat of neoliberalism, that is, ideology, system, and politics, which through poor deregulation, manipulation of the fiscal system, and unfair practices is used to enrich the few at the cost of the many, provoked the expansion of populism—which tries to give people not what they really need for self-realization and satisfaction of rational needs, but what they want in detachment from tough economic realities. It may be very dangerous to combine the illusory ease of financing the mounting social needs from the deficit and the unlimited increase in public debt, which is postulated by the so-called Modern Monetary Theory, MMT, with the implementation of the so-called Universal Basic Income, UBI. For various reasons, these ideas are theoretically false and practically irrational. After all, populism is not the right answer to the challenges of the twenty-first-century civilization, and a peculiar mix of neoliberalism with populism is a simple recipe for a civilization catastrophe.

Humanity faces epochal challenges that result from the overlap of symptomatic mega-trends for contemporary times:

1. Demographic change, especially the aging of the population and extreme stratification of fertility rates.
2. Environmental changes, especially the depletion of non-renewable resources, devastation of biosphere and global warming.
3. Scientific and technological revolution, especially the digitization of the economy and culture as well as automation.
4. Non-inclusive globalization, especially the growing inequalities.
5. The general crisis of neoliberal capitalism, especially structural economic imbalance.
6. The crisis of liberal democracy, especially the accompanying polarization of societies.
7. The Second Cold War, especially the US–China conflict.

Things happen as they do because many things happen at the same time. Hence, the coincidence of these trends distorts the clarity of expectations of economic entities—enterprises and households, producer and consumers, investors and speculators, sellers and buyers, the market and the state—which frequently leads to irrational behavior. The rational is the one who acts in his/her own gain, taking into consideration information at his/her disposal. Yet, quite often, such information are biased, asymmetrical, fragmented, and—as it happens—intentionally manipulated for the ideological reasons or by the groups of special interests. In result, they are emotionally distorted.

We are now in a completely new phase of civilization evolution, in which not only production and classic consumption matter, the level of which is determined by the volume of gross domestic product still maximized in economic policy, this famous GDP. What matters, and sometimes even more unnoticed by the GDP, are phenomena and processes related to individual and social processes of economic activities. This is the time of the beyond-GDP reality, which must be embraced and explained by the beyond-GDP theory of broadly, even interdisciplinary understood economics. Consequently, on this theory—still being developed and barely outlined, to which the considerations presented in the pages of this book aspire to make a modest contribution—must be based wise, not confusing the means with the ends, the beyond-GDP socioeconomic policy and the beyond-GDP strategy for long-term development.

A key element in changing the economic paradigm is to move away from the dictate of profit maximization and quantitative growth of production as a target of economic activity, and to reformulate it, regarding the imperative of subordinating the short-term interests of private capital to long-term public interests. This cannot be achieved without a strong will of the political elites in charge of market economy institutions, since market regulation is crucial for the positive synergy of private interests with social needs. This requires a certain reinstitutionalization of the economy. In democratic conditions, it cannot be done without active involvement of the ruling elites that are shaping the system and running the policies.

Meeting the epochal challenges requires a change in lifestyle, what must be correlated with a different than before way of functioning of the economy. An important rule governing the economy of the future should be moderation, that is, intentional adaptation of the size of human, material, and financial flows and resources to the requirement of maintaining long-term balance and harmony.

Undoubtedly, dealing with the consequences of the devastating Covid-19 pandemic will bring new threads to economic thinking. This great 2020 shock will also affect microeconomic management practices—both at the corporate level, from micro-enterprises and family businesses to large state-owned companies and large transnational corporations entangled in complex supply chains, as well as in the sphere of social and economic policy.

Unfortunately, modern economic thought does not cope satisfactorily with the expectations addressed to it. It neither explains phenomena and processes in a fully satisfactory way, nor does it propose effective methods of dealing with emerging problems, especially at the macroeconomic level, toward the national economy, and at the level of mega-economy, in relation to the world economy at the era of irreversible globalization.

A new pragmatism is coming ahead these intellectual and political challenges. It is an outline of a heterodox theoretical concept within the framework of a postulative trend of economics based on the desire for good economy that responds to the problems of modern times. The new pragmatism is honest economy seeking truth in the sphere of diagnosis as well as efficiency and justice in the sphere of economic activities. It is addressed to both developed countries and emancipating economies, including post-socialist (post-communist) transformation countries.

In this context, the aim of economic activity needs to be redefined. The way in which we measure it determines the direction we are going. Alternatively, in other words, the direction we are aiming at depends on the manner we measure our targets. Due to the tendency to unbalance the economy—what often leads to extensive economic, social and political crisis—and due to objectively occurring environmental barriers, the maximization of a production's size and the pace of its growth should not be anymore the utmost aim of economic activity. The purpose of enterprise in the future implies improvement of the well-being of the population on the path of triple balance: economic, social, and ecological. There are certain feedback loops among these three spheres; it is impossible to balance one of them in the long run without caring about two other.

Under the new pragmatism, economics is treated as a science:

1. Heterodox—the thought flow is free from dogmas and the imperative of staying within the limits of orthodox economic doctrines.
2. Descriptive—analysis and characterization of the state of affairs constitute the basis for diagnosis and the starting point for further considerations.
3. Explanatory—the interpretation of observed phenomena and processes makes it easier to understand why they appear and occur in a different way.
4. Evaluative—the evaluation of ex-post alternative situations and expected ex-ante results compels the search for the answer to the questions whether the past could have been better and whether it will be better in the future.
5. Normative—postulating directions and methods of change for the better following the judgment, what and why appear to be better.
6. Comprehensive (holistic)—observation of all broadly understood economic relations is against reductionism and attempts to build comprehensive theories from fragmentary research results (one size doesn't fit all).
7. Eclectic—combines threads of analysis and synthesis of various economic schools: from classical economics through neo-Keynesianism and institutional economics to development economics and political economy, as well as behavioral and experimental economics, and microeconomics with macroeconomics and global economics.
8. Contextual—analysis and syntheses are not conducted in isolation from reality, in the models of "pure" economics, but in relation to specific, dynamic, variable and complex circumstances, conditions, limitations and possibilities.
9. Multidisciplinary—the analysis of economic reality takes into account the findings and methods of other disciplines of social sciences, especially sociology, law, psychology, political science, anthropology, history and geography.
10. Comparative—comparing economic and technological, cultural, political, geographical and environmental realities in time and space is treated as the basic research method. The scientific process is largely based on comparing events and processes and drawing conclusions from these comparisons.

The methodological phenomenon of the science of economics is manifested in the fact that it is a cognitive process different from other social sciences. Therefore, first, it is about describing (descriptive analysis), then comparing (comparative analysis) and valuation (axiological analysis), and consequently recommending (normative analysis).

Unlike state capitalism, left and right populism, new nationalism and the utopia of collective capitalism and participatory socialism, new pragmatism as a practical economic theory creates opportunities to meet epochal challenges. Economics can be useful. Economics can be advantageous.

The volume consists of new chapters and some research papers published in academic periodicals, in particular in *Communist and Post-Communist Studies*, *Rivista di Economia Politica*, *Polish Sociological Review*, *Business Science Quarterly*, and *Acta Oeconomica*. They cover numerous questions related to the condition of the world economy and its future challenges. While looking into what and why is happening in the economy, a lot of attention is given to its relations with society and polity, environment and security, as well as in sphere of culture and technology.

The train of thoughts presented on the following pages addresses a broad audience, formulating complex insights in, I believe, an accessible manner. The genre is not common, as theory and policy books usually speak to different audiences. In this case, it is more than strictly economic book, since often the considerations are place in the interdisciplinary context. I once traversed Einstein's well-known saying, "Knowledge has a future," and said, "Interdisciplinary knowledge has a great future." Hence, I hope that this book will inspire further debates, because there is something to discuss. Some people are worried that we face an abundance of questions, others are happy that there are still more questions than answers. Better to ask the way than to go astray.

Part I

HOW TO AVOID ECONOMIC DEATH

THE POLITICAL ECONOMY OF PANDEMIC

Chapter 1

Times of Plague

The signs are increasing that the world will be unable to escape the spiral into which it has fallen without a crisis and new revolutions. It would be better to escape this spiral through evolution and universal balanced development but it is both too late and too early for that. What kind of crisis will it be? We do not know. When will it happen? We do not know, but it is only a question of time, because there are more and more contradictions and they are becoming increasingly antagonistic. Overcoming them will take movements on an almost tectonic scale: profound structural changes, the adoption of a new value system, and a different balance of power and allotment of role on the world stage.

Someone will say that there is nothing very revealing in these sentences, and yet, they were couched twelve years ago in the book *Truth, Errors, and Lies: Politics and Economics in a Volatile World*[1] (Kolodko 2008, 340, 2011a, 341). There one can find a warning that in the face of the ineptitude of politics to the challenges of the modern world, an Even Greater Crisis (EGC) will come with time. I used this term to stress the inevitability of a crisis that will be more extensive than it was during the Great Crisis of 1929–1933. "There will come Even Grander Crisis when significant demographic, ecological and political disturbances will overlap with significant economic perturbations. The question is only when and how will its dynamics be." These sentences are not new either; they were written ten years ago (Kolodko 2010). Moreover, a little bit later in the monograph *Whither the World: The Political Economy of the Future*, one can find such cautions: "we're in for a yet greater disaster than the recent crisis and for dissensions building up further, followed by even more exacerbated conflicts, not only economic ones" (Kolodko 2014a, 7), as well as the fact that "we won't escape an Even Grander Crisis (EGC), with all the attendant social revolts" (Kolodko 2014a, 426).

So when today an Internet user asks: "Professor, is this already that EGC—Even Greater Crisis, which you wrote about?" I answer: yes. Things happen the way they do because many things happen at the same time. So, what is happening simultaneously, what we have to see in a long term and vast space, and not just *hic et nunc*? In the trilogy about the world, I write about a Twelve Great Issues for the Future, GIF. Here, I will highlight only a half of them, the most important from the present point of view, by no means disregarding the others.

1. The systemic and structural sources of the previous global financial and economic crisis have not been removed. The greed of the mighty of the world and the compliance of the political elite to their pressure has prevailed (Galbraith 2014; Stiglitz 2019).
2. The influence of neoliberalism, ideology as well as economic policies and meager regulation enriching the few at the expense of the many has not been eliminated. As a result, globalization, which is otherwise irreversible, is still not sufficiently inclusive, which is a sine qua non condition for harmonious development (Harvey 2005).
3. Stopping the processes of devastation of natural environment and global warming is failing (Diamond 2019; Wallace-Wells 2019). Humanity introduces itself to the path to thermal destruction, though it does not have to go to hell at all; it will make it here, on Earth.
4. With certain exceptions, it was not possible to suppress the escalation of income and wealth inequalities, and to set the economy and society on the path of their reduction (Milanovic 2016). Without this, there is no chance of maintaining social cohesion and liberal democracy in the long run.
5. The demographic imbalance is deepening resulting, on the one hand, in huge differentiation of the fertility rates and, consequently, a dysfunctional surplus or deficit of labor, and on the other, a mass migration. Its great waves, reaching tens of millions of people—both refugees from places where it is impossible to live peacefully, and immigrants from regions where it is impossible to live decently—will flow into rich countries.
6. Political tensions are rising due to the inability of conciliatory solutions of the growing transnational problems and the lack of mechanisms to govern the interdependent global economy. The specter of xenophobia and chauvinism, new nationalism and protectionism are rising, accompanied by the Second Cold War[2] and trade war declared by the United States not only against China and Russia, but in certain cases also against its own allies (Klein and Pettis 2020).

Someone may ask: What revolutions? What revolts? Well, first people go wild and then take to the streets. From the Arab Spring to the Black Lives

Matter, from Maidan to Occupy London, from Taksim Square in Istanbul to Wall Street in New York, from Delhi to Santiago, wearing yellow vests in France and T-shirts with a slogan KON-STY-TUC-JA in Poland. There will be more such demonstrations for a number of reasons. One addition among them will be that in most of the places people will notice, in the context of fighting the plague, how much inequality is there. For instance, the fact that in Chicago, where the black people account for 30 percent of the population, but as much as 70 percent of deaths caused by coronavirus affects them, is worth a deeper reflection, isn't it?

In the aftermath of pandemic, more and more dissatisfied people will go out on the streets. There will be no world revolution, but chaos may increase. The world needs new ideas and great leaders—global statesmen—not demagogues shouting *America First!* or *Alternative für Deutschland.* In order to avoid anarchization, which might devastate culture and economy all over the world, new ideas and development concepts are needed, such as new pragmatism—a kind of interface between holistic economic theory and practical economic policy aiming for inclusive growth and sustainable development (Bałtowski 2017; Galbraith 2018; Kolodko 2014a).

We have experienced bizarre times when a Swedish teenager seems to be smarter and more responsible than the American president; when hopes for keeping the global economy on the growth path are placed in China and India, not in the United States and Japan; when many politicians pray for the better future because they are unable to do it without the help of supernatural forces; when entrepreneurs prefer to save rather than invest; when stupidity triumphs over wisdom and aggression over empathy. It is all our human merit.

Additionally, it never rains but it pours. The scourge of pandemic joined the extremely unfavorable coincidence of these mega-trends of modern civilization and globalized economy. Nobody knew when exactly it would come or what it would look like, but it was obvious that it would come. This is not clairvoyance—or rather gloom-mongering—when I wrote in "Truth, Errors and Lies: Politics and Economics in a Volatile World" that we are facing "a growing threat of mass diseases, fast-spreading epidemics . . ." (p. 98) that "it would be the height of naïveté to assume that there will be no new diseases with the lethal potential of HIV-AIDS or SARS. It has to happen sooner or later" (p. 159), adding that "Prosperous countries and those as large as China can cope with such blows; similar epidemics are devastating in poorer countries. They unleash pandemonium there, affecting the quality of life at its roots and diminishing the potential GDP as a consequence" (p. 160), and that "in the contemporary world, there is an increasing need for the global coordination of treatment and prevention policies in the face of the epidemiological threat" (p. 162).

It is not time to regret the roses when the forests are burning. It is not the time to regret the decline in production as it is the result of the struggle for human life. Millions of those whose lives and health are saved due to radical and costly preventive and curative measures are much more valuable than losses caused by the recession, and no doubt than those trillions lost on stock exchanges. Its speculative core is nothing to regret; however, the decline in the value of pension funds and long-term savings of the household sector will be painful. In addition, nothing good is going to happen in the face of a lack of liquidity of a number of businesses and shortage of investing capital caused by the stock exchanges crush.

There are plenty of dramatic microeconomic situations and although it will not be easy, the short-term issues can be handled. Yet, their macroeconomic consequences are going to be very severe. Governments are right increasing public expenditure to support economic recovery and to protect populations and individuals in special need. Depending on the realities, there need to be sensibly pumped billions, hundreds of billions of dollars, often reaching for innovative financial instruments specially created and launched for this occasion.

Longer-term consequences are more important. Undoubtedly, the pandemic caused by disorders in the sphere of production and consumption will leave its mark on the microeconomic behavior of households and macroeconomic performance of transnational corporations as well as on the attitude of economic politicians. Of great importance will be their approach to global supply chains. What is to be feared is the rise of phobia and irrationalism, parochialism and nationalism, particularism and protectionism. We are threatened not only by what cannot be seen—the microscopic coronavirus—but also by what can be seen with the naked eye. Hatred . . .

Racial hatred and xenophobia, Islamophobia, Sinophobia, Russophobia, hatred of "true Poles" or "true Finns" to those of different cultures, Buddhists from Myanmar to Rohingya, Shiites from Iran to Sunnis from the Arabian Peninsula, conservative English to Europeans from Brussels. Aversion to strangers, to others, not from here; those from "shithole countries" and those "rapists from Mexico"; those colorful and these infidels. It harms us all, because it spoils globalization, which is connecting all of us. Indeed, connectivity—this core of globalization—is at stake. No doubt, harmful is Donald Trump's hatred for almost everything that his democratic predecessors did, especially President Barack Obama, with good consequences for peaceful cooperation and inclusive globalization—to engage in regional free trade agreements, to the Paris Agreement on combating climate warming, to an economic agreement with Canada and Mexico, to an arrangement on Iran's nuclear program, to a treaty with Russia on controlling the medium-range missile system, to the prerogatives of the World

Trade Organization, to the multilateralism in global economic and political game.

It is pathetic when the US president, referring to the plague, talks about the "Chinese virus," but it is embarrassing that the spokesperson of Chinese Ministry of Foreign Affairs suggests that it was the US military service that applied it in Wuhan, the first outbreak of the epidemic. In Poland—where hatred flourishes within the post-Solidarity "elite" between Civic Platform, PO, with its right-wing neoliberal feature, and Law and Justice, PiS, with its populist–nationalist mark—we have not long ago heard that refugees are spreading parasites and germs. It is not the refugees who are guilty of the spread of the deadly virus, but some would prefer to close the borders to them anyway; not only temporarily, but also forever and preferably separated by a wall or barbed wire. Moreover, this is happening in more than one place in the world, not excluding countries that proudly regard themselves as supposedly a leading Euro–Atlantic civilization.

DEFICIT OF IMAGINATION

Hard times—and these we currently live are indeed very hard—should also be a period of deeper intellectual and political reflections. Pandemic, with its long-term consequences, is overlapping on mentioned mega-trends, detonating a crisis that has never been seen before. If democracy cannot cope with the challenges arising from such crisis, the resort to authoritarianism will happen more often, and not less frequently. Then, perhaps, there will be less recession shocks, there will be no great migrations of people, there will be no excessively overheated climate, but there will be no democracy either.

Liberal democracy was in deep water even before the pandemic (Deneen 2018), and some argue that for the sake of maintaining the competitiveness of highly advanced economies it would be good to curb it slightly (Jones 2020). It has been so because of expansion of so-called adversary democracy (Mansbridge and Martin 2015) which recently is flourishing in countries as different as the United States and Poland, the United Kingdom and South Korea, Colombia and Indonesia, where the societies are often divided close to fifty-fifty vis-*à*-vis major issues. Now, democracy may suffer even more. On the one hand, its weaknesses and limited ability to solve problems brought by an extremely fast-changing world can be felt (Reykowski 2020). On the other hand, in dozens of countries fighting pandemic, the restrictions on civil liberties imposed with an intent to apply just temporarily may persist even after the conditions for their initial introduction have expired (Economist 2020a).

Hence, what will the world look like after the pandemic? It is better not to ask such questions, because it is impossible to answer them satisfactorily.

The effects of the plague, its scope, depth and longevity of the inevitable economic, social and political crises arising from it, are ex ante beyond estimation. What may seem visionary today may turn out to be a lack of imagination tomorrow.

The most difficult to see is what one cannot see. To look around reasonably, we need not only knowledge but also imagination. Not the one detached from the realities of life, not fantasizing or succumbing to illusions, but the imagination resulting from knowledge born as an effect of critical observation of facts and careful interpretation of occurring phenomena and processes. In addition, a lot is going on. Unfortunately, additionally to other imbalances that disarrange social relations in all their possible cross-sections, there is also a deficit of imagination. The more it is worth to practice it, never forgetting about deepening our knowledge.

It is impossible to overcome the chaos that infiltrates socioeconomic relations if short-term policy is not linked to a long-term development strategy. In the army, they know that there are operational activities, tactics, and strategy and that they must be coherent and support each other. In economics, this is often forgotten or not thought at all, which is particularly due to the naïve neoliberal belief in the market omnipotence. Blinding by the financialization of the economy and narrow concentration on capital markets can be seen similar as the behavior of a woodcutter with a saw in his hand in a situation where one needs a multi-minded forester. A wise strategy must always draw not only from a good understanding of the initial situation, but also use the imagination. Then there are fewer surprises.

Isn't it amazing that actually no economic doctrine questions the need to maintain costly military reserves—human, equipment, financial—and always the governments provide for these purposes public funds, sometimes very generous, despite the fact that their military powers in the overwhelming majority of cases never will be used? Not because a potential aggressor will be afraid of the military power, but because there is not any real enemy which is getting ready to attack. The economy can afford huge wastage, although the balance of power and security can be maintained by a part of the expenses incurred. Unfortunately, obedience to influential military-industrial lobbies and their political and media backers is quite common in the contemporary world. Although it is obvious that no one could have predicted the calamities of the coronavirus pandemic, isn't it amazing that even the richest countries in the world do not keep proper personal and financial reserves and equipment for possible significant deterioration of the health situation in their societies. If in NATO—which is enforcing member states to allocate at least 2 percent of GDP on military expenditure (of course, called "defense")—just 0.5 percent of its aggregated GDP, what gives almost USD 100 billion, would be shifted for healthcare, it would make the 600 million inhabitants of the countries involved in this pact more, not less secure. Isn't it better to maintain rational reserves of medical personnel and medications instead of useless reserves of soldiers and weapons? USD 100 billion per year more for healthcare would make people safer and feeling better not just in thirty countries of NATO but also far away.

Caring for killing the coronavirus before it kills us, one must not forget about the risks that accompany us in other fields. Sometimes this risk is far from here, but in the age of globalization, almost nothing is far away, and certainly not so far as not to worry about it. When defining visions of the post-pandemic future, one must take into account a number of circumstances not related to it, but important due to other reasons. Particularly interesting in relation to the future is that what is not obvious.

The unresolved conflict in Hong Kong may have considerable implications. When its inhabitants believe that the plague is not there anymore, street demonstrations of people wearing masks protecting not lungs against viruses, but faces against intrusive cameras recognizing them, will intensify again. If the demonstrations escalate out of control, they can lead to a condition that Beijing will not tolerate and may decide to use force to restore order. The consequences of such a turn for international affairs, especially for China–West relations, would be fatal. Politically motivated economic sanctions would cause even greater turbulence in the global economy than the ongoing trade war.

If Israel—with or without US approval—bombs Iran's nuclear installations, which the hawks from Tel Aviv have felt like doing for a long time, Iran will respond by blocking the Strait of Hormuz. Then oil will not be at USD 25 per a barrel, a very low price caused by the pandemic, but maybe at USD 125. Either way is bad, because sometimes it is too cheap for someone, sometimes too expensive for many.

If not only Turkey, not coping with nearly four million refugees, mainly from Syria, opens borders with the European Union, but so do also the regimes in Libya—both in Tripoli and the one of the general Haftar—the rising flow of immigrants from Middle East and sub-Saharan Africa will not be stopped. With the overwhelming influx of migrants, it will be impossible to maintain social peace in Europe. If, however, counteracting this wave one resorted to the use of force, it would be time to stop talking about European values. Even more, it is necessary to seek a pragmatic solution to the conflicts in the Middle East and North Africa, and to help it financially, in development (Seck 2020) in order to weaken the growing pressure to escape from there.

If the tensions between India and Pakistan on the Kashmir issue escalate again, and the destructive use of nuclear weapons, which both countries have, will occur, the entire global political scene will be destabilized with strong, unfavorable consequences for economies, also far beyond the Indian subcontinent.

If the uncontrolled logging of tropical forests continues—from Borneo to Congo, from Burundi to Ecuador—and President Bolsonaro does not oppose the burning of thousands of hectares of the Amazon, then as a result each subsequent year will be even hotter than other factors have already determined. This will further aggravate global warming, what inevitably will negatively affect the political climate with its adverse feedback on the economy.

If, taking advantage of the political turmoil caused by the pandemic catastrophe, nationalists in Taiwan will take the lead, and unilaterally declare independence of this territory, China will invade and force the island to join the motherland. Despite the military treaty between Taiwan and the United States, this will not provoke their war with China, but political and economic relations would deteriorate on a much larger scale than it happened between the West and Russia after it annexed Crimea in 2014.

There is almost never such a situation that all good or bad circumstances converge at once. After all, it is always so, that many factors overlap, and that is why the integral feature of strategic socioeconomic analyzes should be their comprehensiveness (Arthur 2015). Therefore, excluding the coincidence of even only these regional crises, one cannot abstract from the risk of their outbreak. More, since they are conceivable and possible, they must be prevented. This is what the politics and polices are for, which in each of these cases, despite the fact that it relates to regional issues, must be coordinated on a supranational, because it has an impact on that what is happening on a global scale. Moreover, for a policy—that by its very nature is oriented at influencing future phenomena and processes—to be wise and effective, also social sciences, in particular economics on which economic policy should be based as much as possible, ought to be oriented for answering questions that the future will bring. Always some part of the future can be scientifically predicted (Morris 2010; Randers 2012), always some part of it can and must be creatively shaped (Krugman 2020).

NOTES

1. Written in 2007, printed in Polish in 2008 under the title *Wędrujący świat.*
2. I coined the term Second Cold War (Kolodko 2019), referring to contemporary tensions and hostilities in international affairs, especially between the United States on the one hand, and China, Russia, and Iran on the other, given that the previous Cold War fortunately was over after the political breakthrough in 1989 in Eastern Europe and the former Soviet Union. Now the previous conflict should be called the First Cold War.

Chapter 2

After the Calamity

Prospects of Recovery and Growth

The situation is volatile as rarely ever. First, we do not know what the pandemic results will be for people. Only millions or tens of millions will fall ill? Or, will hundreds of thousands or millions shuffle off this mortal coil? We don't know how interpersonal relations will be shaped; will there be more empathy, more or less mutual trust, this basis of social capital, more or less tolerance for cultural differences? In more mundane matters, we do not know how much the supply and production chains have been already broken.

We do not know how far and how long the provision of various services has been stopped. Closed restaurants and empty cinemas cannot be counted, but there has been already calculated that two million flights have been canceled; 200 million people did not arrive on time where they wanted and should be.[1] As a result, no major airline will survive without government aid.[2]

We do not know how big, where addressed, in what time sequence implemented, and how effective from the point of view of maintaining economic activity will be record-breaking intervention packages run by more and more governments and by some international organizations. The scale of their determination is also unprecedented, and the famous phrase that *Whatever it takes will be done* spoken in the summer of 2012 by Mario Draghi, then-president of the European Central Bank, regarding efforts to save the euro from falling, is repeated in numerous languages. On a global scale, it can be estimated that only in 2020—and the drama does not end here—the total sums of the support provided by the governments and central banks oscillate within the range of USD 9–11 trillion in total.

We already know that there will be a recession. Not everywhere, but certainly in the largest advanced economies—in the United States and Japan, South Korea and the European Union (in particular, which is important because of their relative weight, in Germany, France, Italy and Spain), in

Canada and Australia. Also in Poland. There is still hope that the recession will not affect all of the poorer countries, because fortunately coronavirus reaches some of them—especially in poor Africa—on a smaller scale. However, through trade, supply chains and capital transfers they are globally integrated with rich countries, and now the latter are pulling them down.[3]

If the plague spreads there, their economies will suffer relatively less than in sophisticated rich countries, while on the human side it would be a terrible cataclysm due to the underdevelopment of the health care system. Enough to mention that in this respect, in Pakistan with more than 230 million inhabitants, health expenditure is per person 200 times lower than in the United States.

Under the conditions of extreme uncertainty, there is a great risk of confusing media panic with the cold-blooded econometric forecast, predictions with warnings, and soft assumptions with hard claims. Thus, more often than not even the information provided by accountable sources must be taken with certain skepticism. It is not easy to accept the warning of Oxfam, the trustworthy NGO, when it claims that "the economic fallout from the coronavirus pandemic could push half a billion more people into poverty." Of course, there is caveat in this opinion, "unless urgent action is taken to bail out developing countries" (Oxfam 2020), but unfortunately such actions have not been taken to the required degree. Well, it is hardly surprising. Since the rich north Europe is not willing to hurry with the help for its neighbors from the south of the continent, where coronavirus wreaks the greatest havoc,[4] it would be surprising if the rich of this world from highly developed countries will be eager to help unhappy people from poor countries by sending them billions of dollars assistance.

There should be no doubt that the obligations of the world's poorest countries must be written off—urgently and unconditionally. They cannot be forced to service their debts toward developed countries and Western banks in a situation where they have to protect health of their citizens and protect jobs of their workers by radical increase of spending, which are not sufficient even in good times. Only in 2020, as many as sixty-nine of the world's poorest countries are due to pay USD 19.5 billion to the governments of rich countries and to the multilateral institutions, and USD 6 billion to foreign private lenders. All these USD 25 billion should be given up, of course at the costs of rich countries' taxpayers and their banks shareholders. What is important, already at spring of 2020 the International Monetary Fund, IMF has made USD 50 billion obtainable in emergency financing and the World Bank has approved a USD 14 billion as response package to the most vulnerable economies (BBC 2020c). These resources ought to be transferred in a form of soft credits and grants to the most in need countries, with the preferences for support to the healthcare systems.

China and India generate about 26 percent of the global gross product (calculated according to purchasing power parity, PPP). Changes in global economic dynamics—an increase or decrease in output—in more than one third depend on these two most populous countries in the world,[5] and therefore the course of affairs there is of great importance. It seems that in 2020 China can still escape the decline in production. However, all this is under a big question mark, so it is not surprising that when some are already announcing a recession, others are predicting growth.[6] This divergence of opinions is not the fault of the methods used for preparing forecasts, because they are econometrically extremely sophisticated, but is a result of walking on statistical quicksand. The model can be very good, while the data entered into it and assumptions are doubtful, and sometimes become outdated faster than an analytical article describing the situation may appear in print.

India—instead of lately expected GDP growth by over 6 percent—will record a recession. It will not be able to come away unscathed from the chaos caused by total blockade of people, announced on extremely short notice (just four hours!). Lasting a few weeks blockade of the great mass of population shocked both the supply and the demand in the economy based mainly on small companies and services, which make up 62 percent GDP. In this poor country,[7] 100 million people are villagers employed occasionally in the cities and nestled in extreme poverty in the slums.[8] The blockade resulted in the abandonment of many companies and, contrary to intentions, pushed tens of millions of people to the streets and roads, because they saw their only rescue in reaching their native villages, sometimes distant hundreds of kilometers from where they stayed. So badly thought out and despite the loud announcements, the unenforceable blockade of people's movement instead of limiting the spread of coronavirus, may increase its transmission, the economic consequences of which may be deplorable.

We do not know in what direction the situation will develop in Africa and Latin America and the Caribbean, but from the global perspective, it is relatively less important, because their economic situation has a slightly smaller impact on the fate of the world, since these continents deliver only about 4 and 7.5 percent of global production, respectively.[9]

We do not know whether the global recession will be 2, 12, or 20 percent, whether production will decline for half a year, and then the economies will rebound and the growth will return, or maybe the declines will be recorded for a year or more. The recession may not last long, but it may take a long time for depression, which is a protracted period of production at a painfully reduced level, accompanied by mass unemployment. Precise determination of the number of the unemployed is impossible, also due to the ambiguity in the definition of this category. According to the methodology used by the International Labor Organization, ILO, before the pandemic, at the end of

2019, there were over 170 million unemployed people in the world, which makes up about 5 percent of global workforce. In other words, we have about 3.4 billion people who are capable and willing to work, but unfortunately, not everyone can find it. We do not know by how many tens of millions—because there will be tens of them globally—the unemployment will increase due to the pandemic.[10] According to evaluation of the ILO, the coronavirus outbreak was expected to wipe out 6.7 percent or one fifteen of working hours across the world during the second quarter of 2020.[11] It is horrendous since this implies that the jobs are lost by the equivalent of 195 million full-time workers.

We do not know how much the public debt will increase because of additional government expenditure and reduced tax and quasi-tax revenues caused by the economic slowdown, and what consequences this will have for the financial markets.[12] During the first 25 days of March, Dow Jones—this most significant stock market index in the world economy—recorded the 5 largest daily declines and the five largest increases in its 135-year history. Before the markets calm down they will often cling to one or the other page. This, in turn, will upset investors and market speculators, but, even worse, will destabilize the expectations of business entities with an obvious negative impact on the real sphere of the economy—employment, production, consumption, and investment.

THE HECTIC TIMES

Up against irritation, it is difficult to behave rationally. Rational is the one who acts in his own advantage, considering the information. However, the information is changeable, doubtful, contradictory and unclear. One can be disappointed even if one follows the rules of formal logic in the decision-making process. On a macro-social scale, decisions are the result of a clash of emotions, political games and rational premises. The latter, unfortunately, played an increasingly smaller role in the past years, after the 2008–2009 crisis, due to the collapse of confidence in the ruling and opinion-forming elites. All in all, not many policy-makers are rational, because it does not result in political popularity and getting votes in elections (Kozminski, Noga, Piotrowska, and Zagorski 2020). Perhaps the shock caused by a pandemic will shift the gravity point in the triangle: emotions>political game>rationality closer toward rationality. Something quite opposite—a rise of various demagogy and quackery, which always appear while facing breakthrough crises—cannot be eliminated either.

Exchange rates will also act jumpy. One should not expect their stabilization for many quarters following the apex of the pandemic. The relationship between the US dollar, European euro and Chinese yuan will be key in this field. Paradoxically, despite the extensive economic crisis in the United States—greater than in China and no milder than in the European Union—the American dollar strengthens during the pandemics. It happens due to international speculative capital, as it were, in difficult times trusts USD more than other currencies.[13]

There is no doubt that the scale of the imbalance of public finances will severely deepen in many countries. Except for extremists, nobody sensible no longer protests against bold, sometimes radical budget deficits. Even monetarist doctrinaires and neoliberal dogmatists, so loud in the years 2008–2010 during the extensive financial crisis (Foster and McCheseny 2014), have gone quiet.

This will also have consequences for economic doctrine and political practice. The colorful, heterodox "economics of pandemic" will develop, both in its descriptive and normative form. First, it will be full of innovative and sensible proposals for the use of economic policies' instruments and management methods, but will also be weeded by various senseless ideas and suggestions. Over time, it will solidify and can form the foundation of post-pandemic orthodoxy.

In the economics of the post-pandemic world, the dogma of an imperative to balance the state budget will calm down. The doctrine of universal inadmissibility of financing the state budget deficit by an independent central bank will fall. Views will be reviewed as to the possibility and the legitimacy of monetizing the deficit through monetary expansion, especially through so-called money printing. Until now, certain central banks, including the American Fed (Ashworth 2020), have used it, now it ceases to be taboo around the world.

Even if inflation accelerates a bit, which in recent years has not been a great problem,[14] it will be an acceptable cost worth to be incurred in order to defend employment and production. Relatively higher inflation will be tolerated as one of the ways of financing public debt's servicing costs. Negative real interest rates of central banks—this anathema of monetary orthodoxy—will be the norm for several years, just as negative government bond yields in some countries may be the norm. This has been happening in Japan for many years. It was similar in 2007–2013, when in rich countries public debt increased from 59 to 91 percent of GDP. Governments have been able to take loans close to zero or on negative interest rates throughout the past decade.

How it will be during the next decade, we cannot be sure, but at least for some time in the leading world economies the real interest rates will remain negative. Since in rich countries, investors are more eager to buy government bonds denominated in their national currencies, so it is easier to finance the budget deficit there. In poor countries it is much harder, the more so because the foreign investors will not be willing to buy their securities. They will have to resort to the so-called financial repression, that is, forcing economic entities to purchase government bonds bearing interest below the national inflation rate. With time, acquiring funds, including capital necessary to finance public infrastructure investments[15] and supporting technological progress as well as innovation of the economy, may turn out to be much more expensive.

One of the most difficult exercise will be freeing oneself from the habit of incurring excessive debt. Yet, international financiers and political and media spheres related to them are particularly interested to continue this behavior. They are the ones who over the last decades have promoted the financialization based on trading in various forms of debt (McLean and Nocera 2010; Wolf 2014; Tanzi 2013).

The great plague in the fourteenth century did not cause such economic havoc (the human one was much larger) than the current one, because credits played a completely marginal role. Nowadays, it plays an excessive role. Who has no debts may come away quite unscathed from the pandemic. Whoever has debts will suffer from break down of the functioning of the company and household. It is impossible to live without a credit institution, and it is not possible to run business, but its scale can and should be reduced in the future. It will be useful even in healthy times. On the contrary, those who have savings are able to manage the challenging situation and weather the time of crisis easier than somebody deprived of any financial reserves.

In practice of the European Union, there are the limits of 60 percent of the public debt and 3 percent of budget deficit in relation to GDP, which according to the Maastricht principles of currency conversion (Baun 2019) and the Stability and Growth Pact, SGP,[16] supposed to be observed by the member states. For the next few years, these regimes will be suspended. Also, the excessive budget deficit procedure (Kolodko and Postula 2018) will not be applied.

As time goes on, governments will also increase the taxes, both indirect and direct ones. In the latter case, of course the higher income groups of the people will have to pay relatively more, thus the raise of taxation progression seems to be inevitable.

We have to be careful to protect ourselves against seizing for money of the left and right-wing populists who will want to grab from the public purse as much as possible, of course under the banner of protecting those in need, even if they can cope alone. One should be yet more careful about the greed of the wealthier people and their influential lobby, organized much better than employees and consumers. We can already see the pressure on the authorities being exerted by the organizations that define themselves as employers, as if employing a worker was a charity, not a profitable business. In the United States, the House of Representatives initially blocked the largest intervention package in history—2 trillion dollars—because according to the original proposals of the White House, a lot of the tax payers money would go to companies doing quite well. On the other hand, before the package was finally adopted and entered into force, there were already voices that it should be at least five times larger. This is nonsense, because then it would reach half of the GDP, which no one can handle, even the United States, at the time when America is becoming great again! Thanks to President Trump.[17]

NOTES

1. Estimate at the end of the first quarter of 2020.

2. American Airlines—one of the richest airlines in the world—already at the end of March applied to the US government for financial assistance in the amount of USD 12 billion. In the first 2-trillion intervention package adopted in March 2020 the US administration has allocated 58 billion to support airlines—a half for subsidies, and a half for loans and loan guarantees.

3. Kristalina Georgieva, the managing director of the International Monetary Fund, on the eve of annual IMF and World Bank Spring Meeting said, "Just three months ago, we expected positive per capita income growth in over 160 of our member countries in 2020. Today, that number has been turned on its head: we now project that over 170 countries will experience negative per capita income growth this year" (BBC 2020a). The IMF says that across the rich world, at the end of 2020 the gross government debt will rise from 105 to 122 percent of GDP (by $6 trillion, to $66 trillion).

4. EU Commission President Ursula von der Leyen offers a 'heartfelt apology' to Italy, saying "'too many were not there on time' when the country 'needed a helping hand'" (BBC 2020b). In turn, Emmanuel Macron, the French president, has pointed that the richer EU members have a special responsibility in dealing with this crisis. He said, "We are at a moment of truth, which is to decide whether the European Union is a political project or just a market project. I think it's a political project. . . . We need financial transfers and solidarity, if only so that Europe holds on" (Financial Times 2020).

5. China and India have approximately 1.4 and 1.33 billion inhabitants, respectively.

6. At the end of the first quarter of 2020, the World Bank forecasted that in the less-developed region of East Asia and the Pacific (except Japan, South Korea, Australia, New Zealand, Taiwan, Singapore, and Hong Kong) the growth rate would fall to 2.1 percent from 5.8 percent recorded in 2019. In the case of China, the prediction still assumed an increase of 2.3 percent in the baseline scenario, and 0.1 percent in a worsening scenario. As a result, in 2020, in the entire East Asia and Pacific region, almost 24 million more people than expected before the pandemic will not get out of poverty, which is defined as a daily income below PPP USD 5.50 (BBC 2020d).

7. The per capita GDP of India is only around USD 2,000, which is roughly 7,200 in purchasing power parity. The world average before the pandemic was around PPP USD 18,000.

8. To put in context, in Dharavi—the most crowded slum of Mumbai, and probably the whole of India—in a small area of 2.5 square kilometers lives not less than 650,000 people.

9. Africa has about 1.33 billion people (the same as India, but the population of Africa is growing faster), and South and Central America and the Caribbean have about 650 million people.

10. By the end of May the number of people registering as unemployed have increased to more than 40 million and the rate of unemployment were approaching 15 percent, the highest level since Great Recession in 1933. For comparison, as a result of the financial crisis in 2008, a total of 9 million jobs were lost.

11. This average of 6.7 percent is the resultant of 26.5 percent in agriculture, 14.5 in retail, and 13.9 in manufacturing, at the higher end of the spectrum, and 1.6 percent in finance, 4.1 in health, and 4.6 in accommodation and food, at the lower end of it (ILO 2020).

12. During the first quarter of 2020, the Dow Jones Industrial Average and the London's FTSE 100 saw their biggest quarterly drops since 1987, plunging 23 and 25 percent, respectively. The S&P 500 lost 20 percent, its worst performance since 2008.

13. At the end of 2019, the sum of currency reserves of all countries was the equivalent of USD 11.08 trillion, of which 60.9 percent were held in USD, 20.5 in euros, 5.5 in Japanese yen, 4.6 in the British pound, 1.9 in the Canadian dollar, 1.7 in the Australian dollar and only 0.15 percent in the Swiss franc. In the Chinese yuan, RMB, central banks hold approximately USD 222 billion, i.e. the equivalent of about 2 percent of global currency reserves.

14. Apart from exceptions, such as Argentina, Sudan, Angola, Turkey, and especially the hyperinflation cases of Zimbabwe and Venezuela.

15. How much of additional, launched by the response to pandemic crisis public money should be directed for infrastructure investment and how much for support of private business to protect the jobs, is another disputable matter. Some authors argue that allocation for the business sector will be more efficient (Frydman and Phelps 2020).

16. Because of the insufficient effectiveness of SGP, it was significantly modified using "Economic six pack" (Schaechter, Kinda, Budina, and Weber 2012). It has helped to control the extent of budget deficits and public debt of EU member states. Now, in the aftermath of pandemic, its fiscal rigors will have to be relaxed.

17. Based on the article published in Kolodko (2020c).

Chapter 3

Politics and Policies in the Post-Pandemic World

Definitely, the generosity of President Trump, who a few weeks before the coronavirus severely attacked the entire United States, spoke about the threat of the pandemic as "the democrats' hoax," is supposed to favor his reelection. The political logic is that since the economic situation deteriorates in each subsequent month until the elections, the resulting political losses must be offset as much as possible, in all possible ways, by vast transfers of public money too. Of course, concern for "American people" will be always declared, even if their fate is not necessarily the most important.

The Law and Justice government is showing similar generosity in Poland to ensure the reelection of President Andrzej Duda. His opponents think—and not without a cause—that during the next few months, certainly until the postponed election, the economic situation will deteriorate. Therefore, political moods will deteriorate as well, resulting in growing dissatisfaction with those in power, including the president seeking reelection, and will act in favor of his opponents. The government's answer will be to spend public funds with a lighter hand, the more so because the pressure of both, the numerous activists who declare concern for human fate and the few rich men concerned about their own fate, will be enormous. The government will yield to them. Therefore, the later elections take place, the more expensive it is for public finances.

Democracy does not come cheap.

It is therefore worth understanding how expensive preelection periods are, those previously established, as well as those in many countries extended due to quarantine and radical restrictions on the movement of persons. A lot of money will be wasted and squandered on such occasions under beautiful, of course, slogans—both pro-human and pro-business. How much, no one can estimate, but many can argue about it. They do already.

In these contexts, four flows of funds will pour out of the sack of money created by the fiscal authorities and central banks. We are not able to distinguish exactly these flows from each other, yet they can be generally described:

1. A stream of public spirited and socially justifiable resources to protect people's health and life and to uphold the standard of living of those most affected by the crisis and those who cannot cope with it without state aid.
2. Economically justified outlays backing financial liquidity in the economy and stimulating production, service, and investment activities as well as employment through various reliefs and subsidies supporting supply and demand.
3. Resources which are grabbed by populists indifferent to hard economic realities and subsequently transferred to poorer groups of the population in much bigger extent than it is objectively necessary.
4. Flows captured by strong business lobbies that are unscrupulous and for which every opportunity is good to profit at someone else's expense.

The mutual relations of these streams are dynamic and flexible, and diverse in different countries. While we are trying to imagine their sum, and planning ex ante the proper flows of money in political practice, its true value will only be known in time, ex post. In other words, we cannot estimate exactly the proportions of these streams, but we understand that they depend on the following:

- The ideology behind the ruling parties.
- Practical strength and determination of governments in implementing the chosen strategy of socioeconomic policy.
- Condition of social cohesion.
- Business ethics.
- The balance of power of particular interest groups.

While it is worth to support the policy creating the first and the second stream, it is necessary to resist the leakage of the third and the fourth. The political struggle around this will be extremely brutal. It is already.

The fundamental questions that would have to be asked anyway—and which the crisis provoked by the coronavirus pandemic only highlights—concern the shaping of state and market relations; democracy and centralism; multilateralism and unilateralism; the role of international organizations, both governmental and nongovernment; and above all the dilemma coordinated global policy and inclusive globalization versus unfortunate clash of civilizations.

It is becoming increasingly common opinion that after the pandemic the world will never be the same as it used to be. Similar opinions appeared after each crisis, also after 2008–2009 (Legrain 2010; Posner 2009), when many believed that it must be different. Well, that is not true and it did not necessarily happen. The world can remain quite similar as it was, because the interest groups, which benefited most from the recent reality—sometimes even shamelessly and cynically preying on it, was it avaricious neoliberalism, or the corrupt state capitalism—will do everything possible to return to the status quo ante. It will not be easy, so let us hope that they will fail, because it would be a disgrace to go back to the political and economic disorder that prevailed in the world prior to the current mess. Then what?

First, the Even Greater Crisis—this unique period of conflicts and contradictions, chaos and anarchization of globalization resulting from the overlapping of the mega-trends characteristic for the modern world—will last for certain time. Despite this, globalization will prove to be irreversible. Liberalization and integration of national economies as well as commodities and capital markets, and albeit with a delay and to a limited degree of labor force, in one interconnected worldwide market will stand the course (Kolodko 2002; Rodrik 2011; Stiglitz 2007). This will happen not without glitches, but it will endure primarily due to the attractiveness of free trade and the benefit of global supply chains, as well as due to the impact of the current phase of technological revolution on deepening internationalization of production and services.

Nor can one fail to notice the enormous importance of culture's globalization (Pieterse 2019; Zelizer 2011). Watching "foreign" movies and reading books written "elsewhere," listening to songs composed "far away" and traveling over there, if there only is enough money—all this is unstoppable. "Foreign," "elsewhere," and "far away" in quotation marks, because already in the pre-pandemic world these terms seemed to be more meaningfully similar to "native," "in the same place," and "near" than contradicting them.

So the question is, which way will it go? Both in national and supranational systems, where mechanisms of policy coordination within the UN Organization and the G20 should be increasingly important,[1] and the game will be about rearranging relations between the following:

- The state and the private sector.
- Politics and the market.
- Regulation and supervision.
- Safety and welfare.
- Having more and feeling better.
- Freedom and spontaneity.

In this sense, indeed, the world will no longer be as it was. It is not anymore.

The incomplete globalization syndrome may deepen. It manifests itself in the inconsistency between the advancement of economic globalization and political globalization that is not following it, or even retreating due to the Second Cold War. For several years, when new nationalism becomes apparent, tendencies to protectionism and the desire to loosen external economic connections have been manifesting. Now for some time they can become even stronger and turn into ill-advised isolationist and autarkic impulses.

On the one hand, all these can push many countries toward the orientation not so much on globalization as on regionalization. On the other hand, it may weaken the processes of regional integration where they had advanced a lot in the past; the European Union is a special case here. Its further fate, in the shadow of the coronavirus pandemic, will be of great importance for the future of the world.[2] This is not because it makes the sixth part of global production (still considering the Great Britain which is leaving the group), but because as the most advanced regional integration process it will be worthy or not of imitation in other parts of the world.

In the follow up of the Great Crisis of 1929–1933 not only fascism and Nazism, militarism and Stalinism developed, but also the creative New Deal had emerged. This shows that both bad and good things can arise from the catastrophic economic collapse. The later World War II resulted in the division of the world into two great opposing ideological, political, and economic blocks. In the shadow of their confrontation was the mass of poor people in the so-called Third World. Today, the situation is different because this "third world" has over 85 percent of the world's population, which provides over 60 percent of world production. They cannot be pushed further into the "emerging markets" category promoted by neoliberalism, because by now they have emerged sufficiently and are visible on the world stage as increasingly emancipating economies and polities (Kolodko 2014a; Lin 2012a). This time they will have much more to say, contributing significantly to the post-pandemic world new order. When thinking about the concept of such order and then implementing it, one need to listen not only to the sounds coming from London and Washington, Paris and Tokyo, Berlin and Seoul, but also from Abuja and Ciudad de Mexico, from Jakarta and Cairo, from Bangkok and Istanbul, and especially from Beijing and Delhi. Moreover, let us do not forget about Moscow.

Geoeconomics will constantly intertwine with geopolitics, thus the interdependencies and feedbacks occurring in these areas must be carefully observed. The great dangers will be there, because in the absence of unambiguous, clear global leadership for primacy, in such unstable world growing China and the relatively weakening United States will be increasingly competing (Brown

2017). Friendly competition would be fine, yet hostile confrontation will be devastating. This is especially dangerous because losing their significance at the time when they were supposed to be *First! & Great again!*, the United States can behave impulsively, aggressively, and irrationally. To a certain extent, it could be seen already. China's response most likely will be calm and pragmatic but it is also far from sure. What's important is that China will not give up its Belt and Road Initiative (Maçães 2018; Kolodko 2020b), but will be even more eager to push it further with a new impetus as soon as the pandemic will be behind us. While certain countries will welcome it with the invigorating support, some others will approach it with a reservations and suspicions because it may diminish their international influence (Obbema 2015; Economy 2018). It will spark.[3]

WINDING PATHS OF THE FUTURE

In the future, we will wander more than once. Apart from the first path, an unlikely return to the past, to the disgraced "business as usual," the second path is capitalism of limited democracy. Of course, there is some rationality in transferring certain areas of public affairs to be resolved by competent and efficient technocrats. Nevertheless, in the contexts discussed here, limited democracy implies that the ruling elites and their servile bureaucracy dominate certain areas of public discourse and the decision-making procedures based on it. In this case, one must be very careful that the temporary restrictions imposed on the movement of people and information, goods and capital—including intellectual capital—does not become permanent. More and more countries already goes into such direction: Russia with President Putin and Turkey with President Erdogan, the United States with President Trump and the Philippines with President Duterte, Egypt with General as-Sisi, who came to power in a military coup, and Congo with President Tshisekedi, who exercises power with the support of the West, although he was by no means elected in a democratic way so much praised by the West, or Myanmar, whose system is defined in its constitution as "disciplined democracy," and Hungary with Prime Minister Orb*á*n who proclaims the idea of "illiberal democracy." We definitely need discipline and democracy in the future world, but not necessarily "disciplined democracy."

The third path is the spread of Chinism—a mono-party system in which meritocracy rules, with ownership pluralism in the economy and a flexible system of synergy of the power of invisible hand of market and the visible hand of state (Kolodko 2018, 2020b). This is not a proposal for highly developed countries, but it may become an increasingly tempting offer for the ambitious emancipating economies, in particular in Africa, southern Asia and the Middle East, and on a smaller scale in South and Central America due to traditionally strong American influence there. It may prove to be an attractive political model, because China has not only been very successful in managing incredible economic growth during the past four decades, but also in a fight with the coronavirus pandemic is coping better than democratic countries. This occurrence is impressive and it has a positive meaning in the politics.

The fourth path—the best one—is inclusive globalization based on cooperation between social market economies, to which as many countries as possible should evolve in the post-pandemic world. Of course, with its own culturally embedded characteristics. It also requires appropriate synergy of the market forces and state policy, as well as a new style of international coordination. The functioning of economies must be based, to a greater extent, on new pragmatism, taking into account the imperative of moderation and caring for triple—economically, socially and ecologically—sustainable development. Then there will be more harmony, empathy and tolerance, and less exploitation, injustice and hostility.

The chance to take such a path is increased by the fact that, apart from conservative and nationalist-oriented politicians, there are also such liberal leaders as the president of France, Emmanuel Macron, who

> "says he hopes the trauma of the pandemic will bring countries together in multilateral action to help the weakest through the crisis. In addition, he wants to use a cataclysm that has prompted governments to prioritize human lives over economic growth as an opening to tackle environmental disasters and social inequalities that he says were already threatening the stability of the world order. But he does not hide his concern that the opposite could happen, and that border closures, economic disruption and loss of confidence in democracy will strengthen the hand of authoritarians and populists who have tried to exploit the crisis, from Hungary to Brazil" (Financial Times 2020).

The president of France could not say this because of political correctness, we must say it because of the substantive correctness: also to the United States under the presidency of Donald Trump.

The future will be a combination of these four paths; none of them will get the upper hand, and none will become universal.[4] Their heterogeneous system will be fluid and conflictual. Obviously, its shape will depend on a huge mass on how the pandemic will eventually go and how the Even Greater Crisis will unfold.

No matter which path will prevail in one country or another, everywhere, although with unequal strength, the changes in the use of artificial intelligence, robotization, e-learning and remote work will rise. The fight with the pandemic accelerates such changes. The scope of population surveillance based on modern technologies will increase significantly, and not only in the authoritarian states. In democratic countries, the range of surveillance will be the subject of constant disputes in public discourses and in politics, but it will increasingly turn out that what is technically possible (and in the future yet more will be possible) will break through politically.

In the post-pandemic world, the relative strength of individual countries and regions will change in favor of emancipating economies. This is good news, because income inequalities between countries and regions may decrease, which in turn may weaken emigration trends and international tensions that build up against this background.

The role of some international organizations must increase, in particular the World Trade Organization, the International Labor Organization, and the World Health Organization, WHO.[5] The UN Organization and its agencies will be thoroughly reformulated to expand their prerogatives. The role of the emancipating economies in the international organizations will be on the rise following the growth of their economic weight.

Good news is also that in this wandering world there is still a lot of beneficial happenings, including the sphere of constant improvement in the quality of human capital and enormous scientific and technological progress. The plague temporarily closed billions of people at home, but thanks to the dynamic development of the Internet platforms, millions do not have to commute to work, because it turns out that they can perform their tasks while remaining at home. On the one hand, this can fundamentally change the way of working, on the other, it radically shortens the daily, several-hour lasting busy time, which also includes commuting. Smaller traffic jams, less crowd in public transport, more hours each day to enjoy life. All this does not compensate for the shortages of political capital—the ability to meet the challenges, counteract against the conflicts of interests and solve the problems—but creates opportunities for improvement, even when the fatal pandemic is still raging. It is all the more important to be careful not to make mistakes on other fronts. All art is to know in advance what a mistake is.[6]

NOTES

1. The group of the countries known under the acronym twenty actually consists of not twenty, but forty-three states. This is because it consists of nineteen countries and the European Union with twenty-seven national economies. The EU includes Germany, France and Italy, which due to their international rank sit in the G20 directly. Thus, this structure represents forty-three countries: nineteen individually and additionally, twenty-four treated collectively within the EU. Counting around

two-thirds of the globe's population, they produce nearly 90 percent of gross world product.

2. At the one moment of many tensions during the struggle with the pandemic the "Spanish Prime Minister Pedro Sánchez has even warned that if the EU fails to come up with an ambitious plan to help member states saddled with debt by the fight against coronavirus, the bloc could 'fall apart'" (BBC 2020e). Italy's prime minister, Giuseppe Conte, has similarly warned: "The European Union risks failing as a project in the coronavirus crisis. The EU must act in an adequate and coordinated way to help countries worst hit by the virus" (BBC 2020f).

3. By the way, it is interesting that while in the past—during the peak of tensions of the previous Cold War—the Americans took advantage of the charms of Warsaw and in the years 1958–1970 in the Myślewicki Palace in the royal park in Łazienki there were meetings of their ambassador with the ambassador of Maoist China, now Washington has commissioned Georgette Mosbacher, US ambassador to Poland to ruthlessly attack China. She did so on a popular Polish website, insinuating that "their [China's] government is to blame for this pandemic" (Mosbacher 2020). Liu Guangyuan, the Chinese ambassador to Poland, responded immediately to this criticism by saying that "the US authorities called for 'isolation' of China, while claiming that the epidemiological situation in China could help accelerate the return of the manufacturing industry to the United States" (Liu 2020). The dialogue continues.

4. Certain authors believe that the world of the future will consist of one and only one capitalist system, yet with two types being distinguished: liberal meritocratic capitalism led by the United States, and political capitalism inspired by China (Milanovic 2019). However, one should have to be aware that the reality is already more diversified and richer than just these two models. The post-pandemic future will diversify it even more.

5. Unfortunately, to the long list of people, things and institutions he doesn't like, at the most difficult times President Trump added also the WHO. "He said he would consider ending US funding for the UN agency and accused the WHO of being 'very China-centric' and said they 'really blew' their pandemic response" (BBC 2020g). He later blocked this funding, and shortly thereafter he informed the UN and the American Congress that he was withdrawing the United States from WHO. Formally, this is to take place after a one-year notice period, that is, on July 6, 2021.

6. Based on the article published in Kolodko (2020c).

Part II

FACING FUTURE DEVELOPMENT CHALLENGES

Chapter 4

The New Pragmatism, or Economics and Policy for the Future

There is no end to history, after all, just as there is not any to divisions and differences in viewpoints between the proponents of progress and reaction, between the wise and the foolish, between the young and the old, because there are ongoing conflicts of interest and antagonisms between the poor and the rich, between the United States and China, between neoliberalism and state capitalism, between old ideology and new pragmatism. Between the evil and the good.

However, even though it does not end, history does not stand still. Aldous Huxley (Huxley 1952, 259) beautifully expressed this: "The charm of history and its enigmatic lesson consist in the fact that, from age to age, nothing changes and yet everything is completely different." Indeed, nearly everything is different, but is it better?

When arguing over the ways leading to a better future, there is no need to settle the dilemma of which of the imbalances threatens humanity more: the environmental or the social one? The economic imbalance, though serious, is not the biggest threat. However, we cannot live in peace and develop economically without managing the situation on all three fronts—and still, the list of challenges does not end here.

TOWARD A BETTER FUTURE?

How do we reconcile a practical approach to the economy with an uncompromising attitude? Can you be both an economic pragmatist and a man of principles? Is it worthwhile? It is both possible and worthwhile. If we want the world of the future to be a world of peace and of reasonably harmonious development, and we do want that very much, we need to introduce new values to economic reproduction processes, but, at the same time, we should not, even for a moment, forget pragmatism, which is the fundamental, indispensable feature of rational resource allocation. We need a pragmatism that favors multiculturalism and comes from a system of values that promotes participatory globalization, inclusive institutions, social cohesion, and sustainable development.

There is no inconsistency here, because the supreme values guiding the economic activity process in a society and its economic goals are identical. In both perspectives, what matters most is a threefold sustainable social and economic development in the long term. "Threefold" stands for the following:

(1) *Economically* balanced development, that is, one relating to the market of goods and capital, investment, and finance, as well as that of labor.
(2) *Socially* sustainable development, that is, one relating to a fair, socially accepted income distribution and appropriate participation of basic population groups in public services.
(3) *Environmentally* sustainable development, which is one relating to keeping proper relations between human economic activity and nature.

Therefore, there is no need to sacrifice fundamental principles at the altar of short-term economic or tactical matters. Meanwhile, we need a practical strategic activity to be governed by those principles. This imperative determines the path of evolution of the political economy of the future. Good economics is more than a description of the world; it is also an instrument to change it for the better.

Income relations have a major significance for a long-term economic growth. The latter is particularly stimulated by balanced income distribution. This conclusion is based on comparative studies of long time series and is irrefutable.[1] Economic growth is more durable in countries with a relatively low degree of income inequalities. Furthermore, income relations there had more impact on the dynamics of economic growth than trade liberalization and the quality of political institutions did (Berg and Ostry 2011). This very observation shows on what development policy should we especially focus in the future. Namely, on the fact that what plays a key role is economic institutions, in the behavioral rather than in the organizational sense, which is rules of conduct, or rules of economic game, and the distribution relations. We cannot build welfare on exploitation, while it can be built on profit produced under the conditions of inclusive political and economic institutions.

Of great importance is the possibility to achieve two goals at a time, which stems from the fact that one of them, socially sustainable income distribution, is, at the same time, a means of achieving another, namely economic growth. Neoliberal economic thought and economic policy based thereon has failed to comprehend this interrelation and that is why, by causing a major crisis, it annihilates itself (Roubini and Mihm 2010). This is also beyond the grasp of the economic thought behind various varieties of state capitalism and that is why there is no bright future ahead of it (Halper 2010). It is time for the new pragmatism.

While not underestimating the rivalry between *neoliberal capitalism* and *state capitalism*, it is not this dichotomy that will have a major importance for the future. The shape of the latter will be determined by the result of the confrontation between these two varieties of contemporary capitalism and a social market economy in the form of the new pragmatism. In this battlefield, neoliberalism, trying to regain its strength and position, and state capitalism, which is hostile to the former, will be pitted against the concept of genuine social and economic progress. Its benefits should be available, as widely as possible, to the masses rather than only to narrow cliques following their own particular interests and to their well-paid lobbyists in the world of politics, media, and "science." No system where a vast area of economic inconvenience is called a "margin" of social exclusion, and, at the same time, a narrow margin called the "elite" swims in excessive wealth, has a great future.

It is interesting that in the literature on economics, one-sided or even tendentious interpretations of development processes can still be found and are still promoted. They attempt to reduce the problem to a dichotomy between private and state property, or, from another angle, between individual and collective property, or to a confrontation between the market and the state, or laissez-faire and interventionism. If the choice was as simple as suggested by these alternatives, we would not have so many challenges to face and we would not need that many economists.

It is astounding to what extent some people confuse concepts and categories of development economics, trying to talk themselves and others into believing that it is the Anglo-American style neoliberal capitalism that is characterized by the greatest degree of political and economic inclusiveness (a European would say cohesion). Some go as far as to suggest that compared to anything else in history, from the Roman Empire to the China of the Ming dynasty to the Soviet Union in all of its periods, or, these days, from Argentina to Turkey to Vietnam, it is virtually devoid of any elements of exploitation and, supposedly, it is the wide participation of large social masses that is the source of the high development level achieved over there (Acemoglu and Robinson 2012).[2]

It is symptomatic that even the International Monetary Fund, the stronghold of economic orthodoxy for many years, concedes that the policy meant to overcome the crisis in highly advanced countries, both in the United States and in the European Union (EU), should focus more on increasing tax revenues (mostly from the more affluent segments of the population) than on cutting budgetary spending (mostly addressed to the less affluent segments). Let me hasten to add that an increase in fiscal revenues does not always and everywhere have to be tantamount to a tax increase, as this goal can be achieved also by eliminating exemptions and exclusions, and by ensuring a more efficient tax collection. When such orientation is adopted, pro-growth changes in the structure of the final demand take place and the scale of income disparities decreases, which is conducive to limiting both the causes and consequences of the crisis. Likewise, in emancipating economies, an income redistribution that leads to reduced inequalities, promotes economic growth in the long run.

INCOME DISTRIBUTION AND ECONOMIC GROWTH DYNAMICS

Moreover, beyond a certain national income level, a greater increase in social satisfaction can be achieved through distributing it more evenly than through its quantitative increase. This is a major hint for economic policy. Well, actually not only for the policy, but also for the education system. The better people understand it, the easier it will be to follow that direction. At the same time, there is a risk involved, as a policy based on such a thesis may turn out to be populist rather than pragmatic. This is all the more difficult because the output growth is quite easy to measure. When it comes to human satisfaction, on the other hand, such estimates can be easily manipulated (OECD 2013).

We can perceptibly increase this satisfaction by reducing the Gini index by a certain fraction of a point, instead of pushing the traditionally measured GDP up by several percent. The economic policy of the future will have to resort to such a course of action more and more often. This will be all the easier because, on the one hand, the absolute output and consumption level is growing, and, on the other hand, the present scale of income inequality is higher than before. In other words, when it comes to inequality, there is ample room for reduction. In poor countries, the traditionally defined economic growth, or an increase in the volume of output, is what will count most for many years to come. Conversely, in most rich countries, except for social market economies that are characterized by a low inequality level, the most important method will be a properly oriented change in income proportion.

We should take resolute measures against unjustified inequalities, especially those resulting from pathologies of distribution. They weaken mutual trust between people, which affects social capital, a very desirable component of development processes. If various professional and community groups place no trust in one another, if society does not trust the authorities, and the feeling is mutual, if entrepreneurs are mistrustful of one another, social capital will erode instead of growing. In the economy, like in a family: even if there is enough money, but trust is in short supply, things are not going well.

What about capital accumulation? After all, it is necessary for the economy to run properly, mostly to invest in modernizing the existing production capacities and to create new ones. Is not a shorter ladder of income going to weaken the propensity to save, and thus to create capital, and invest in a better future? Not at all. If that was to happen, we should not reduce the income differentials. However, apart from exceptional situations, this is not the case. There is no empirical or theoretical evidence to prove that in economies with a flatter income structure people save and invest less. It is enough to examine the course of relevant capital formation processes in Austria, France, the Nordic countries, and other countries with similar characteristics in this respect, to learn that more egalitarian societies were able to save no less than countries with a more elitist distribution.

This is also corroborated by conclusions that are easy to draw when comparing the so-called "big government" economies with those where the government is "small." Well, in several decades (1960–1995), in countries with a small, around 30 percent government involvement in national income redistribution (and, consequently, with higher inequality of distribution), the rate of investment or the percentage share of investment in the GDP was 20.7 percent on average. At the same time, in countries with a high scale of budget redistribution, with around 50 percent government involvement in the GDP (and, consequently, relatively lower inequalities in the income distribution), the investment rate was 20.5 percent[3] on average. No difference at all. You can have the same capacity for capital formation, which determines economic growth in the future, with a no less balanced income distribution, which co-determines satisfaction with the present state of economy. And that is an important guideline for the new pragmatism economic policy. That is what things should be like in the future.

The continuous growth of human needs, with the attendant irresistible desire to satisfy them, is a double-edged sword. It overcomes many barriers and, by permanently stimulating the economy, is an indispensable link in the extended reproduction process, or economic growth. At the same time, it's a devastating force as it can dull the mind, spoil preferences, favor reprehensible qualities, and, as a result, contribute irrational elements to resource allocation.

The perennial growth of consumption aspirations is a great problem. The huge crisis at the turn of the first and second decade of the twenty-first century only slightly toned it down and deferred it a bit. It is also a product of a specific system of values. Ever since a couple of centuries ago, humanity has broken the chains of simple reproduction, when the same volume of production and consumption conditions were reproduced from one period to another, and moved to extended reproduction, where it produces more and more from one period to another—appetites are hard to quench. In the old times, one needed just enough to ensure similar living standards to those one had a day, a year, a generation before; now the more it is, the better. Is it really better though? No matter how much we produce, how much we consume, we want more. They say that appetite comes with eating, so economic gluttony is rampant, and with it, economic obesity and many resulting social pathologies. The economy needs a healthy diet, just like one is necessary for a well-functioning body. The economy of the future needs moderation.

Even though the degree to which needs are satisfied is growing, needs themselves are growing even faster. As a result, even though economic growth continues, the gap between needs and satisfying them is widening. Even though one has more, things are worse. This is, in essence, a psychological problem, but one with significant economic consequences. And political ones, too. I once referred to this syndrome as a paradox of a lower level of satisfaction of needs at a higher consumption level. How to solve this problem? Well, it should be clear that we need to solve it or else there will be no end to the chase for producing more goods, while getting no satisfaction from consuming more. This is environmentally devastating and causes social disturbance, so what is the point in it?

The current logic of the society-wide reproduction process is that of autonomously growing needs to own and consume various goods, which stimulates growth in their production. At the same time, income, for which one can purchase the goods produced and services provided is rising, too. So are the needs themselves, which, in the age of consumerism, are usually higher than their satisfaction level. Therefore, a certain tension persists, which is both the driving force behind economic growth and the cause of discontent with the existing situation. If needs grow faster than the economy that fulfils them, individual and social frustration grows, too. There is only one way to overcome this syndrome: to slow down the rate at which the needs are rising.

Theoretically, one can call for accelerating the production growth rate, but, for the reasons we already know well, it is virtually impossible, and it is not recommended from an ethical point of view, either. Furthermore, the essence of the current reproduction mechanism is such that an accelerated economic growth causes yet greater acceleration of consumption appetites and, again, the system is facing the same syndrome, but then there is more of everything, including more problems.

NEEDS AND DEMAND

While it is economic nonsense to call for a zero growth (Jackson 2011), it is a social nonsense to call for letting the issue of all consumption needs to take its course. The economic tradition assumes that needs are unlimited and basically it does not deal with this category at all. It focuses on studying factors that drive the effective demand, that is, only on needs that can be satisfied as they are supported with real purchasing power. If you want to have the latest iPad, that is a need. If you have the means to buy it, that is demand. Consequently, if you want it but have no means to buy it, you are of no interest to narrowly defined economics, and when you finally find the money to spend on it, only then do you become an object of economic study.

We could narrow down our approach and deal exclusively with ways to create demand so that we can sell what we can produce. However, it is better to broaden the field of reflection and find the answer to the question of which needs to stimulate and how, in order to motivate people to become educated and work more efficiently, which must result in a higher income and, consequently, in a higher demand. This alone shows us that modern economics cannot help but deal with mechanisms to drive the needs and with ways to satisfy them. This is dealt with, among others, by behavioral economics and some socially oriented currents in economic thought.

It is indispensable to study needs, their nature and structure, priorities, and preferences, to be able to control the development of the real sector of economy. A major part of needs becomes demand, as time goes by. A lot of needs that marketing tries to identify at the microeconomic level and that experimental economics examines, should be considered a potential demand. There is no market for them yet (they take the form of "window shopping," that is walking through shopping malls to see what is available and to dream of what you could buy if you had the means), but one can emerge one day. Naturally, it will not only depend on time, but also on the increasing real income of the buyers or on a change in their consumption preferences. Therefore, some of the needs are a potential demand that will become a real demand and one needs to know, beforehand, what real supply we will have to balance it with. If it is about a new smart-phone type, we need to leave it solely up to the market. If it is about healthcare protection or motor industry development, it will not hurt if the state, as well, takes account of the implications of the imminent changes in its budgetary and investment policies.

Certainly, with time, we will want something else as we will have something else. And we will know something else. Being under constant pressure from the gap between needs/desires and satisfaction/possession, we will be motivated to look for an extra portion of income as higher spending will be required to improve our standard of living. Being unable to have more and better things today, we will strive to have more and better things tomorrow. Therefore, the economics of the future is not an economics of a state, but an economics of changes. Rather than tell us how things are and what depends on what in production, distribution, and exchange, it says how things will be and what will depend on what.

The issue is very complex from an ethical, psychological, social, economic, legal, and political perspective. We cannot, after all, forbid people to desire to have something, neither can we order them to want something. This would be an Orwellian reality. Naturally, there are exceptions, in which the situation must be under control, especially where we deal with the negative external effects of consumption, as in the case of drugs, guns, or uncontrollable gambling. Needs of that sort must be stifled in the interest of the public, so we must undertake organized efforts to prevent them from spreading. Some needs may not be irresistible.

Which of them and who should decide that? Views are divided. The prohibition in the 1920s in the United States did not work out. Still, would a liberalized soft drug market fail, too? What would the loosened regulation of the pornography market bring? Its expansion, for sure. That is why, because of the values we cherish, the lawmakers, nearly everywhere, introduced restrictions, which mitigated an escalation of needs in that respect (it would surely be immense if it were not for the formal limits), but, at the same time, it set black market mechanisms in motion, and created the need to penalize such markets. However, a slightly higher tolerance to "soft" drugs in the Netherlands caused the demand for harmful "hard" narcotics to go down. The experience of Denmark suggests that the liberalization of the pornography market contributed to a lower sexual crime rate. From the point of view of the intended cultural and educational goal, the use of only rigorous prohibitions has a limited impact and sometimes comes with adverse side effects. This is not the way.

Which is the way, then? The market will never rise to meet this challenge on its own, so we need relevant social organizations, and especially the state with its regulations and human capital investment, because the higher the resulting social awareness, the greater the ability to shape one's own needs in an intelligent way. It is worth adding that education has a fundamental impact on the type of needs we have. As education increases, needs move toward cultural goods and services. It does not have to be the case if only income increases, without a corresponding education increase. This has specific consequences for the economy, which should adapt the structure of the supply offered to the resulting changes in the structure of the effective demand. Let me refer to the classic example: less vodka, more books. It is worth limiting the former need, while the latter is worth promoting with the use of fiscal instruments, among other things.

If we asked an educator "how," he would say: through education and upbringing. A priest would have no doubts that it is all about conscience that shapes desirable habits and behaviors. A psychologist would suggest that we cultivate proper individual traits of character. A sociologist would recommend creating attractive social interaction models that provide an alternative to consumerism.

What should an economist do? A neoliberal one knows: leave matters to their own devices and keep talking rubbish about how every shoeshine boy can become a millionaire or, in our day and age, how every business school graduate can turn into an ultra-rich man; as long as he really feels like it and has no scruples. Meanwhile, an honest economist will approach the matter in an interdisciplinary and pragmatic manner. First, he will try to learn as much as possible about all of the above disciplines, to be able to propose a set of long-term measures within the entire development triangle formed by values, institutions, and policy. Moreover, surely, not for a moment will he forget that what people want depends not only on what they already have, but also on what they know.

After all, we cannot bridge the gap between subjective needs and the objective possibilities to satisfy them, with the former growing faster than the latter, unless we redefine human desires, both individual and social, accordingly. It cannot be bridged without relevant regulations that block the expansion of "wrong" needs and favor the "good" ones, if only by stimulating the interest in sports activities or book reading. We will not be able to bridge it without resorting to a specific policy where what matters most is not to allow an excessive social diversification in terms of income and property.

As long as all neighbors drove to work in a Fiat, the neighbor from around the corner would not need a Mercedes. When he can see that a couple of them have also upgraded to such a vehicle, he starts to feel the same need. The demonstration effect is at work here. In an individual case, it can motivate people to improve their skills and to work even more efficiently and for a higher salary. In a macro-scale, it leads to a situation where, even though the national income almost doubles every decade or so, people complain that things are as bad as they have always been, or they are even worse, although before they used to commute to work on a crowded bus or subway.

Once again; this is by no means calling for any demotivating egalitarianism, but for acknowledging the significance of a socially sustainable income distribution. It consists in a diversification that fundamentally reflects the contribution of individuals and groups to the national income generation, while guaranteeing their participation in the income at proportions that promote both efficiency and justice, or, if we look at it from a different angle, private entrepreneurship and social cohesion.

Travel broadens the mind. Let's see what it can teach us. Common sense tells us we should be in favor of as many people as possible having a personal tablet. A lot of them have one in the United States, quite a few in Poland, a bit fewer in Russia, much fewer in China and almost nobody in Cuba. Whoever has been there has seen this. If we studied social attitudes carefully, it would turn out that the highest dissatisfaction with not having a tablet (yet) can be found in Poland where there are ten times as many of them, pro rata to the population, as in Cuba, where relatively fewer people are dissatisfied with this specific issue. It is because such a need has not developed yet over there, not only because the network is underdeveloped, but most of all because there is no demonstration effect at play. Such a need will emerge over there, as well, but there is no point in blowing it out of proportion if there are no realistic prospects of satisfying this need, or of the need transforming it into demand in a reasonable time interval. There would be hardly any use for it, while the disappointment would be huge. With time, when people can afford to buy tablets, as they will produce them themselves or they will sell something else abroad at a profit to have means for importing them, the need will develop by itself, without TV spots, full-page newspaper advertisements, or huge billboards that stimulate sick emotions rather than healthy efforts.

Both with respect to individuals and entire nations, what we need is ambitions. Not those aiming higher than you can reach, but realistic ones. Without them, it is hard to get far and climb high. On the other hand, it is not good for ambitions to be excessive, as then the disappointment of being unable to satisfy them can be depressing. An excess of ambition can hinder rather than promote development. Leaders, at all levels, should, in particular, have ambitious visions rather than naive illusions. These, however, must be aspirations embedded in an actual cultural and economic potential rather than just populist promises.

It is natural that societies and nations aspire to at least catching up with a richer neighbor, if not with Japan right away. Mexicans dream of the United States, Slovaks wish things were as good at home as they are in Austria, Estonians compare themselves with Finland, while the Vietnamese are planning to outdo Thailand. Once I was even asked at the PNG University in Port Moresby, when things in Papua New Guinea will be the way they are in Australia (never, in a foreseeable future), and recently a Cairo-based journalist wanted to know what I think about Egyptian politicians who announce that their country will catch up with Turkey in seven years. Well, it is sheer megalomania, as it would require doubling the Egyptian GDP per capita in this seven-fat-years period (unrealistic assumption), on the assumption (also an unrealistic one), that Turkey would experience a complete stagnation due to seven lean years.

The wish to match those who are better is one of the major driving forces in eliminating development gaps, but if we plan tasks that are impossible to complete in a given time frame, people may get discouraged. It is worth being an ambitious realist or a pragmatist. Poland may one day reach the GDP per capita of Germany, just like the Irish managed to do with that of the UK, or South Korea almost of Japan, but this cannot happen over one generation, and considering the not-so-good policy of the recent couple of years, even two or three might not be enough. There is no telling. While Spain managed to get close to the GDP level enjoyed by the French (USD 36,000 per capita at PPP in the years 2012–2014), the Portuguese (24,000) did not catch up with Spain (31,000). The resulting implication for economic development policy is: aim for what you're strong enough to achieve. If you can, increase your strength, but you should not aim beyond your potential, because then your goals will not be matched by the possibilities to achieve them.

It is not about limiting human needs, but about endeavoring, by all possible means, to maintain a harmony (which is necessary to ensure social satisfaction) between needs, both the old ones growing in strength and new ones emerging, and realistic, economically reasonable possibilities to satisfy them. Also, in this case, just like with the future growth rate, it would be good to leave more room for development to societies from emancipating economies,[4] with a relatively lower increase in needs in rich countries. To a certain degree, this is already happening, as, again, it is similar to gluttony: at some point, you have had enough of even what you like and you cannot have any more of it.

MEANS AND ENDS OF DEVELOPMENT

If, in a broad perspective, it all boils down to maximizing, in a long term, the level of social satisfaction with economic activity, we need to look at the new pragmatism from the angle of the objectives of social and economic development, its essence, and method.

Fulfilling needs in a way that satisfies people is a development goal that is in line with the guiding values of the new pragmatism. A GDP growth is a means to an end rather than an end itself. It is high time for the highly developed countries to move away from maximizing the income, mostly from driving the gross domestic product as high as they believe they can. If half a century of ever-increasing incomes did not increase the life satisfaction of rich Americans, why make so much effort and incur extra costs in the form of extended work time, while devastating the natural environment even more? (Bok 2010)

Incidentally, something interesting is going on in this respect, as even during the US presidential campaign in 2012, there was relatively less talk of quantity, and more of quality, less talk of the output growth, and more of other aspects of rational resource allocation, such as financial and trade balance, provision of public services, employment, although still not enough about culture and environment. This was due, to a great extent, to the specific nature of the time of crisis, but, partly, also to the evolution of mentality. It is good, because we are standing on the brink of a fundamental redefinition of social and economic development goals. In the future, the goal will not be to just maximize income, but to distribute the fruits of such growth in a way that increases people's true satisfaction; nonmaterial values will be another goal.

It is estimated that if income proportions in the United States were like those in Scandinavian countries (which I consider to be a totally impossible future, taking into account American values), the sense of mutual trust among people (additionally strained during the crisis and the 2012 electoral campaign) could increase by as much as 75 percent, and the number of people suffering from mental disturbance and obesity could drop by two-thirds. The number of teenage mothers would drop by half, and the number of convicts by three-fourths. Overall, people would live not only longer, but also more happily as their working hours could be reduced even by one-sixth, or a total of two months a year (Wilkinson and Pickett 2010). If these estimates are exaggerated as to specific indices, and surely they are, they still speak volumes.

The United States is not the navel of the world and will never again have the same capacity to impose its values on others that it had right after the end of the Cold War. Still, changes taking place there are having an impact not only on Americans, but also on other places in the world where many people still idolize the United States. After all, a great majority of opinion-forming books in economics and other social sciences are published in English, right there, in the United States.

In this context, maybe it is a good thing that the volume expansion in the form of a traditionally defined economic growth weakens once the GDP threshold of 20,000 dollars per head is exceeded. Even if it turns out that under the conditions of the present scientific and technological revolution the dynamics slow down at a higher level, let's say at 30,000 dollars at today's prices, we will have to be glad as this will mean a higher chance of survival for the natural environment and more time for continued technological progress that will reduce the excessive consumption of nonrenewable resources. So maybe we should rejoice that with the slower volume growth economists and politicians will give more attention to other aspects that co-determine the quality of life and the resulting life satisfaction.

I suggested a different economic progress metric, that I called *Integrated Success Index* (ISI) (Kolodko 2011a). It depends only partly on GDP, since the value of this composite index is co-determined by other factors. In detail, the aggregated value of ISI is composed of the following:

(1) Gross domestic product—40 percent.
(2) Subjective well-being related to the overall life satisfaction, including the standard of social services, and projections of its future prospects—20 percent.
(3) An assessment of the state of the natural environment—20 percent.
(4) An estimate of free time and cultural values that fill it up—20 percent.

This suggestion, quite an arbitrary one, is not about details, but about the line of inquiry. Whether we emerge unscathed from the present mess is contingent upon the imperative to redefine economic development goals. Therefore, while not insisting on ISI, which is just a general concept rather than an operational metric, at this point we can advocate the widest, possibly universal use of the inequality-adjusted human development index (IHDI), already being applied by the UNDP for international comparative analyses. The time has come to demand that politicians take this matter seriously.

Let's imagine that the desirable and absolutely possible future is approaching fast and in the US House of Representatives, in British Parliament, in the German Bundestag and in the Spanish Cortes, in the Brazilian Senate, and even in the Chinese National People's Congress, deputies are discussing the ways to increase the value of human capital and to improve the social tissue by limiting income inequalities. Let's imagine that the idea on how to increase IHDI is the main point of dispute between White House contenders in the 2020 election in the United States or when deciding, with the door kept more ajar, on the composition of the Politburo of the Communist Party of China in 2022 (it will exist and it will be in power). Let's imagine deputies to the Sejm of the Republic of Poland and the Russian Duma, who, rather than squabble over how to interpret historical circumstances or whether or not to limit sexual minorities' rights, argue over the direction of institutional solutions and over the macroeconomic policy instruments which lead to increasing IHDI; if only because they know that this is one of the things their future political fate will depend on. Is it that hard to imagine? Is it still just political and economic science fiction?

ECONOMICS OF MODERATION

To make it happen, especially to cause concepts and proposals of the economics as a normative discipline to be followed by relevant measures of political economy, it is indispensable to grasp the essence of the economics of moderation, which is what the new pragmatism is all about. The economics of moderation means adapting the volume of human, natural, financial, and material flows to the requirement to keep a dynamic balance. Turbulent transformations of the last several decades are caused both by acute imbalances in various fields, and by their outcome. What we are surrounded by is an economy of a permanent imbalance as there is always either too much of something or too little of something else. A surplus of something is available, while there is a constant shortage of something else, and yet a good economy should be that of moderation. Hence, what is also indispensable here is a thought that promotes such a desirable state of affairs, namely the economics of moderation.

In the future, we need economics of moderation rather than that of excesses, imbalances, and crises. All of those will happen more than once to humanity and the interconnected global economy as well as to the national economies, but it should be an exception rather than a rule. What should be the rule is to know where to stop and adapting to real economic growth opportunities; moderate-income disparities rather than extremes that wear out vast numbers of people and lead to new revolutions; toning down the marketing folly, which creates needs that are utterly detached from the realities of effective demand. Last, but not least, what should be the rule is not overdoing it when transforming more and more pieces of Mother Earth into goods that are meant to be sold at a profit by their manufacturers, although possessing and using them no longer improves consumer satisfaction.

There is a shortage of some raw materials and budgetary incomes, while we have an excess of garbage and all kinds of debts contracted by households, companies, entire countries. A technology to produce clean and renewable energy is missing, while there is a surplus of technologies for producing weapons of mass destruction. There is an abundance of banks with excess liquidity, willing to grant loans to naive consumers, while there are not enough loans for small enterprises as it takes more effort to monitor them. In many countries and regions, there is an evident surplus of people who cannot be properly nourished, while somewhere else areas that were prosperous until recently are becoming depopulated. In some economies, in the wake of the speculative bubble on the real estate market, too many houses and apartments were built, which are now standing empty and becoming dilapidated, as there are no buyers, while there is no shortage of people over there who have nowhere to live and are camping out. In some industries, there is not enough workforce, while in others, it is excessive. In some places, surplus food goes to waste, while somewhere else, there is not enough of it to meet elementary needs. In some hospitals, doctors sit idly by, as there are not enough patients who can afford the treatment, while in others people die as there is not enough staff to save lives in time.

In developed countries, there is an oversupply of consumer goods on the market, and a shortage of the population's effective purchasing power. In consumerism-tainted societies, there is an indisputable excess of needs, while a shortage of economic capacity to satisfy them is evident. While an overwhelming majority of us is constantly short of funds to buy what we really need, many entrepreneurs are afflicted by surplus productive capacity that they cannot exploit in a cost-effective manner as there are no buyers for goods they could manufacture. One might say maliciously: there is constantly too much or too little of everything, depending on the angle from which you look at it. In other words, there is nearly always both too much and too little of nearly everything. Of economists, too.

The greatest deficit in contemporary economy is most palpable where we need to be moderate. Moderation is generally in short supply. In the future, however, there should be as much of it as possible. Moreover, this is one of the fundamental canons of the political economy of the future. It is necessary to create mechanisms for balancing economic flows and resources. One might say, again: that is nothing new. Well, in the approach suggested here there is a lot of new content, as it does not rely on the deceptive assumption—typical of some other trends in economics—that market money mechanisms are capable of solving the problems of deficiencies and surpluses, which is dynamically balancing the economy. If they were, we would not be going through a time of turmoil, as we are, but would be enjoying an age of prosperity.

Once, at another stage of civilization and at a much lower level of overall development, in some countries attempts were made to solve this syndrome by adopting a bureaucratic supervision over economic processes. Theoretically, this was meant to eliminate wasteful overproduction crises that are characteristic of a badly regulated capitalist economy, while in practice it led to the emergence of a socialist economy with its inherent structural shortages. The Hungarian economist Janos Kornai saw shortage as the main constitutive feature of that system and called it the "shortage economy," while for its theoretical description he coined the term "economics of shortage" (Kornai 1980). Almost all countries involved, except for Cuba and North Korea, managed to get out of such an inefficient system and there are no fears anybody will be tempted again to try using statism and command central planning as instruments of balancing the economy.

However, overcoming the shortage syndrome by the post-socialist transition economies by no means solved the problem of the lack of overall balance. Also, countries that never experienced shortages typical of real socialism are plagued by a number of deficits. There is, sometimes, a shortage of exports, of budget revenues, sometimes there are not enough professionals in a given field, and at other times, it is certain precious metals that are lacking. Not to mention common sense. There is a constant lack of time, although it is wasted on a massive scale by society as a whole. At the same time, there is always too much of something. Probably nothing in this world is as permanently out of balance as the economy.

Let me say right away that this will also be the case in the future, because such is the intrinsic nature of the economy. Mechanisms for balancing demand and supply flows are working, for better or for worse, in a short term and so are, even in longer time intervals, mechanisms for balancing certain types of needs and possibilities to satisfy them; still, balance can be reached only temporarily. The natural condition of the economy is a permanent imbalance with momentary episodes where lines of supply and demand, output and sales, income and expenditure cross each other. This is true of reality; in theoretical models, on the other hand, balance comes as easy as making relevant assumptions, and what should cross in illustrative diagrams will always cross exactly where it is expected.

That is nothing to wring our hands about, because market economy, also by its intrinsic nature, has corrective mechanisms, too, though they are imperfect. When the deviation from the balance is too high, forces are activated that correct the disproportions. The problem is that very often they do so too late or not strongly enough, or they miss the point of balance, by going from lack of something to excess or the other way round. Obviously, it raises overhead costs of resource allocation and reduces its efficiency. Therefore, market corrections must be sometimes triggered, some other times speeded up, and yet some other times reinforced, curbed, or even blocked; they need regulating. Who else than the state should do that?

It is necessary to use state interventionism to assist market corrections of the intensity of flows (income and expenditure, supply and demand, supplies and market) and of changes in resources (property, savings, stocks). It would be good to end ideological disputes on that matter and focus on which intervention techniques to use. If they are inadequate, you can do more harm than good because interventionism is a risky business. To avoid the resulting errors, neoliberalism suggests throwing out the baby with the bathwater: not to interfere with market processes as they have the capacity to self-adjust or to automatically balance themselves. State capitalism proposes not to throw out the baby, but to keep the dirty water, too, excessively interfering with resource allocation, on many occasions, which reduces the achievable efficiency.

The new pragmatism calls for a well-balanced role of the state and a suprastate economic policy coordination, which is meant to correct, or, when necessary, to strengthen market processes. It says, wash the baby, pour out the dirty water, and if it starts to wash itself one day, perfect, but we can never do without washing. Therefore, we need to optimize the scope and instruments of state interventionism, while bearing in mind not to confuse the means of economic policy with its ends. The constant care to ensure balance in all of its sectors is an issue of great importance, but it is still a means the policy uses to achieve the end, which is development. The balancing of the economy is meant to foster rather than curb it.

Well, but each action causes reaction. Teams of experts, mostly lawyers at large corporations that can afford it, rack their brains over how to be compliant with the law that is, with the constantly changing regulations, and still come out ahead. Business must be profitable, legal, and ethical—these are the three sacred principles of the new pragmatism. Business should be ethical, it does not have to be profitable, and it will be compliant with the law because we are the ones to establish it—these are the features of state capitalism. Business must be profitable and legal, and it may be unethical—these are the three canons of neoliberalism. How eagerly and, to a great extent, how effectively, it can, in nearly any situation, promote the interests of specific groups, especially those of the financial circles, is illustrated by the attempted legislative amendments and by the results of those adopted in response to the crisis in the United States after 2008 (Suskind 2011). As a result, in many cases, attempts to improve regulations cause their quality to deteriorate, from the point of view of the general public interest.

DESCRIPTIVE AND NORMATIVE ECONOMICS

It is a cliché that we need to take care not to let the state that intends to improve the market spoil it even further. There are cases where the state ruins the chances of achieving the desired results. After all, not only the market errs; governments and central banks can be wrong, too. In addition, they often are. Governmental regulations, and in the era of irreversible globalization intergovernmental and worldwide ones are, to a growing extent, often established to address challenges of the past.

Meanwhile, it is about the future. Regulations are meant to help avoid blunders, errors, oversights, scams, frauds which can happen in the future rather than those that already occurred in the past. For these we should apologize, reprimand, dismiss, punish, and put in prison. It is like the case of accidents and disasters, after which technical inspection is tightened, while it should have been done beforehand, limiting the causes of potential tragedies. An airplane crashed, so they check the technical condition of all those that have not, while it would have been enough to check some before the crash. A great flood broke the dike that had not been monitored for years and afterward all the dikes are inspected, while it would have been enough to check, in advance, the crucial points to avert the disaster.

Systemic state interventionism is supposed to examine fundamental shortcomings of the market and remedy excesses in the field of the overly unequal income distribution, rather than try to take over the allocative functions of the market. Interventionism must refrain from socializing private losses. In the future, the growing complexity of market processes may make it easier to misuse interventionism for one's own ulterior motives. Ironically, these days there are more and more, rather than fewer and fewer ways to pass the costs of private capital failures on taxpayers. This is one side of the coin.

There is another one, too. In all types of market economy, but certainly to a greater degree and more often so in state capitalism than in the neoliberal one, clientelism is rife, where state regulations and government policy serve the purposes of political, bureaucratic, and business cliques rather than correct market deficiencies. This has as much in common with a decent interventionism as neoliberal frauds do with honest business.

This can be defied only by a society that is well organized in a state with strong institutions, one founded on progressive law and order. That is why neoliberalism wants a "small" government or a "cheap" government because what is small and cheap is poor and, consequently, weak. If a government can be relatively smaller without weakening its intervention functionality, we should by all means follow that direction. If it is not possible, it has to be "bigger" or "more expensive," because precious public services, also those that safeguard law and order, have a higher price than goods of poor quality.

Therefore, if somebody wishes ill to market economy, he should wish it an unbridled freedom as then it will be only a matter of time before its future becomes uncertain. Yet who wishes it a good future must advocate proper regulation and harmony between the market and state interventionism. In the long term, and on a macroeconomic scale, what can help in this respect is developing strategic indicative plans using the rolling wave method. These are plans in which, as time goes by, the time horizon progressively moves by the corresponding period, so that the perspective ahead of us does not get shorter. In the world of the future, countries and regional integration blocs that can make better use of this instrument will get the upper hand. Unlike in private capital corporations, which often prefer to keep their strategic plans secret (and every self-respecting corporation has plans), in states and regional integration agreements they are part of the knowledge of long-winded intentions and do not harm competitiveness in any way. Actually, by causing an overall mobilization, also among competitors, it can favor development even more.

It is worth noting at this point that without a proper strategic plan, the United States will be unable to cope with improving its public finances, which are in a pitiful state, and the EU will be unable to sort out its backyard when it comes to finance, either. This is understood by the Chinese, who approach the problem from the other end, in a way. They still rely on macroeconomic five-year planning, but it is no longer command-based, but rather strategic and indicative. From one period to another (currently in 2021–2025 already the fourteenth five-year plan is to be implemented), this is a less and less planned and more and more market-oriented economy. Indicative planning is also used in India, which has not abandoned this instrument of controlling the development of economy, while continuing to deregulate the same, for over a decade now, calmly and rationally, without neoliberal excesses.

Against this backdrop, it is easy to note that the new pragmatism is in keeping with the compensation hypothesis, which says that the more advanced globalization, the "bigger" government, or that the public expenditure to national product ratio is rising (Garrett 1998, 2001). Naturally, the goal is to relativize the sum total of expenditure to the gross world product, or to the sum total of gross domestic products of all countries. After all, there will be among them also those where the good cause of sustainable development is better served by reducing such expenditure (adjustment according to the efficiency hypothesis), but there will also be those where it requires a greater scale of fiscal redistribution.

One of the attributes of the method presented here is that it provides a deeper identification of mechanisms and of the impact of processes that lead to future conditions rather than simply forecasting those conditions. It is about showing a dynamic path to the future, or ways to achieve the intended goals, and not just a static future. Valuable methods, used in economic reflections on the future to arrive at correct conclusions and right decisions, include variant projections, alternative scenarios, foresight thinking, as well as microeconomic experiments where they are applicable.

Such a methodological approach by no means totally eliminates the risk of mistake, but it limits its scale. The reason is that unpredictable events are more likely to occur than unpredictable processes, especially in the long term. Many of the latter are anchored in the past and are already happening. Future events are not there yet and some of those currently forecasted may not occur at all, while quite many of the future processes have already been launched and are underway.

The new pragmatism expresses a strategic approach to the future. It is no stranger to global visions or to warning forecasts, but in principle; it has a pro-active approach to the future. Good economics is not only about describing the world; it is also an instrument to change it for the better. Considering the long-term development trends, it is worth developing strategies to help orient them the way we wish them to be, which will make it easier to solve more than one problem and avert more than one economic disaster.

Hence, the new pragmatism is a normative consequence of a descriptive perspective, which I presented earlier as the *Coincidence Theory of*

Development (Kolodko 2011a). It emphasizes the significance of a given concurrence of development determinants, which is always specific, but varies over time and space. This is the very concept succinctly conveyed in the sentence "things happen the way they do because a lot happens at the same time." This rule will be always applicable in the future. Starting by describing, analyzing, and interpreting what happened in the past and what is taking place in the present, we arrive at evaluating and postulating measures that are expected, in the future, to give rise to a specific bundle of phenomena and processes, whose resultant is the desirable direction and pace of social and economic development. The determining factor will be coincidence, or correspondence and togetherness, the overlapping and interpenetration of various components, and that is the multilayer, heterogeneous "philosopher's stone" which might, in the future, allow us actions that would be otherwise impossible.

CONCLUSION

As for the future, even more interesting than alternative scenarios or extrapolations of various trends, is the political economy of the future which addresses the critical question of how the contradictions, surfacing from various economic activities, will arise and by what institutions and policies' coordination mechanisms, on the worldwide scale, they might be mitigated. The greatest challenge for the future is to find a way of the governance of globalization, since despite the recent crisis, it remains an irreversible process.

What I call the "new pragmatism" is a policy-oriented theoretical approach looking for the set of values, institutions, and policies that ought to sustain a balanced growth of the world economy in the long run. "New pragmatism" is eclectic, multidisciplinary, and dynamic. It also pays great attention to the multi-culture aspects of social and economic development, since the future requires continuing opening of societies and economies, and their peaceful cooperation will not be possible without a tolerance based on multi-culture.[5]

NOTES

1. This is discussed at length by Wilkinson and Pickett (Wilkinson and Pickett 2010). See also the remarks on this issue in the recent book by the Nobel laureate Edmund Phelps (Phelps 2013).
2. See its review in *Acta Oeconomica* 2014/1.
3. I say "consequently," suggesting the obvious relationship between a relatively greater scale of budget redistribution and a relatively lower scale of inequalities of income distribution. This is the case of the state with inclusive institutions and a

relatively high level of social cohesion. However, it is possible to have a state with a "big" government, the benefits of which are not available to masses, but are instead reaped by the so-called elites, often corrupt ones. It is a common situation in state capitalism economies.

4. "Emancipating economies" is a category which I substitute for the widely, and often cloudlessly, used "emerging economies," a term that, in essence, refers to objects rather than subjects of a process. The "emerging" angle is mostly about new capital markets emerging for investment by rich countries, while the "emancipating" angle focuses on societies that are striving to secure a better position in a global game of the future. See more in part II of this book and in Kolodko (2014a).

5. Published in Kolodko (2014b, 139–160).

Chapter 5

Imperative of Heterodoxy

Gone forever are the days when sitting in his office, a great scholar could create a new theory, which revolutionized thinking about economy. It was possible in the eighteenth and nineteenth century, maybe for the last time in the twentieth century, in the time of Keynes, but it is no longer viable in the twenty-first century. The fundamental work that has had the greatest impact on the evolution of economic thought in the twentieth century is, written in 1935 and published a year later, Keynes's work on the mechanisms of a market economy and impact mechanisms on the economic situation. Now, due to the huge variety in economic matter, he could not write such a work or would have to stop at too high level of generalization. Analogies with other disciplines have caught my eyes, because these are not Edison and Eastman times, this is not the time for inventions of geniuses from the garage. This is the time of large R&D centers and interdisciplinary, huge, expensive, multi-year programs. However, glimpses of genius always happen and they are very handy. If they also appear in the area of the economy—it is good for us.

These considerations give the irresistible conclusion that the economy of the future must be heterodox. Times of orthodoxy, expressed in homogeneous schools of economics, also proclaimed uniqueness, are gone forever. Recalcitrant economists, who insist on their models, as the only legitimate and, worse, applicable to every seemingly similar situation in time and space, more often are wrong. Examined matter is complicated—the reality which surrounds us everywhere, environmental, economic, social, cultural and political and technological reality—and therefore relations within it, which want to understand and try to describe it, are complicated. Embracing what is going on, requires multi-threading, leaving the traditional mainstream economics (some with pleasure use an Anglicism—mainstream economics), and using heterodoxy in place of worn-out orthodoxy. You do not have the old, sacred canons, because reality has changed qualitatively.

Future economy will be less and less mathematicized and formalized, and in relatively increasing extent will be embedded in a cultural context. In the twenty-first century academic textbooks proportions of words and patterns, as well as narrative arguments and charts will change in favor of the former—contrary that has happened in the twentieth century. The departments of economics and business schools will need to teach more anthropology and cultural studies. Not at the expense of mathematics and econometrics, but next to them. This opinion in the future will be more and more obvious, today's suggestion will become tomorrow's canon.

Some economists put in particular their hopes into behavioral economics coupled with traditional macroeconomics, seeing as the first can become an instrument of improving the latter. If something creative emerges from this, perhaps there would be fewer mistakes in macroeconomic policy. Nevertheless, it can also give rise to an economic Frankenstein, which will lead us astray. Not from today and from yesterday I believe that without a better understanding of the behavioral evidence of rationality shortage, we cannot comprehend the ground of errors in economic policy. However, I have no doubt that it cannot be set to optimize policy decisions based on behavioral models of rationality and irrationality of behaviors. A good economist can explain the errors of the American central bank Fed (Federal Reserve System), which has not blocked rising evidence of the economic crisis, as well as which policy we should carry out to avoid similar mishaps in the future, without relying on sophisticated models of behavioral economics. Once again, we may be threatened by triumph of form over content.

Behavioral economists are tempted to assume that, because we are so often not rational, rather than insist on the fact that we should be rational and theoretical generalizations should be done based on this, it is worth to try to model alternative theories of irrational or not fully rational behaviors. This is supported by computerization using more and better data on the one hand, and the achievements of other sciences, from physics to neuroscience, on the other. This may give rise to neuroeconomics. Just do not get upset.

Maybe in the future theoretical economics will become simply an instrument of empirical economics? Do we follow in this direction? There is an increasing number of situations in which you do not need to make assumptions about the object of research, because you can rely on the extensive factual empiricism. In the United States they say that all the information can be found somewhere on one hard drive. In fact, it is not all even there—and still too often we do not know on which one—but empirical field of research in comparison with what was and is, is rapidly expanding.

Moreover, it is interesting to see how the story comes full circle and once again, like in the days of central planning, placing high hopes in the giant supercomputer capabilities. While it is already getting harder and harder to meet veterans of centralized economy era—dreaming about such computational power that today has the Titan supercomputer that could provide optimum planning—there are more and more economists that believe that a centralized computer calculations will in future serve to slow down, and even to eliminate market failure. In some way this will happen, but this direction of evolution of economic thought is not promising too much, because computers will count, and economists again miscalculate.

Some things you need to observe other count, while others invent. Significant economist of his time Vilfredo Pareto (1848–1923), to the output of whom we even turn today, said that if it is the price of tomatoes that he do not know—which is a parameter necessary to solve the complex multilevel system of equations—he sends housekeeper to the market to check out how much are the tomatoes. Now it is not sufficient to just look at market trading, then put the data into a sophisticated computer model and insist on results. We should also doubt and constantly circulate between empiricism and theory, not just knowing how to count, but also not forgetting what and why is counted.

It is not far to the next observation. Economics must be interdisciplinary. This statement may at first glance strike. How to be an interdisciplinary discipline? Yes, but maybe now we should talk about economics not as a social science discipline, but simply about interdisciplinary economics, or, if you prefer, about an interdisciplinary approach to the study of economic processes. The reason is that many—more and more—happen on the meeting. And there is the most interesting. At the meeting of the economy and society which examines sociology, social psychology, anthropology, history, at the meeting of society and politics we examine the political science and sociology of power, at the meeting of the economy and the environment, which studies the ecology, at the meeting of the economy and culture, which studies, among others, anthropology, the relations of the economy and technology, being particularly the interest of management science, moreover, which is the part of economics. These meetings are more. In order not to lose sight of what is important, you have to look for appropriate set of lenses, not just the glass of one scholar in the traditional, narrowly understood economic speech. If we agree that thinking has the future, then let us agree to the fact that interdisciplinary thinking has a great future. In general and in particular, in relation to the management and investigating its economics.

Chapter 6

Emerging Markets or Emancipating Economies?

As for the so-called emerging markets, not only should we not get too easily excited by this seemingly attractive concept, which, sadly, happens to too many economists but also, on the contrary, we need to defy it. The term "emerging markets" was proposed not so much in relation to a society that allocates its resources as in reference to a very narrow category of financial markets in those economies. Therefore, it is a very objectifying approach: it's not people that matter but their money. A neoliberal economist will probably even applaud it but somebody oriented toward a social market economy must oppose. Looking at countries that are trying to narrow the gap in development level, one needs to treat them as subjects and see the people while counting the money.

Hence, I suggest we abandon the term "emerging economies," that is that we no longer limit ourselves to analyzing further and further countries whose financial markets have widened enough to "emerge" internationally as a result of liberalization and now offer the opportunity to speculate. They emerge as a place to strike good deals, not necessarily for the benefit of people from those markets but sometimes at their expense and surely for a speculator's own benefit.

Looking at things from the perspective of development economics and political economy of the future, I suggest we talk of "emancipating" economies. It's a huge difference compared to "emerging" markets as this time they are treated like subjects rather than objects. While in the case of "emerging markets" society is something less significant, a part of the game revolving around speculation, money and profits, in an "emancipating economy" society becomes crucial. The lynchpin here is a society that allocates its resources. Obviously, one existing in market economy conditions, in financial environment, without turning its back to the unavoidable market speculations and pursuit of gain but also without submitting to them as the master of the whole system.

What does it implicate for the future? How may the position of respective country groups in the world evolve? Will the earlier division into "three worlds" disappear completely and will the present division into "two worlds" of highly developed countries and "emerging markets" fade away? Will the future course of globalization contribute to these differences vanishing gradually?

To reduce the conflict potential of the present phase of globalization, the greatest possible number of less advanced countries must emancipate. The world composed of pieces so diverse that in extreme cases production capabilities and the resulting standard living in the richest countries is over a hundred times higher than in the poorest ones, is unsustainable. If we were to keep up such a scale of imbalance, the world would have to tumble down. Destabilization, revolutions, wars would be unavoidable. In other words, with present situation maintained in the long run, a dark future would start to turn from possible and undesirable into an unavoidable one.

A reasonable response to that challenge is the emancipation of countries and societies on their way up, both those getting out of the erstwhile "Third World" and those originating from the "Second World," in most cases already industrialized and characterized by a relatively high standard of human capital. In the latter case, that of countries undergoing post-socialist transformation, it should be easier as their societies have a per capita GDP which is about 50 percent higher than the world average and human capital is of a relatively high standard. While the average income for humanity as a whole stands at around USD 12,000 (measured at PPP), for the 126 million in European post-socialist countries, including post-Soviet Baltic states: Estonia, Latvia, and Lithuania, already part of the European Union, it's approximately USD 17,600, and for nearly 280 million people living in the remaining former Soviet republics, it's about USD 12,400 (in Russia with a population of 138 million, it's 17,000). Therefore, for over 400 million people living in Central and Eastern Europe and former USSR, this gives an average income at PPP of slightly over USD 14,000.

When it comes to the quality of human capital, measured most often with the human development index, HDI, this part of the world looks even better and more than one country can already feel emancipated, and free of insecurities. The richest of post-socialist countries, Slovenia (with a population of just two million and so having hardly any impact on the regional average) ranks only thirtieth in the world when it comes to per capita GDP (USD 29,000 at PPP), while it ranks as high as nineteenth in terms of human capital, with an HDI of 0.844. If we adjust the index for inequality in income distribution, the way UNDP, UN Development Program, has done since 2011, then Slovenia goes up to the tenth place, between Switzerland and Finland. At the opposite end of this spectrum is the poorest post-socialist country, Tajikistan, with a per capita GDP of merely USD 2,100 and an HDI of 0.607, is not even among the top hundred countries listed. To show these countries from this perspective compared to the whole world, let us mention extreme global HDIs: the list begins with Norway and Australia with indexes of 0.943 and 0.929 respectively and ends with the Congo and Zimbabwe with very low HDIs, 0.239 and 0.140 respectively.

Let's explain that UNDP, starting from 2011, changed its methodology for HDI calculation. These days, it is slightly more complicated, but probably more adequate as a consequence. Earlier on, a relatively simple composite coefficient was in use, whose final value was determined in equal measure (one third each) by per capita GDP (at PPP), by the education index measured with literacy ability and gross enrollment rate and by population health assessed with life expectancy index. In theory, the maximum of this measure equals to one. It is also the case of the present method, which would happen if three conditions were simultaneously met:

(1) Full enrollment rate and no illiteracy.
(2) Average life expectancy of 83.4 years, which is an extreme level recorded in a data series for the years 1980–2011.
(3) A per capita GDP of USD 107,721, also at the highest level for the years 1980–2011.

At present, HDI is still a resultant of three partial coefficients but it is calculated as a geometric average (or a cube root of their product), rather than as their arithmetic average.

In addition, the coefficient calculated this way is adjusted for inequality in income distribution, which gives IHDI (inequality-adjusted Human Development Index). In the event of a perfect equality, IHDI would be identical to HDI. In reality, those indexes deviate from each other the more the bigger the inequality in income is. Consequently, while in the egalitarian Sweden HDI is 0.904, and IHDI, taking account of distribution ratios, is 0.851, in South Korea, which is only slightly less developed in general, relevant indexes are 0.897 and 0.749. While in Poland HDI has increased to 0.813, like it has in Chile, where it amounts to 0.805, IHDIs in these countries are 0.734 and 0.652 respectively, as the disproportions in income distribution are greater in Chile than they are in Poland. Human capital indexes in terms of HDI are similar but, all in all, considering income relations, living quality is better in Sweden than in Korea and people have it better in Poland than in Chile.

Incidentally, it is a food for thought that on the African continent it was Libya that could boast the highest HDI (0.755 in 2010), one of the countries where the "Arab Spring" rebellion unfolded the most dramatically. Let us hope that this index will not fall as a consequence of the political and economic transformations taking place. This incident, not isolated anyway, demonstrates clearly that even though HDI and IHDI are definitely better metrics for evaluating the level of social and economic advancement level than per capita GDP is, it is still an imperfect indicator that ignores a number of factors that co-determine the quality of life and human satisfaction with it. Or lack thereof.

Considering the smaller gap between highly developed countries and economies undergoing a post-socialist political transformation, especially the European ones, the latter have greater chances for emancipation than countries from other parts of the world that are still lagging behind. Economies integrating with highly developed countries as part of the European Union can be especially hopeful. Together with Croatia, since mid-2013 there are eleven countries like that but, over time, there will be more of them. Leaving aside post-Soviet republics, whose accession remains an open question, all post-socialist European countries should join the European Union. Such is the logic of temporal and spatial coexistence of historical processes taking place on the European continent: regional transnational integration and post-socialist systemic transition.

Full integration, manifesting itself, most of all, in an institutional convergence, is a good way to catch up and reduce differences in development. Though the integration makes this process faster, this may take a long while, even up to several generations. That is how long it took to level the differences between the rich north and the less affluent south of the United States, which took a century and a half since the end of the Civil War; meanwhile the process of bridging the gap between the south and north of Italy continues to this date. This is why Balkan economies, which managed to join the EU in the first decade of the twenty-first century, will emancipate faster than those that will not be accepted into this bloc until the third decade.

This has specific implications for the processes involved in integration, which can already be viewed as an instrument of emancipation in other world regions, from Latin America and the Caribbean to Sub-Saharan Africa, North Africa, and Middle East, to South Asia and South-East Asia. The more economies become regionally integrated the easier it will be for them to improve competitiveness, the faster growth rate they will reach and the easier it will be for them to bear the costs of development. Their emancipation, with a society treated as subject rather than object, will be mostly expressed in a better quality of market institutions so a better regulation of the economy, from the perspective of growth dynamics. Thus defined emancipation process will result in an ever-growing general development level, a higher living standard and a greater social satisfaction.

Undoubtedly, for emancipating countries these processes must continue for many, many years to come while following on the path of fast economic growth. In this case, there will be no development and progress without a significant increase in output. What does "fast growth" mean? It is not an absolute but rather a relative term. "Fast" should be defined as emancipating economies growing twice, three times higher than rich countries that enjoy a GDP per capita of over USD 30,000. This means a growth dynamics of almost the double of the world average. In terms of quality, fast growth is a rate which provides economies at a medium level of development with a chance to achieve the present level of highly developed countries over the span of one or two generations and, in a similar time horizon, underdeveloped countries with a chance to achieve the level now typical of medium level countries.

Let us emphasize the power of the compound interest here. To double the income level in just one decade, an average annual growth of 7.2 percent is enough. To double the output level in twenty years, you need to maintain an average of 3.5 percent rate. In the former case, after half a century the income is 32 times higher, in the latter it is also higher, by an impressive 460 percent. Let me stress, right away, that, in the economic practice, the dynamic of the former kind is impossible in such a long period on a macro-scale, while a fivefold increase of output in five decades under very favorable circumstances should not be ruled out. Certainly, this observation does not hold good for the world as a whole as maintaining such a high growth rate for the whole fifty years is neither possible, nor desirable. There are emancipating countries that are able to double their income and, at the same time, consumption, which is neither automatic nor the same, in just one decade, for example, Taiwan in the past and Vietnam recently.

Chapter 7

Socialism, Capitalism, or Chinism?

The dispute over the essence of the Chinese system is not new, at least beyond the borders of China itself as over there it's been consistently, for three generations already, declared that we're dealing with socialism. At most, this word would be accompanied by adjectives, which changed over the years, or synthetic descriptions would be added. When I was in China for the first time, in 1989, I had no doubt that it was a socialist state, though that socialism was different from the one I knew better from Central and Eastern European, CEE countries and the Soviet Union. When I visit China these days, I do sometimes have doubts if it's still socialism, and, at the same time, I have no certainty that it is already capitalism.

So what are we dealing with? Is it simply a period of transition from one formation to another, in this case from socialism to capitalism, or is it a different system, which deserves a name in its own right? A quarter century ago we used to joke in CEE countries that while the erstwhile transition from capitalism to socialism was possible, at least up to a certain point, a transformation in the opposite direction—from socialism to capitalism—is impossible, just as it's possible to turn a stallion into a gelded horse, but the reverse cannot be done. However, it certainly proved doable, at least in the post-socialist economies, which became part of the EU.[1] China, though, is following its own path. Where has it brought the country, where is it leading to?

ECONOMY—SOCIETY—STATE

The literature on capitalism and socialism is enormous. There is no need to discuss it here, though it's worth pointing out that throughout the entire time those systems functioned and confronted each other in practice, for most of the twenty-first century, different meaning was attributed to those same terms, especially in intellectual, scientific, ideological and political debates. Such confusion in definitions and the lack of methodological discipline continue today. No wonder then that there has never even been a consensus in theoretical discussion as to what capitalism is, and especially as to what socialism is. For definitions of capitalism, we would usually content ourselves with defining it as a socioeconomic system based on private capital aspiring to maximize its profits (or, in other words, on predominance of private means of production) and free market exchange, whereas things were—and still are—more complicated with socialism.

The problem becomes muddled for many reasons, major one being the confusion resulting from watching the same matter from different perspectives or different matters from the same perspective. So for a political scientist, of key importance are the observations and interpretations of the ways power is gained and wielded, and of the functioning of the state and its institutions, whereas, for a sociologist, the heart of the matter is the society and the mechanisms governing interactions of its component population groups. An economist, in turn, focuses mostly on observing and analyzing the recurring economic phenomena and processes and on explaining them, and if we go further—to normative (prescriptive) economics—on formulating recommendations for economic policy and growth strategy. Meanwhile, all three use the same terms: capitalism and socialism, though they do not mean the same. These words correspond, first and foremost, to an economic regime, but they also involve obvious references to society and culture as well as to state and law. In fact, not only the economy can be capitalist or socialist, so can be the society and the state.

Of key importance is the fact that we once had real socialism, or the one functioning in practice—from the Soviet Union to China, from Poland to Yugoslavia, from Vietnam to Cuba, from Cambodia to Ethiopia. Let us emphasize right away that even in those countries it differed, sometimes quite significantly. Furthermore, it differed not only in space—say between Mongolia and Hungary or Albania and Czechoslovakia—but also in time, say between Poland of the first half of 1950s and the second half of 1980s. Nevertheless, we had the same theoretical socialism, referred to by some—especially in the Soviet Union—as the scientific socialism. This was socialism that was meant to be, that should have been there but somehow was always in short supply.

By the way, speaking of real socialism, it will not be amiss to digress that it's the same with real capitalism. The one existing in practice, entangled in crises, economic disasters and political manipulations, scandals over negligence and dishonesty, the insurmountable distance between the declared goals and the practical targets, differs so much from the one described in textbooks, or—if you will—the apology of this regime is at such great variance with the reality, that we need an innovative theory of contemporary capitalism (Heilbroner and Milberg 1995; Ormerod 1997; Stiglitz 2007; Csaba 2009; Kolodko 2011a; Phelps 2013; Galbraith 2014; Tirole 2017), which would eliminate the chasm between what takes place in the real world and what is written about it in books. Hence, what I call the new pragmatism (Kolodko 2014a; Bałtowski 2017; Galbraith 2018).

After all, reality differed from the theoretic perspective, and sometimes so much so that subsequent editions of the same academic works, being unable to ignore reality, were increasingly unlike the earlier editions. It will suffice to compare textbooks of *Political Economy of Socialism* by European authors published during one generation—in the 1950s and 1970s. Oddly and importantly enough, they differed between one another much more in Poland and Hungary than in Bulgaria and East Germany, GDR. The reason is, most of all, that due to various reforms that loosened the straitjacket of nationalized and centralized economy, the face of real socialism was significantly changing in the former two countries (also in Yugoslavia, which followed a different, but still socialist path) and, coupled with those changes, its reflection in political narrative and scientific descriptions evolved as well. In countries that were less susceptible to reforms, the most orthodox ones being the Maoist Albania, incidentally the poorest country in Europe, and Romania, textbooks could be republished without major changes.

Therefore, there are different countries—with their state, society, culture and economy—that are referred to as socialist. Let's pass over, on the one hand, the fact that the Nazi Germany once was created by a party which, though fascist in nature, had the word "socialist" in its name, embellished with the addition of "national." On the other hand, socialism is associated by some with something positive, namely with the social market economy of Scandinavian countries—Denmark, Finland, Norway and Sweden. In this context, to distinguish them from the CEE economies and from the Soviet Union, in western literature, more often that of political sciences than the economic one, the latter group is referred to as communist states and economies. This further complicates the deliberations, as in this case we would have at the same time three socioeconomic regimes: capitalism (e.g., Italy), socialism (e.g., Sweden) and communism (e.g., the former Czechoslovakia).

This is not a convincing perspective, for a number of reasons. Well, communism also has many interpretations—from the specter haunting Europe according to Marx and Engels, outlined 170 years ago in the *Communist Manifesto* (Marx and Engels 2011) to the so-called war communism in Russia a hundred years ago, to the utopian regime of abundance of goods and services and social justice, expected to supersede socialism one day. Throughout all the years of the Cold War, which was, after all, mostly waged on the ideological and political front, and thus it embroiled in its battles social sciences including economics and sociology, the reality east of the Elbe river was called "communism" in the West, though in the East the term "socialism" was predominant. So the two terms were used to describe the same environment.

Curiously enough, in most CEE countries hardly anyone called the socio-economic reality of 1945–1989 "communism," as the same was only to dawn one day (Walicki 1995), whereas since 1990 the term "communism" has been used quite universally with reference to the socialist era of those years and "post-communism" for the contemporary period, after 1989. I myself had dilemmas about that but they mostly stemmed from addressing some of my works to the western public. Hence the title of one of my book contained the word "post-socialist" (Kolodko 2000a), and that of another, "post-communist" (Kolodko 2000b), though in both cases it's about the same period following the real socialist era. Interestingly, a decade earlier, János Kornai (Kornai 1992) following his lecture at Harvard, put both these words in the title of one book: *The Socialist System: The Political Economy of Communism.*

Even though science, with its rigor and methodological and substantive clarity, should be the one to define the categories we use and interpret, and explain the phenomena and problems we study, and then impose the correct terminology on mass discussions, frequently the opposite is true. While newspapers should more often use the language of academic circles, it is academia that borrows the language of newspapers. Certain terms, sometimes uncritically and without much thought, diffuse from the popular parlance into the scientific discourse and become widespread (Wheen 2004). That was the case of the term "post-socialist" or "post-communist." The attendant confusion lead to a situation where in 1990s all of the republics of the former Soviet Union were treated as "post-socialist" even those with a much lower share of private sector than in Polish economy in the 1980s, which accounted back then for no less than 20 percent of the GDP, and obviously nobody would refer to it as post-socialist. It's nonsense, when in 2018 we hear that Poland or Hungary—countries with relatively free markets and liberalized economies three decades ago—were communist in 1988, and Turkmenistan, having a lower share of private sector now than Poland and Hungary had back then, is a capitalist country. Unless we go on to add that it is a post-Soviet state capitalism, a unique new category on the taxonomic map of economic systems (type 1001, with post-Soviet characteristics).

In the meantime, nearly all post-socialist countries, including China, which itself still does not admit to be one—have been crammed into another category, mindlessly overused both by political commentators and in research papers: that of "emerging" markets. So here we are emerging—in Croatia and Vietnam, in Russia and China, in Kazakhstan and Serbia, in Armenia and Slovenia. So far only Poland has emerged, since it

> will no longer be ranked by FTSE Russell as an Emerging Market (FTSE Emerging All Cap), but as a Developed Market (FTSE Developed All Cap Ex-US). This will place the country together with 24 other nations including Germany, France, Japan and Australia. Poland is the first Central and Eastern European economy to be upgraded to Developed Market status. (Emerging Europe 2017)

Thus, emerging market is no longer socialism with its lack of free market mechanism, but it's not yet capitalism with its mature market. When approaching the issue this way, the socialism–capitalism antinomy loses its validity because what matters is whether the market works or not. Instead, the discussion shifts from the plane laden with heavy ideological and political baggage into the plane of more practically oriented disputes. Hence there is less emotion and political intransigence in the debate as to whether not only in the present-day China, but also in countries such as Uzbekistan or Azerbaijan, we are dealing with a reformed planned economy or a market economy, on the one hand, or, on the other hand, is this still a state economy or already a private one.

That's why further on I pass over those taxonomically important dilemmas and, not to complicate things even more, I will only make a side observation that one of US presidential candidates in 2016, Bernie Sanders, calls himself a socialist, while Emmanuel Macron, elected president of France in 2017, used to be the minister of economy in the government of the socialist president, François Hollande. None of them, with their political views, would have been accepted into the parties that held power in CEE until 1989, or into the so-called Communist Party of China at present. I say "so-called" because what kind of communist party is it if it openly accepts or even endorses the attributes typical of capitalist economy, such as private capital's pursuit of profit, high unemployment rate, major areas of social exclusion and huge income inequalities, much higher than in many capitalist countries.[2]

This by no means exhausts the confusion over the application of the terms "socialism" and "socialist," as there once was the idea of utopian socialism, spawned, among others, by the French Henri de Saint-Simons (1760–1825) and Charles Fourier (1772–1837), and the attempts to implement it, for example, by the same Fourier in the *La Reunion* colony in Texas or by the Welsh Robert Owen (1771–1858) first in New Lanark in Scotland, and then also in the United States. It is fitting to add that there is no shortage of utopian socialists also these days, though, due to the past disgrace of the real socialism, and the current poor social resonance of the leftist program, they get almost no traction. This is shown by the miserable results of the recent elections in European countries, where parties with a socialist orientation—also Labor and Social Democratic—used to do in the past quite well.

Finally yet importantly, presently we have hybrid and poorly performing, or even crisis-prone systems, which are called socialism by their detractors, authors and proponents alike. I'm not talking here about the caricature of socialism as practiced by former president of Zimbabwe, Robert Mugabe, who, in the beginning of this century, declared his willingness to introduce centrally controlled economy, while in fact his policy allowed extremely corrupt state capitalism to boom; rather than that I mean the more noteworthy Latin American experiments, such as *socialismo del siglo XXI* of Hugo Chávez and his successor as the president of Venezuela, Nicolás Maduro, or *socialismo del siglo XXI* in Bolivia, Ecuador and Nicaragua.

These are mixed systems, pervaded with elements of a policy associated by some with socialism, but in essence it is a socially oriented capitalist economy, which functions in less economically developed countries. José Mujica, once a Tupamaros guerilla, later (2010–2015) leftist president of Uruguay, says that

> There's a fundamental problem there—you can't make socialism by decree. We on the left have the tendency of falling in love with whatever it is we dream about, and then we confuse it with reality. (Anderson 2017, 42)

Maduro himself, seeing how wretched the results of the Venezuelan version of *socialismo del siglo XXI* are, concludes:

> Speaking about the working class, Marx said that time was needed to change history. Marx was right. It's a long struggle. (Anderson 2017, 53)

It takes longer than there is a time for it.

While discussing the choice between alternative: capitalism or socialism with respect to the poor (GDP per capita of USD 7,200 according to purchasing power parity, PPP) and small (population of 11 million) Bolivia is certainly engaging, with respect to China, quickly getting richer (GDP per capita of USD 15,400 according to PPP) and populous (1.380 million citizens), it is fascinating. Bolivia will not affect the fate of mankind. There is no way China won't affect it (Halper 2010; Kissinger 2011, 2014; Shambaugh 2016; Kolodko 2017a).

SOCIALISM AND THE SHORTAGE ECONOMY

In a textbook socialism, effective central planning ensured economic equilibrium, however in the real one, as experienced by hundreds of millions of people, this equilibrium was by no means there. In fact, it was an economy of systemic shortages; there was a permanent surplus of the flow of demand over the flow of supply, with all of its negative consequences. This applied both to the sphere of production (enterprise sector), where shortages disrupted the continuity of production, contributing to efficiency being lower than in the alternative scenario of equilibrium (Kornai 1971), and to the sphere of consumption (household sector), which took an especially heavy toll on the population. The scale of shortages was varied and temporally and spatially diverse. These were less acute in countries that did not experiment with even partial price liberalization, and, at the same time, had rigorous wage and price control in place, in Czechoslovakia and GDR, and the most severe as a result of inconsistent reforms in Poland in the late 1980s (Kolodko 2000a).

Shortages occurred in all socialist countries, that is in economies based on predominance and sometimes even omnipotence of state ownership, central planning of the volume and structure of production, and the wage and price control. The supply of goods, both products and services, was insufficient from the perspective of the requirement to balance the demand. Of course, the scale and intensity of shortages and their changes varied for respective goods.

The word "shortage" was, in principle, foreign to economics textbooks in real socialism countries until Kornai (Kornai 1980) gave it a status of one of the fundamental categories of centrally planned socialist economy. Furthermore, he pointed to the inextricable link between those two economic categories—socialism and shortage. If there is socialism, there are shortages. If there are shortages, there is socialism.[3]

Though in no economy of the CEE region, let alone in the Soviet Union, insisting on heavy industry and engaging in high armament expenditure, shortages were successfully eradicated, periodically there were times where the supply of consumer goods was relatively suitable and close to equilibrium. This was not full-fledged consumer's market that would ensure sovereignty of the same, but this was not yet a drastic economy of shortages; this was a producer's market, which, with a relatively limited supply offered, it dictated to the consumer how to behave and what to buy.

The situation of full, ideal market equilibrium occurs—only theoretically—at market-clearing prices; all supply (Ψ) is sold, all demand (Π) is satisfied:

$$\Pi_1 = \Psi \tag{1}$$

Producer's market is a situation of a slight surplus of the flow of demand over the flow of supply, at times resulting in inconveniences such as forced substitution (for example buying a couch with burgundy upholstery, not with the desired beige, or warm rather than cold beer), wandering from one store to another in search of the wanted item, which will be found in the end, or buying a lower quality product. Or:

$$\Pi_2 > \Psi_2 \tag{2}$$

Consumer's market means consumer's advantage over the producer, supplier and seller. One can pick and choose, be fussy or even bargain before the purchase is concluded. This is a situation where we are not yet dealing with structurally excessive stocks and wastage of goods because they get sold in the end:

$$\Pi_3 < \Psi_3 \tag{3}$$

When the excess of demand over supply is high and structural, meaning a permanent inability to buy the desired goods and when the extent to which buyers' time is wasted can no longer be tolerated, we are dealing with an economy of shortages:

$$\Pi_4 > \Psi_4 \tag{4}$$

And the other way round; when all the goods supplied to the market can no longer be sold—despite various marketing efforts and huge advertising expenses—and part of them goes to waste, we are dealing with an economy of surpluses:

$$\Pi_5 < \Psi_5 \tag{5}$$

These variants can be schematically illustrated in figure 7.1.

Crossing the fluid boundary from the producer's market to shortages was much easier than the returning process. It was also difficult to cross from the producer's market to relative balance. In Hungary, the latter, with the elements of the consumer's market, was successfully achieved due to pro-market reforms after 1968, and in Poland in the early 1970s, incidentally, thanks to a great degree to the loans quite eagerly granted by the capitalist West. Therefore, consumer market's symptoms were strengthened at the cost of generating an external imbalance resulting in a growing foreign debt until it became impossible to service it in the coming years.

By the very essence of real socialism, which dogmatically took care to ensure that prices should not be too high and intentionally guarantee access to products and services to all population groups, pricing reforms could not have been effective. They partly consisted in the state raising prices to a level that balances demand with supply, and partly in deregulating prices and

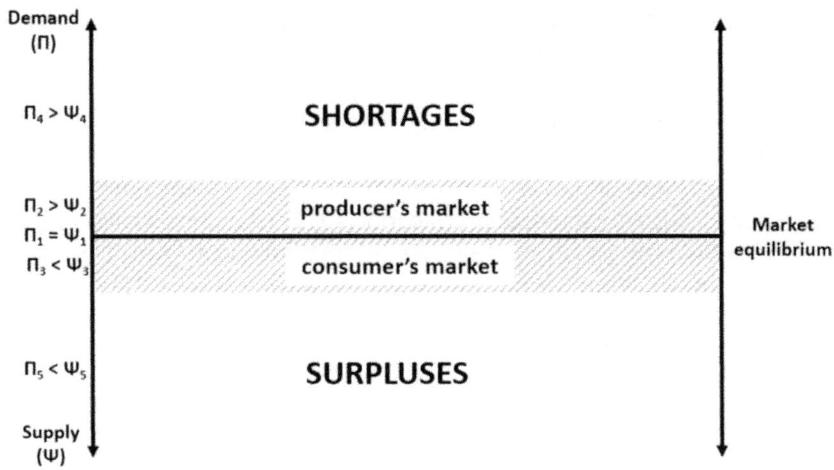

Figure 7.1 Producer's Market and Shortages versus Consumer's Market and Surpluses.
Source: Author's own.

allowing them to be driven by free market mechanism. When the unavoidable price increase was accompanied with moves to partly compensate the increased living costs, it was called "price and income reforms." This type of policy, which mainly dealt with the sphere of consumption as in the production sector the state's pricing rigor was much stricter, was able to temporarily improve the situation on the quasi-market. It reduced the symptoms in the form of shortages, without eliminating the causes of this systemic disease (Kolodko 1986; Nuti 1986).

Worse yet, in economies gradually moving away from the orthodox socialism model characterized by a high degree of decision-making centralization and strict bureaucratic price control[4]—a process that was in place, with varying intensity, already from 1956, especially in Poland and Hungary, less so in Bulgaria and Czechoslovakia—the tentative reformatory measures in the form of partial price deregulation led to price increases rather than to the elimination of shortages. Kornai wrote:

> There is a casual relationship in one direction: the shortage strengthens the tendency towards (upward) price drift. But there is no casual relationship in the opposite direction [. . .]. A constant price level, a fall in price, and a rise in price are equally compatible with the permanent maintenance of the normal intensity of shortage. Norms of shortage are not eternal, but no price change, in either direction can on its own alter them in the long run. (Kornai 1980, 498)

In addition to the repressed inflation, typical of state price control,[5] open inflation emerged, as well. The former resulted in households accumulating forced money savings, and the latter in price inflation, as it was a classic increase of the general price level.

Meanwhile, in socialism that underwent reforms, both those ailments occurred at the same time; something unknown to free market economy, something unheard-of in capitalism. For this dual inflation syndrome, partially open, partially repressed, I coined the name shortageflation (Kolodko 1986), per analogy to stagflation (Haberler 1977): the coexistence of stagnation, that is, slow production growth and the attendant growth of unemployment and inflation, which are known from capitalism. The scope of stagflation is conventionally measured as the sum total of unemployment (U) and price inflation (CPI) rates:

$$SF = U + CPI \tag{6}$$

whereas the severity of shortageflation is expressed by the sum total of shortages (SH) and price inflation (CPI):

$$SHF = SH + CPI \tag{7}$$

Comparing the rates of stagflation, SF, and shortageflation, SHF, controversial as it is, makes great sense (Kolodko, McMahon 1987). In the former case, it's about choosing between the inflation rate and the unemployment rate, which dilemma is described by the Phillips curve (Fisher 1973), while in the latter, between the rate of price inflation and the rate of suppressed inflation resulting in shortages, which is described by the shortageflation curve.

Without delving here into the methodologically complex issue of measuring shortages, it is reasonable to confront those two processes—as these are not so much situations as processes happening over time—because they

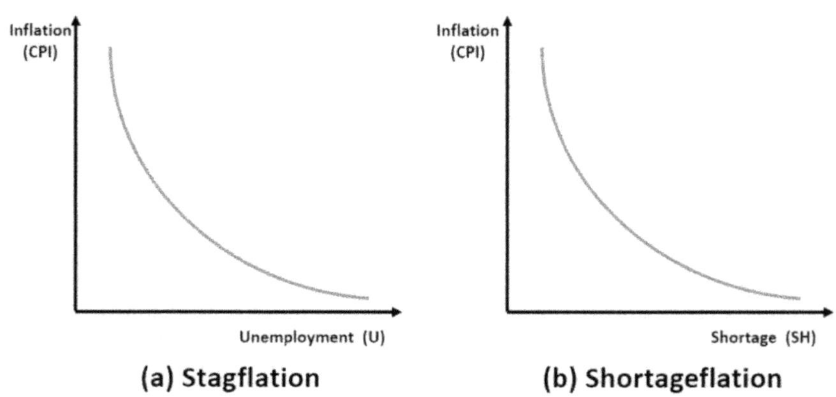

Figure 7.2 Stagflation and Shortageflation. *Source*: Author's own.

show the systemic shortcomings of capitalism and socialism. Kornai refers to that in his book entitled *Dynamism, Rivalry, and the Surplus Economy. Two Essays on the Nature of Capitalism* (Kornai 2014), when favoring capitalism as the lesser of two evils, because a system which, by its very essence, involves permanent overproduction with the attendant unemployment, is far from ideal. This is the real capitalism, which, in practice, cannot find the ideal that exists in theory, that is, full employment. In real capitalism, it reaches at most the so-called natural rate of unemployment.

Protesting against queues and high prices, or shortageflation, and suggesting a transition to a free market economy, which quickly turned out to be a capitalist economy, many people, I guess the majority in socialist countries, including many economists,[6] did not realize that they were in favor of substituting structural unemployment for structural shortages. What happened is that post-socialist countries, dreaming of a balanced economy, one free of inflation and unfamiliar with shortages—a bit like Alice in Wonderland going through the looking glass—moved from the right-hand side of the diagram, from the disagreeable alternative between open (price) inflation and suppressed inflation (shortages), to the left-hand side, to differently disagreeable alternative between price inflation and unemployment.

There is no way to stop at the intersection of the X and Y axes—without inflation, without shortages and without unemployment. So Kornai is right in saying that capitalism is the better of two evils, being a system which, admittedly, does not guarantee dynamic equilibrium as it is characterized by permanent surpluses and underuse of manufacturing capacity, and, most of all, by unemployment, but, in turn, ensures a higher economic efficiency than

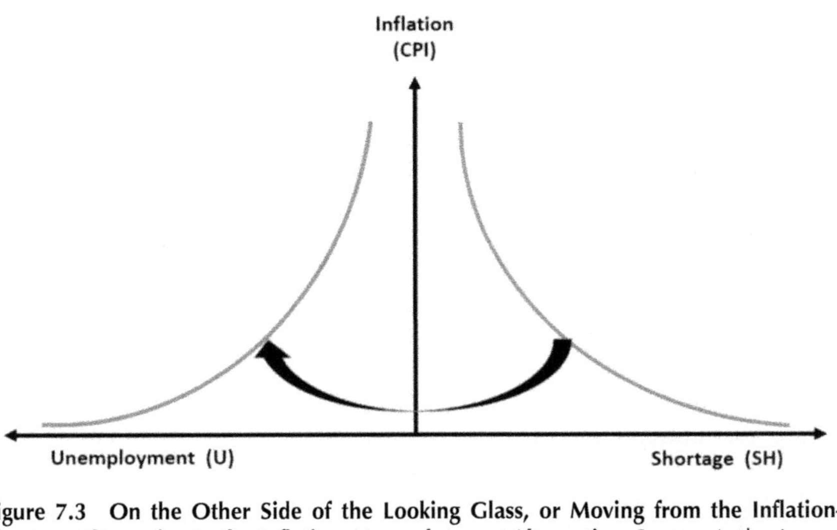

Figure 7.3 On the Other Side of the Looking Glass, or Moving from the Inflation–Shortage Alternative to the Inflation–Unemployment Alternative. *Source*: Author's own.

shortage-plagued socialism, and, thus, a better long-term economic development and higher standard of living for the population.

When I look for a one-word answer to the question about the causes of the fall of real socialism, shortageflation is precisely that word. This syndrome was eating away, like cancer, this already not-too-healthy body of nationalized, overly centralized and bureaucratized socialist economy, in the end turning the lack of social acceptance for this regime into its utter renouncement. Shortageflation would so strongly erode the efficiency of the enterprise sector and reduce the households' satisfaction with the volume of consumption, even though the same was growing in line with the overall economic growth, that not only did the societies of those countries stop to support the system; their elites abandoned their attempts to reform it as well. The futile efforts to streamline the socialist system were replaced by departure from it, or a system transformation.

Kornai provides an accurate diagnosis of the causes of shortages in socialism, demonstrating that they have their source in the phenomenon of soft budget constraints (Kornai 1980, 1986, 1990). Price manipulations—more often bureaucratic than liberal ones—were of little avail if they were not accompanied by the systemic hardening of budget constraints, adjusting the financial flows going into enterprises and households to the economy's supply capacity. In the framework of state ownership of means of production, supply of money was adjusted to demand for money, and the former was generated to the extent that could not be offset by the supply of goods. If the state ownership is a fundamental and, according to orthodox views, inalienable characteristic of the socialist economy, then shortages, too, become its intrinsic feature.

In our day and age, there is basically a consensus that in the case of real socialism it was the state ownership of means of production that caused the soft budget constraints, and these, in turn, caused inflation—more or less repressed or more or less open, depending on time and place, so depending on the systemic and political context. That was the reality, but did it have to be inevitably so? While Kornai claims it did, Nuti has his doubts. He believes that, theoretically speaking, market-clearing equilibrium prices could have occurred in socialism without the need to introduce the regime of hard budget constraints (Nuti 2018). And if it wasn't successfully achieved? Then it resulted from the deficiency of the economic policy rather than from the essence of the system.

In the Soviet Union and in socialist economies of Central and Eastern Europe the attempts were made but failed. Meanwhile, in China—as well as in Vietnam and in the very poorly developed Cambodia and Laos—it worked. So isn't Kornai wrong because market-clearing equilibrium prices are possible also in socialism? Where it works, does it happen with hard or soft budget constraints in place? What follows from the evolution of the Chinese economic system? Is it socialism with a balanced market, or, more accurately, a consumer's market, since the flow of supply exceeds the flow of demand, or is it capitalism, with a market characterized by overproduction and unemployment,[7] with still partly soft budget constraints?

SOCIALISM WITH CHINESE CHARACTERISTICS OR CORRUPTED CRONY CAPITALISM?

The case of China, the country accounting for nearly a fifth of global output, at PPP, is iconoclastic for at least two reasons. First, if this is socialism,[8] then eliminating shortages in its framework has proved possible, without changing the system. Second, if this is capitalism, then it can exist and, in economic terms, virtually thrive without democracy.

These days, in China one can buy both a bowl of rice and the latest Ferrari model; it's enough to have money or the purchasing power, which is balanced on the market by the supply. Furthermore, China successfully got out of the economy of shortages without stepping into the shortageflation, which devastated the economy of European socialist countries so much, even though, yet, it has not managed to fully harden budget constraints. This is best evidenced by the mounting debt of the enterprise sector, fluctuating around 170 percent of GDP. Most of this debt is amounts payable by state-owned enterprises, SOEs (or companies with a majority state shareholding). So the case of China shows that it is possible to break free from the shortage syndrome by creating a liberalized price system and elastic price policy while maintaining a significant SOE sector. Let's add that in that perspective, SOEs function amid hardened, though still not hard budget constraints. Like between white and black, there is a whole palette of colors and shades between soft and hard budget constraints.

Free market economy is the necessary but not sufficient condition for democracy. Political correctness also calls for preaching the opposite view that democracy is an inalienable attribute of free market economy and that, by its essence, it favors efficiency and, consequently, the economic growth, though, in itself, neither the market eliminates dishonesty, nor democracy precludes stupidity. Leaving political correctness aside, as it does not apply in science, which looks for truth, those propositions have to be at least brought into question, if not dismissed outright. Actually, economic growth is promoted by right decisions taken both at the microeconomic scale, managing enterprises where nobody is concerned with democracy, and at the macro scale, running the economic policy, which, in the contemporary Western-style capitalism, incessantly is entangled in democratic disputes. It's not enough to be right (and those rulings because of democratic elections often are not), one also needs to have majority.

Experience shows that democracy in itself by no means guarantees that and often it virtually complicates the process of taking the right decisions. It's no accident that the financial crisis of the turn of the first and second decade of the twenty-first century was caused by the country where liberal democracy reigns supreme—the United States. It doesn't follow from this that democracy should not be cherished; it should be, as it is a value in itself, even when it makes it more difficult to take rational economic decisions. It doesn't follow, either, that lack of democracy favors economic growth. It can happen but it doesn't have to. And these days it happens rarely.

It is hard to quote other examples than Singapore (not a democracy until recently) and still a few relatively successful Middle Eastern states such as United Arab Emirates, Qatar, Oman or Kuwait, where market is functioning pretty smoothly without democracy, and, which must be emphasized, this happens with a clearly dominant role of the state sector. However, the fact that it has been this way does not mean that it will continue also in the future. The Arab Spring from the beginning of this decade has failed, but in some geopolitical zones there are even more than four seasons.

In China, even though its political system is not democratic as it is actually authoritarian, good things do happen; for over a generation the country has enjoyed an economic growth that, every decade, more than doubles the value of production and consumption. In terms of economic growth, the Middle Country is the greatest success story in the history of mankind. Something like that has never, at such a scale, happened in the past, and never will so much happen for so many in the future. The case of China confirms that of crucial importance to the dynamic, long-term social and economic development is the proper synergy between market and state, a creative harmony of the market spontaneity and state regulation. In addition, what "proper synergy" means depends on the context. There is no single universal rule; each country has to work out their own synergy, taking account of the cultural, historical, geopolitical and environmental context (Kolodko 2014a).

Using the ownership relations as the decisive criterion, Kornai believes that we have had capitalism in China since dozen years or so. According to the data provided by the Organization for Economic Co-operation and Development, private sector generated a greater part of the national income as early as in the end of previous century, in 1998.

If such dynamics of structural ownership changes were to be maintained, at present we would have an overwhelmingly greater part of assets, and consequently, also production, employment and budget revenues related to the private sector. However, it's not the case as the pace of private sector expansion was made to slow down in the last decade or so. In a way, it's

Table 7.1 Proportions of Private and State Sectors in China (percent of value added, by form of ownership)

	1998	*1999*	*2000*	*2001*	*2002*	*2003*	*Change*
Non-farm business sector							
Private sector	43.0	45.3	47.7	51.8	54.6	57.1	+14.1
Public sector	57.0	54.7	52.3	48.2	45.4	42.9	-14.1
Of which: State-controlled	40.5	40.1	39.6	37.1	35.2	34.1	-6.4
Collectively controlled	16.5	14.7	12.7	11.2	10.1	8.8	-7.7
Business sector							
Private sector	53.5	54.9	56.3	59.4	61.5	63.3	+9.8
Public sector	46.5	45.1	43.7	40.6	38.5	36.7	-9.8
Of which: State-controlled	33.1	33.0	33.1	31.2	29.9	29.2	-3.9
Collectively controlled	13.4	12.1	10.6	9.4	8.6	7.5	-5.9
Economy-wide							
Private sector	50.4	51.5	52.8	55.5	57.4	59.2	+8.8
Public sector	49.6	48.5	47.2	44.5	42.6	40.8	-8.8
Of which: State-controlled	36.9	37.1	37.3	35.7	34.6	33.7	-3.2
Collectively controlled	12.7	11.3	10.0	8.8	8.0	7.1	-5.6

Source: Kornai 2008, 149 (after OECD 2005).

natural as the fewer assets there are left to denationalize, the slower the private sector is growing. That's one aspect, and the other one is that the policy of the Communist Party of China deliberately limited the scale of privatizing state assets, being of the opinion that keeping them in the state's possession or at least under its control will better serve the state's strategic goals which, according to the party, boil down to developing and strengthening socialism rather than dismantling it.

One can estimate that private sector's share is presently not much higher than it was a dozen years ago; maybe it fluctuates over two-thirds of GDP. The official sources say that private business generates over 60 percent of the Chinese GDP and provides more than 80 percent jobs. Fragmentary data of the National Bureau of Statistics inform that in the first half of 2017 private sector investments grew by 7.2 percent compared to the first half of previous year, representing 60.7 percent of total expenditure. At the same time, the considerable importance of the state sector is emphasized by the Chinese authorities. The value of SOE assets exceeds 150 trillion RMB (USD 23.1 trillion), which is the equivalent of Chinese GDP for two years (according to the current market exchange rate), and SOE investments in research and development account for 25 percent of total R&D expenditure (China Daily

2017a). China Public Private Partnerships Center, promoting the practical usefulness of public private partnership, PPP, reports that in 2017 over 13,500 PPP projects worth 16.3 trillion RMB (USD 2.5 trillion) were implemented.

There are no grounds to question those data, especially because we do not have any better. It must be emphasized, though, that because of the Chinese the taxonomy of forms of business ownership has become even more complicated. The solution to the dilemma of how to define state- and private-owned is often a matter of convention. The matter is greatly complicated here as in many cases it's hard to judge clearly: are we dealing with private or state ownership? That's because even in this area there's a spectrum of in-between and mixed forms. The differences between the state-owned and the private are not clear-cut, the distinguishing features of those categories are being blurred, and the boundaries are becoming fluid. In this context, a special focus is placed not only on the traditional perspective on ownership forms, but also on changes in the sphere of management and in state corporate governance. It is possible that actual corporate governance over somebody's formally private ownership is exercised by the state, and it cannot be ruled out that a state-owned enterprise (more often one with mixed ownership) is managed by a private company, which mostly takes care of its own earnings rather than of the state's income and of furthering its other purposes such as employment, environmental protection or contribution to social cohesion.

It's symptomatic that when I was looking for current data necessary for relevant analysis, one of the Chinese economists told me: "As the public and private sectors are gradually mixed together, China no longer emphasizes the ownership in most industries and stopped publishing related statistic information. Therefore, it's not easy to calculate their share of GDP. Many researches use enterprise number, fixed-asset investment, taxes, main business income, and total assets of industrial enterprises in public/private sectors."

The multitude of forms of ownership in China—including the hybrid ones which some authors qualify as private while others prefer to see them in the group of SOEs—is illustrated by the data demonstrating the size of employment and its changes in the years 1978–2016 in different types of enterprises. Nowadays, the Chinese government's statistical administration distinguishes ten types of ownership:

1) state-owned units
2) collective-owned units
3) cooperative units
4) joint ownership units
5) limited liability corporations
6) shareholding corporations ltd.
7) private enterprises

8) units with funds from Hong Kong, Macao and Taiwan
9) foreign funded units
10) self-employed individuals.

Without thorough analyses and certain compromises on definition, in some cases it is impossible to explicitly decide if it is private property, or state-owned one. Such oversimplified alternative is no longer reasonable.

It's worth adding that in that time—from the breakthrough reforms launched in 1978 by Deng Xiaoping (Vogel 2013)—a major part of China's economic growth resulted from increased productivity of nonagricultural sectors of the economy. However, such enormous economic success would not have been possible if it weren't for the substantial changes in agriculture, where work efficiency also increased significantly, but for much smaller scale than in industry. Both of those processes were accompanied by the greatest migration in history, during which hundreds of millions of peasants left the countryside and moved to the city. Currently, urban population already represents the majority of Chinese population, 58 percent. Nevertheless, what mattered even more to the economic growth than the shift in population from agriculture to industry was the shift in ownership of the means of production from state-owned enterprises to private companies (Lardy 2014; Cheremukhin 2015).

That implies that still as much as 42 percent of the Chinese population lives in the countryside, or, more accurately, in the rural areas. Do they live in capitalism or socialism? Both. Altogether, 314 million people work in agriculture; that's 40 percent of the country's workforce. Yet agriculture contributes less than 9 percent of GDP, which shows how low labor productivity is. One reason for such backwardness is that, due to ideological concerns rather than economic arguments, the farmland is still collective. It is regarded as a socialist type of property and as such cannot be traded at the market and cannot become a source of income for the farming population. There is no such thing as agriculture's profits from selling the land or derived from it capital gains due to the rising nonagricultural land prices, which definitely would influence the farming land prices if only it was commercialized. Interestingly, despite the enormous boom in the sectors of industry and not-agriculture services, the fall of the farming population has recently slowed down. If in the decade of 1997–2006 it declined by 100 million, in the following ten years, 2007–2016, it shrank only by 28 million. In other words, while in 1996, 36.3 percent of the country's population was farming, this ratio declined to 22.8 percent twenty years later.

Kornai formulated his view of China as a capitalist economy a decade ago, founding his reasoning on the data on the rapid growth of the private sector, which as early as in 2001 reached a majority position in the national economy (Kornai 2008). I myself maintained back then that upon joining the World Trade Organization, WTO, in 2001, "*China committed itself to a full-fledged market economy*" (Kolodko 2011a, 229), and later I concluded that to do so it's only possible for a capitalist economy (Kolodko 2014a, 146–70), in particular Chapter XIV: "*An Asian Era with the Euro-Atlantic Civilization as a background?*," which some authors disagreed with on principle, claiming that actually the case of China proves that one can be at the same time a full-fledged market economy and a socialist one.

When speaking of full-blooded market economy, I meant its more sophisticated and institutionally advanced form than the one achieved so far by China. It turns out that the path to a mature market is longer than we might think. The WTO still has not accorded to China the status of a market economy and, though a great majority of WTO member states are in favor of it, and rightly so, it's hard to expect it since president of the United States, Donald Trump refers to China, together with Russia, as a rival power. Also, the European Union is still reserved about granting formal market economy status to China.

While those with a more skeptical opinion on the Chinese economic, social and political reality point out to practices in breach of the WTO market economy standard such as exchange rate and currency market manipulations, restrictions on organizing free trade unions and strikes, huge corporate debt and excessive production capacity in some sectors, others emphasize rescuing hundreds of millions of people from poverty and allowing, also by using market mechanisms, a wider range of society to benefit from the economic growth. Some focus on the authoritarian, and at times, oppressive political system (Ringen 2016), others argue that rather than that, it is a functional meritocracy (Bell 2015). While some are afraid that the great program of the so-called New Silk Road[9] is a manifestation of Chinese imperialism, others emphasize assistance offered by China to poor economies in their struggle to overcome backwardness, often one resulting from prior capitalist exploitation. Some get overenthusiastic about the advancement level and international competitiveness of Chinese private high-tech companies, others showcases of intellectual property violations that are far from being isolated.

Hence, we have doubts as to how to define the contemporary Chinese system. Kornai didn't have any as he concluded that even though this was still a deficient market, over a decade ago it was already capitalism. He derives this declaration not only from relationships between core economic sectors, state and private ones, but also from the fact that shortages have been eliminated. His judgment is clear: there are not any in China as it is already capitalism with hard budget constraints, which is demonstrated by the predominance of private sector in the economy.

Opinions on that matter are divided among Chinese economists. An overwhelming majority of them publicly supports what the party declares.

Many of them, privately, are aware that there are more and more capitalist fundamentals in their surrounding reality. Still, they approach the issue less ideologically and more pragmatically. Call it what you will, the important aspect is about efficiency and competitiveness rather than ideological and political disputes. WTO may continue to unjustly claim that it is not a market economy but it is a market with Chinese characteristics, whose essence—and, obviously, the supremacy—the West is unable to fathom.

The issue needs a broader perspective, as the share of private ownership in the economy is by no means the only criterion for declaring socialism or capitalism. An equally important question relates to the nature and function of the state, and those can vary for different levels of private production and employment. In specific cases, their share of GDP may be relatively higher in country A than country B, but, at the same time, the nature of the state, its functions, tasks and activities may determine that there are more elements that are typical of socialism. To settle the matter, one needs to take a broader look around. In particular, it's necessary to assess the scope of the state's interference with the economy. From this perspective, several types of states can be distinguished.

In addition to the classical socialist state, four models are identified (Block 1994):

1) public goods state,
2) macroeconomic stabilization state,
3) social rights state,
4) developmental state.

Without going this time into an in-depth analysis of those models, their names themselves lead to the conclusion that all these attributes are present in China. The two former spheres—provision of public goods and concern for macroeconomic stabilization—are unquestionably a matter of state responsibility also in capitalism, something even neoliberal economists must concur with (though they will surely argue with their social-liberal colleagues over the scope of public goods). The latter two spheres—the area of social rights and developmental policy—are associated with the prerogatives of a socialist state. Or, which further complicates the matter, with state capitalism (Bremmer 2010). This shows how fluid the distinction is in some cases. Certainly, from such perspective China falls into the category of socialist economy, unlike Middle Eastern style state capitalism, such as the one in Saudi Arabia, or Central Asian one, as in Kazakhstan.

Anyway, on the long path from orthodox socialism to liberal capitalism, one that is longer than it seemed ex ante, there are many intermediate stops, the most significant ones being market socialism and state capitalism. To confuse the scene even more, they partly overlap; in this same place and time interval, something already is there and something else not yet.

WHITHER CHINA AND WHAT BUSINESS IS IT TO OTHERS?

China is actively getting involved in reforming the floundering global governance system (Lan 2017). If globalization is irreversible—and that's the case—the imperative for the coming years is to re-institutionalize it (Kolodko 2004). Undoubtedly, China will play a major role in this field, though it will definitely not be a "globalization with Chinese characteristics." It's striking that at the same time the American president being sworn into the office on the steps of the US Capitol, shouts *America First!*, at the Global Economic Forum in Davos the president of supposedly communist China declares that his country champions free trade and new-era globalization—not the one promoted by neoliberals, which enriches the few wealthy at the expense of many poorer ones, but one that is multilaterally beneficial.

In addition, this time, the Chinese imported a slogan from the West, talking of a *win-win* globalization. Cynics add that this *win-win*, which incidentally sounds nice and kind of familiar in Chinese, will mean 2:0 for China, but the idea is to have an inclusive globalization, in which China will undoubtedly play one of the leading roles in the coming decades. This is one of the purposes of the *One Belt, One Road* program, envisioned with so much flair, and engaging both the state and private business. It is neither socialist, nor capitalist, but surely it's practical.

The globally growing economic power of China is clearly visible from many angles. Not everybody realizes that the essential change in the structure of major corporations that has taken place over the past decade or so, toward more than doubling the number of state-owned enterprises among the top 500, was mainly due to the dynamism of Chinese companies.

While in 2004, out of 49 SOEs listed on the Fortune Global 500 (meaning they accounted for 10 percent of the list), 14 were Chinese companies, in 2016 in the group of 101 globally important state-owned enterprises (now they represent already 20 percent of that group) there are as many as 76 Chinese companies. Moreover, the question, again, is: is this a sign of expansion of socialism or state capitalism?

However, the system evolution and the policy followed as part of it in the Middle Country will be subordinated to something else than creating international power of China. What is and will be, in the foreseeable future, of greatest importance is an improvement of the internal economic situation. The Chinese expression *mei hao sheng huo*, which can be translated as *better*

Table 7.2 Number of State-Owned Enterprises from Selected Countries on the *Fortune Global 500* List in the Years 2004–2016

Country	*2004*	*2006*	*2008*	*2010*	*2012*	*2014*	*2016*
China	14	22	32	52	72	78	76
India	4	5	5	5	5	5	4
Russia	1	2	3	3	3	4	3
France	6	4	4	3	3	3	3
Japan	2	2	2	2	2	2	2
Brazil	2	2	2	2	2	2	2
Mexico	2	2	2	2	2	2	1
Germany	6	4	5	3	2	2	1
South Korea	1	1	1	1	2	2	1

Source: Fortune Global 500, CNN Money (subsequent years).

life or *happier life*, was used fourteen times by the Chinese leader Xi Jinping in his opening report at the nineteenth National Congress of the Communist Party of China in October 2017. He emphasized that

> China's socialist democracy is the broadest, most genuine, and most effective democracy to safeguard the fundamental interests of the people [. . .]. We should not just mechanically copy the political systems of other countries. (Xi 2017)

Dissociating himself from the *one size fits all* rule, typical of the neoliberal Washington consensus, he added with the characteristic Chinese imagery:

> Only the wearer knows if the shoes fit or not. (China Daily 2017b).

While rightly saying "no" to having too large or too small shoes imposed on them, and being aware of its own memorable achievements and strength, and at the same time sensing the needs of other countries looking for an effective path to development, China suggests that it may lead the way and that it will be a socialist one.

> Xi's vision of "a great modern socialist country," which aims for socialism's triumph over capitalism, not only guides China to avoiding the middle income trap but is a reference for the governance of other socialist countries. (China Daily 2017b, 7)

At the congress of the party he leads, Xi Jinping said:

> The path, the theory, the system, and the culture of socialism with Chinese characteristics have kept developing, blazing a new trial for other developing countries and nations to achieve modernization. It offers a new option for other

> countries and nations who want to speed up their development while preserving independence; and it offers Chinese wisdom and a Chinese approach to solving the problems facing mankind. (China Daily 2017b, 8)

China is eager to borrow from abroad not only cutting-edge technologies but also popular mental shortcuts or symbolic slogans. No wonder then that the state president and the chairman of Communist Party of China rolled into one outlined a roadmap for the coming decades (Zhang 2017). By condemning on principle one of the worst sides of the Chinese real economy, which is more associated by external observers with capitalism than with socialism, namely the wide-ranging corruption for which as many as 1.4 million people (*sic!*) were punished in various ways in the last five years, Xi Jinping indicated how in two giant steps China is to become in 2050 "a great modern socialist country." "Socialism with Chinese characteristics for a new era" is already there, a "great modern socialist country" is under construction. Unfortunately, from party documents and official governmental materials we will not learn more about what these two giant steps should be about, except that soon, in 2020, there will be a "moderately prosperous society in all respects," then, after 2035, a "socialist modernization" will be carried out, and in the following fifteen years, by 2050, a "great modern socialist country that is prosperous, strong, democratic, culturally advanced, harmonious and beautiful" will be created (China Daily 2017b, 5).

If we assume that we already have a social market economy in China (Berger, Cho, and Herstein 2013) or, as preferred by Chinese authorities, socialism with Chinese characteristics for a new era, then such an ambitious vision, of course with many reservations, may be worth considering. If we assume, however, that what we have there is capitalism with Chinese characteristics, or even an utterly corrupt crony capitalism (Pei 2016), then we are faced with quite different questions.

I believe that deliberations such as capitalism versus socialism, with respect to China are becoming less and less fertile and lead us astray. If every economist agrees with the view that the ownership of means of production is of key importance to the way economy functions, then every good economist must agree that of no lesser importance are culture, institutions and policies. This, on the one hand, confuses the picture and the object of the analysis, and on the other hand makes the analysis easier as it enriches the field of observation by adding new elements. After all, things happen the way they do because a lot happens at the same time.

Meanwhile, one cannot but agree both with some Chinese economists (Lin 2004, 2012a; Huang 2017) and with critical external observers (Jacques 2009; Moody 2017), who show the *differentia specifica* of China and try to explain what and why is happening there without resorting to the regime categories: socialism and capitalism. I myself am inclined to go in that direction, when formulating the theoretical outline and practical recommendations for new pragmatism also for China (Kolodko 2017a). In fact, resolving this dichotomy in a clear manner is not the key to understanding the heart of the matter in this case; the key is this typically Chinese commentary: with Chinese characteristics. Hence, a toughening of ideological and political position is even more interesting in a situation where new grounds for dialog are opening in intellectual and academic community. We heard from the Chinese leader at the congress of the ruling party that "Socialism with Chinese characteristics is socialism and no other -ism" (Berthold 2017, 31).

I believe that the capitalism versus socialism disputes are, on the one hand, a specific legacy of the Cold War period which real socialism evidently lost, as real capitalism evidently won it. However, this does not mean the end of history (Fukuyama 1989), as history will be with us for as long as we are surrounded by conflicts of interests and the attendant clashes. It is good, as it will make economists always needed because wherever there are conflicting interests, there's room for their research and activities. Also, this does not mean those two regimes must be inevitably in constant confrontation, whose fetters are so difficult to mentally break free from.

Some time ago, there were lively discussions over three alternative systemic megatrends and transformations:

- divergence,
- subvergence
- convergence.

The first one was supposedly a case where the opposing systems, capitalism and socialism, coexist and the challenge was to make this coexistence peaceful. In the second case, one system was to dominate the other and though many believed for some time that socialism would be the dominant one, it happened otherwise. In the third case, a systemic convergence was to occur, with each system drawing on and assimilating some elements, including culture, from the other and thus they would become alike over a long historic process. Certainly, it partly happened as various aspects of capitalism were adopted by socialism and vice versa, certain feature of socialism trickled into real capitalism and settled there. This applies especially to the social reorientation of this regime, which is, these days, so different from what Dickens described in *Oliver Twist* or half a century later Reymont in *The Promised Land*.

INSTEAD OF CONCLUSIONS

No doubt, China has significantly reduced public ownership, though it is still dominant in banking sector and a blurred division between public and private sectors exists. It is no longer egalitarian, the way it attempted to be during the Mao times. It has limited economic democracy and participation. It is exposed to internal and international market discipline. It has retained extended control over economic performance through traditional instruments of market economic policy (Tinbergen 1956), such as fiscal and monetary policies, interest and exchange rate management, price setting and SOE investments as well as some forms of direct controls. Hence, it seems justified to claim that China is the economy in transition from successive forms of socialism to market capitalism (Nuti 2018b). However, how long "transition" can last? In Central and Eastern European post-socialist economies it has taken a decade or two. So what about China? Will it take a generation or two? Or maybe an entire century or two?

During the landmark visit of American president Richard Nixon to Beijing in 1972, Zhou Enlai was asked by Henry Kissinger about the impact on his country of the recent student uprising in France in 1968, calling it "French revolution." China's prime minister thought that he meant the French Revolution of 1789 and, although 180 years had passed since, he replied: "*It's too early to say*."[10] In addition, that wasn't the first time when the Chinese showed their unique ability to look at things over very long periods, from the perspective of historical processes. It is similar now; it is too early to assess the impact of the Soviet Union's collapse and post-socialist transformation in Central and Eastern Europe on the China's course into the future.

These days, China is the one undergoing a sort of convergence. It is experiencing a process of gradually infusing the social and economic reality with fundamentals associated with capitalism, but capitalism is being opposed or sometimes pushed out by elements associated with the mentality typical of socialism. One can say that a hybrid in the form of socialist capitalism or—if you will—capitalist socialism is developing there; a sort of Chinism. It sounds like *contradictio in terminis*? A contradiction in terms? By no means; we are just stuck in the mental trap of a sharp but also false alternative: socialism or capitalism—*tertium non datur*. Meanwhile, something systemically different, though, in its nature not entirely devoid of elements of those both systems can be born.

While not giving up on specific values, differing in diverse places of this wandering world, which always guide human beings and societies in their economic activities, and bearing in mind the imperative of caring for dynamic balance, what matters most from the economic point of view is effectiveness and pragmatism. That's what Deng Xiaoping meant when he said: "It doesn't matter if a cat is black or white, as long as it catches mice."

Tertium datur.[11]

NOTES

1. There are eleven CEE post-socialist countries, which are now the members of the European Union. The Czech Republic, Estonia, Hungary, Latvia, Lithuania, Poland, Slovakia, and Slovenia joined it in 2004, Bulgaria and Romania in 2007, and Croatia in 2011.

2. Gini index in the United States stands at ca. 0.4, whereas in China it is around 0.46. Though for methodological reasons and there being no precise data, these measures are not exactly comparable, it can be assumed that they reflect quite accurately the disproportions in the income distribution of the world's two largest economies.

3. Shortages occurred exceptionally also in capitalist countries, including the United States and Japan, and especially the Great Britain during World War II (Charlesworth 2003). This was caused by the administrative measures adopted to suppress the inflationary price rise. Such shortages were accompanied by vast rationing schemes.

4. I mean prices in the strict sense, that is, monetary expression of the value of consumer products and services exchanged on the market rather than prices in the broad sense, also inclusive of the price of labor, that is, wages, the price of money in the future, that is, the interest rate, and the price of foreign currency, that is, the exchange rate.

5. Contemporarily, it can be observed in its extreme case in North Korea, on a lesser scale in Cuba as well as in Venezuela and Zimbabwe.

6. It's worth recalling that the authors of the infamous shock without therapy in Poland at the turn of 1980s and 1990s announced the unemployment would amount "only" to 400,000, and then—allegedly, after one-year moderate recession with a 3.1 percent GDP decline—it was supposed to stabilize or even reduce. Actually, unemployment was growing for five years, exceeding 3 million, that is, over 18 percent in 1994 (Kolodko and Nuti 1997). At the end of 2017, after periodic ups and downs, the rate fell below 7 percent, amounting to slightly over 1 million.

7. The official unemployment rate in China is 4 percent but it is certainly higher as a lot of those migrating from the countryside to cities find no job there but are not registered as unemployed. Thus, they are not included in the official statistics.

8. In the West, China is still most often nonsensically referred to as a communist country, both in professional literature and in political commentaries. This error stems from the simple-minded practice of equating a single-party system with a communist state, and a meaningful role of the state sector with a communist economy.

9. The New Silk Road, or OBOR, that is *One Belt, One Road*, as it is known under the official name, is a vast infrastructure investment program supposed to facilitate the trade between China and its foreign partners to the west, south, and north. The program addresses sixty-five countries in Asia, Middle East, North and East Africa,

and East Central Europe (so-called *16+1 Initiative*, including sixteen post-socialist countries: Albania, Bosnia and Herzegovina, Bulgaria, Croatia, the Czech Republic, Estonia, Hungary, Lithuania, Latvia, Macedonia, Montenegro, Poland, Romania, Serbia, Slovakia, and Slovenia.

10. That popular story about Zhou En-lai omits an important clarification, given years later by Chas Freeman, the State Department interpreter, to the effect that Kissinger's question was translated as referring to the student uprisings in France in 1968, not to 1789. When Zhou's answer came back, Freeman decided that the misunderstanding was "too delicious to invite correction."

11. Published in Kolodko (2018).

Chapter 8

Look to the Horizon and Beyond

When we observe the world economy, we see that there is a different economic growth and development in different parts of the world and in different countries. The political correctness suggests that we are supposed to say that the more democracy we have in a country there is a more robust economic growth there. Yet that is not the case. There are examples where democracy or liberal democracy—since there are different types of democracies—are supporting economic growth, but we have also seen cases where democratic procedures are making economic expansion more difficult. One may see this problem through a prism of efficiency of a decision-making process. Let's take an example of, for instance, China, which is not a democracy but an authoritarian system, yet the decisions are made in a fast and accountable way, they are reasonable—and I would say most of the time it is a rational economic policy, though not a democratic one.

If now we take, for instance, the United States, especially under the Trump presidency, it is hardly rational and is even simply stupid what Trump does or what Trump economics implies. So one may say that an authoritarian regime is better for an economic expansion than a democratic one, but that is not true, because an authoritarian regime does work in China but does not work, for instance, in Egypt, in Saudi Arabia, in Congo, and in some other countries, so it depends on very many factors, and the political regime, the political system, the political culture, the political institutions are very important for political performance, for economic growth, for social and economic development, but that is not a leading or a decisive factor. Also important are institutions, that is, the rules of the game and the culture.

Therefore, the case of China, which I call Chinism and which is neither capitalism nor socialism, is a different system, a unique one. Chinism is an authoritarian political regime, yet a meritocracy; most of the time people in charge are professionals, they are technocrats. It cannot be claimed, for instance, about the current US administration. The lead negotiator at the trade negotiations between China and the United States, Mr. Robert Lighthizer, is a lawyer, but he is ignorant in economic matters. And what Americans are insisting on, is hardly rational from an economic prospective, because if they want to get rid of a too big fiscal deficit or trade deficit, they have to raise domestic savings and not attack China, because a current trade balance is a multilateral and not bilateral problem.

Therefore, it depends. Political correctness says democracy is good for everything, yet democracy is a value per se, and for that reason I am very much in favor of a democratic regime, of a democratic system, of liberal democracy—but if it is supported by a proper leadership. To be successful—and it is my experience in Poland where I was four times deputy prime minister and minister of finance—one has to have a vision, not an illusion. A vision is something complex, accountable, dynamic and long-lasting. Second, one has to base a development strategy on a proper economic theory. It is supposed to be not a merely knowledge-based economy, it is supposed to be also knowledge-based policy and politics. Thirdly, we have to have good leadership.

For the global economy, the biggest challenge is no doubt the climate change. This long-term problem must be addressed gradually in the long term. If we are talking about 1–2–3 years or even 3–5–10 years, we can survive the climate change but we cannot survive it for 1–2–3 generations. To be responsible, accountable, and successful we have to act now—year after year, country after country.

Hence the question is, what kind of leadership do we have? We have better leadership, with all of its problems, in France than in Italy. We have better leadership, with all the caveats, in Germany than in Spain, in Mexico than in Brazil, in Indonesia than in the Philippines. Moreover, especially from the point of view of inclusive globalization, we definitely have better leadership in China than in the United States. So, professionalism and leadership, which very much depends on vision, may be good or bad within a given ideological or political system.

Going back to basic economics, it's the question of rebalancing the world economy. Globalization is an irreversible process, even if Mr. Trump does not understand it and even if he dislikes it, even if current US administration—not only, but mostly United States, as the United States is critically important—dislikes it. If there is a new nationalism in some smaller countries, one may not care too much, but the United States is a leading economy in the world, and its unilateralism, protectionism, nationalism, and likeliness of trade wars are contributing to severe international and global problems.

What is globalization—in an economic sense (as there are other aspects of globalization such as culture, security, and environment etc.)? It is a historical and spontaneous process of liberalization and integration which brings separately performing national economies into one interconnected, intertwined worldwide economy, global economy. What happens here, be it Indonesia or Russia, depends on what happens elsewhere, whether in Canada or Israel, and that is making some influence still elsewhere, be it Nigeria or Argentina. We are all connected because of many factors, of which the most important is the supply chain. Now China is moving up within the global supply chain, is upgrading herself to more technologically advanced industries, what makes the United States nervous. However, the global economy is interconnected, and trade war does not bring much.

The question is about rebalancing the world economy, because some countries have too much of savings while others do not have enough savings. There is a surplus of savings in China, Japan or Germany, while there is a lack of savings in the United States, France, or Poland. So some countries are importing capital whereas others are exporting it. Thus the problem of economic imbalance, both trade and current accounts, is a very big challenge for the ongoing globalization.

There is one way, Mr. Trump's way, which is irrational and which in a longer run will be harmful for the US economy. In mid-January, the so-called Phase One Agreement between the United States and China has been signed. China accepted it because it gives more time to cool the tensions down. My reading of China's approach is that they decided to take time. To be exact, it's been decided by the leadership, which is constant, as they do not change it in a democratic way like they do in the United States, and they do not change it in a weird way as they do it in Russia, where in the morning Mr. Medvedev is a prime minister and in the afternoon somebody else takes the post. Therefore, we have a spectrum of political systems and a spectrum of economic regimes.

Hence, in the short run, the challenge is the flow of capital, including speculative capital, and efforts to regulate financial flows all over the world, on a global scale. That may be done either by the IMF—or we need some coordination within G20, of which partners are not only the biggest and richest Western economies, but also India, China, Brazil, Mexico, Russia, and Indonesia. It is very difficult, but it is possible. I am not an optimist but just a pragmatic rationalist, and I know that each and every of these problems has a solution. We are not doomed to have another great crisis if there is a proper effort to govern, because in our lifetime, as a result of a historical process of globalization, the global economy has emerged and we do have an interconnected global economy. Nevertheless, we do not have interconnected global politics and policy. We do not have a governance mechanism in the interconnected world economy—unlike on the national scales. It is a very long shot to address such challenges in working, pragmatic manner.

I cannot see a good solution for short-term problems like trade imbalances, currencies volatility, flight of capital—without a long-term approach and long-term view. If one wants to solve a problem which one is confronting today or tomorrow, one must from time to time to look to the horizon and even beyond. Hence, the best solution to the current problems, including climate change and migration that is linked somehow to these processes, is a long-term approach. In the richer countries the rate of growth, measured traditionally by the rise of GDP, must be brought a little bit down for the purpose of leaving more ecological space and room to catch up for the developing countries. Relatively speedier growth there will also encourage people to stay there. Otherwise they'll be leaving the poorer countries trying to get not only to the rich West but, for instance, from some Central Asian republics to Russia which is a Big Brother and a richer country for them, or from Mozambique and Zambia to South Africa and Botswana, or from Laos and Cambodia to Thailand and Malaysia.

As for the less developed countries, a complete, full extension catching up with the most developed ones, there will never be a situation when everybody is as rich as Switzerland, Norway, New Zealand, or Canada. Yet it seems like we would like to have all over the world a level of consumption of the United States which now has a GDP per capita of roughly $60K. In the United States, there are 330 million people, whereas globally there are 7.6 billion of us. Therefore, if one would like to have the standard of living or level of consumption which is approximate to the standard of living at the US level, one has to have the US GDP per capita. Let us presume, from a theoretical viewpoint, that it would happen. Then, having the US labor productivity, we would have to have as many resources per capita as there is in the United States. However, for 7.6 billion people, even if all of them use the current US advanced technology, it would require resources three times larger, than we have on the entire Earth. Therefore, simply due to the natural barrier it is impossible. Of course, the technological progress will contribute a little bit to meeting this challenge because consumption and output become less material- and energy-demanding and we need less energy and resources for producing products, yet it will not be enough for everybody to catch up with the richest countries.

While observing what is going on in developing countries—which I would rather call emancipating or catching up economies, and not emerging markets, what sound quite instrumental—one see that outward-oriented policies of liberalizing and opening up go together with domestically oriented development policy, which must be contextual from geoeconomical and geopolitical as well cultural perspectives. Globalization is a good thing for development as it fuels the growth of countries lagging behind—if they have a proper strategy to use globalization to their advantage. China has such a strategy, while Saudi Arabia—not necessarily. Russia, which is not a good player in globalization and in promoting expansion of its economy internationally, is actually somewhere in between. Mexico is growing faster than the United States, so it is catching up. Poland is growing faster than Germany, so it is catching up. Estonia is growing faster than Finland, so it is catching up. Indonesia is growing faster than Japan, so it is catching up. As a result, the distance between the poor and richer countries is now much shorter than it was ten, or twenty, or thirty years ago.

Some would say there is more inequality in the world due to globalization. Well, not necessarily. Indeed, not only in Russia and the United States, in China and Brazil there is too much of inequality, yet at the same time in certain countries—unfortunately, quite a few—inequality has been going down, for example, in Poland or in Morocco. The complex pictures show that there while there has been increasing inequality within countries, the gap in average income between the countries—say, between Hungary and Austria or Albania and Greece, of Vietnam and South Korea—is now smaller than twenty years ago. That is again a positive result of the globalization, liberalization, of the transition to the market economy in post-socialist part of the world.

Therefore, some countries have been much more successful, for instance, Poland, because there was a realistic vision, a proper economic policy based on a proper economic theory and, most of the time, a good leadership.

As for Russia's hardships in economy, they are due, to some extent, to political arrangements because Russian democracy is still somehow limited and it is not a full-fledged liberal democracy as there is a low exchange and competition of different options of economic policy. The main cause for Russia's somehow lagging behind in taking advantage of the indispensable global economic game, is the resource curse, because it relies too much on its natural resources. True, over the last two, three of four years, the non-energy sector has been growing faster than the energy sector based on oil and gas. Nevertheless, definitely, a recipe for the success of Russia in the future is diversification of the real sector and diminishing dependence on energy. It is easy to take the cream, especially if there is a good price for oil and gas. Sometimes bad news is good news. There are mounting problems in Venezuela and Nigeria, in Libya and Iran, and in many other places. All that sounds good for Russia as most likely the prices of oil and gas will go up. Unfortunately, the importing economies will pay more, while Russia sells them more profitable. This factor is not a good motivation to work hard to restructure and diversify the economy. That is one of the causes why Russia is not very successful in engaging in the globalization game. The second reason is the influence of oligarchs in Russia's economic and political matters.

Many factors contributed to the success of economic reforms in Poland, and one of them was the fact we could avoid an oligarchization of the economy. We knew since the beginning that we wanted to join the EU that is not an option for Russia. Nevertheless, the diversifying its economy and engaging its industries in the global supply chain are certainly options for it. Yet Russia has to be supportive for FDI and open some industries, which are still relatively closed for foreign investors. That is what China has managed much better, and now because of that it is being accused by the United States of stealing intellectual property.

I was saying twenty-five, fifteen, five years ago that China did even better than us in inviting direct investments to the sectors and industries they wanted to restructure, make more competitive and develop. Foreign direct investments brought new technologies. China's approach was simple: if you want to invest in China, you are welcome, but you should share your technology and show your managerial and marketing skills; you will get access to our market, but we will get access to the world market through increasing our competitiveness due to technology you bring. Now Mr. Trump says China was forcing foreign investors to share their know-how, but that was not a blackmail; it was business, indeed, not "as usual," but a different one—"with Chinese characteristics." Such policy and macroeconomic governance contributed a lot to the diversification of Chinese economic structure and enabled China to become a powerhouse in the global economy. Now they export capital but not in the way it is done in Russia—by buying expensive properties abroad. China invests in industries including hi-tech, and now it exports more capital than comes there from abroad.

Thus the question is, how are countries involved in globalization in a successful way? Definitely, Germany does it much better than Italy, Poland much better than Ukraine, the United States does it pretty well too, but without taking care of complexity. The answer to all challenging questions is complexity.

When I first became deputy prime minister and minister of finance twenty-five years ago, I was very much critical of so-called shock therapy which I called shock without therapy since there were too many avoidable shocks and not enough sufficient therapies. Therefore, I came up with a program called "Strategy for Poland." A journalist asked me to summarize in 30 seconds, what was the difference between "Strategy for Poland" and "shock therapy." The answer? "Strategy for Poland" is a complex medium-term structural reform and developing policies program, based on an orthodox economic theory, addressing not only the issue of dynamic economic growth, but also social and ecological balances. A large difference between my strategy and what was done before is that we are not confusing the ends and the means.

I had the privilege of having known Yegor Gaidar. We were together in Erasmus University in Rotterdam in 1991 when he got a call from Russia's president Boris Yeltsin who asked him to join the government as finance minister. Gaidar was trying to the very end, not understanding all the aspects of this paramount challenge, to liberalize and stabilize the economy. He didn't appreciate enough the institutional aspects of the great change and was behaving wrongly, thinking liberalization and stabilization constitute a critical step toward a market economy. No, the institution-building is such a step.

In 1990, 500 Days program of transition to market economy was presented in Russia by Grigory Yavlinsky. When I came back to Warsaw from a meeting held at Moscow at that time, I organized in the Research Institute of Finance, of which I was the director, a conference that I called "In 500 Days to Hyperinflation." And I was right. Market economy is basically about institutions and rules of the game—of course, based on the dominance of private property. Therefore, a very tricky part of a transition is sensible privatization. Nevertheless, what Russia did wrong in the 1990s under President Yeltsin's administration was denationalization and privatization that was not linked with demonopolization and unfortunately fueled the emergence of oligarchic structures which are very much engaged in politics since.

What is the difference between Russia and Ukraine? Both systems are corrupt and oligarchic, but in Ukraine oligarchs say to policymakers: do what we want—and they do. Moreover, in Russia policymakers say to oligarchs: get out of politics and do your business—and they do. We may need big business, but not an oligarchic one. Therefore, oligarchization of Russian economy that occurred in the mid-1990s was a critical moment when Russia actually started to lag behind.

In Poland, a transitional recession was just three years or twelve quarters. It lasted form second half of 1989 through first half of 1992 and during this period, the country lost a little bit less than 20 percent of its GDP. Not much if compared with the transitional contraction in Russia, too much if relative to unavoidable fall of output under the Polish realities of that time. It happened due to the wrong, ideologically and not pragmatically driven policy. The liberalization was too radical and stabilization measures had been overshot. Set of policies based on the Washington Consensus was proclaimed: deregulate as much as you wish; privatize as much as you can, the faster the better; be tough in a fiscal and monetary way, and the market will do the job. No, the market will only come up with recession and hyperinflation. You need inclusive institutions, supervision of the markets. What is necessary is a creative synergy between the power of invisible hand of market and the power of visible hand of the government.

As Poland and Hungary were reformed since 1989 toward market and democracy much more than anybody else, it was relatively easy to jump toward the transition to a full-fledged market economy. Besides, since the very beginning, there was a consensus in Poland that the country was going to join the EU. That required implementing certain reforms, so influence was at some moment coming from the outside, from the EU, but it was in line with our free independent wish to join the European integration process.

In Russia, there was much more hesitation about where to go. People knew they were leaving the Soviet Union behind and going to a better future. Nevertheless, what does a better future imply? To this end, there are so many views that are quite often contradictory. Hence, the case is to be discussed more because there are solutions to these problems; let us find them.

As for Russia, there is all the time too much of the power of the government and not enough of the power of the invisible hand of the market. The new pragmatism—while stressing that the economic problems always ought to be seen in contextual framework—requires a triple balance: an economic one but also ecological and social ones. We do not need 200 economics for 200 national economies, but it is impossible to have a one-size-fits-all economics for all of them in this intertwined, extremely complex global economy. We need a contextual approach. The basics of economy is always the same one but particulars and details—they depend on legacy, geopolitics, geoeconomics, culture, legacies from the previous system.

Chapter 9

Chinism and the Future of the World

INTRODUCTORY REMARKS

For some time, opinions have been more and more expressed that a new era is inevitably coming, in which Asia and especially China will dominate the world. Not necessarily. However, certainly the relative importance of China—due to the enormity of its still growing economy and population size—will be increasing. This has its obvious not only economic but also political implications. In an era of irreversible globalization, none of the world's great problems can be solved without China. It is therefore necessary not only to compete with it, but also to cooperate creatively. The sooner the culture of such cooperation develops, the sooner its supportive institutions are developed, the better for development of the global economy.

In the world of the future, human capital and technology will be decisive for the competitiveness of knowledge-based economies. In themselves, however, they may not be enough to promote sustainable development. A political and economic system that favors the formation of capital and its efficient allocation is also indispensable. The Chinese system is still evolving, so the question arises as to how much it will be able to face the growing challenges.

POPULATION AND HUMAN CAPITAL

The time of quantity will never end, but now the time has come for next generation quality. Today, and even more so in the future, economic successes will depend less and less on the possession of natural resources, tangible and financial assets, and increasingly on human capital. Since the dawn of time, economy has relied on knowledge, but never has so much depended on knowledge resources as it does now. It is knowledge and the skills in leveraging it in production and exchange processes that will determine which economy is at the leading edge. The competitiveness of economies increasingly depends on knowledge, of what China is fully aware. Accordingly, the country invests in knowledge and technological progress ever more time and funds. Chinese universities are working their way up the global ranking lists, though they are far from the top positions. Those are occupied nearly entirely by US and British schools (only one continental European university is among top ten: Swiss Federal Institute of Technology in Zurich) with MIT, Stanford and Harvard on the podium, but Tsinghua University already ranks sixteenth, and Beijing University, twenty-second (QS 2020). In top engineering school rankings, Tsinghua is already right after MIT and experts say it is a matter of years before it becomes a world leader. The results of this cannot yet be seen, for example, in Forbes list showcasing the most valuable brands, where the remote ninety-seventh place went to the only Chinese company on the list, indeed the most known and significant on the global, not only economic, scene—Huawei (Forbes 2020). It wedged in between Danish Lego blocks and US John Deere tractors. Meanwhile, in a much more important ranking, having specific implications for decisions on investments and purchase orders, namely in the Global Competitiveness Index compiled by World Economic Forum, China ranks twenty-eighth, after Malaysia and Iceland and before Qatar and Italy (WEF 2019). The list starts with Singapore, the United States, and Hong Kong. Interestingly, in terms of competitiveness, China is ahead of all other BRICS countries—Brazil, Russia, India and South Africa—and most European Union countries.[1] However, economy serves people, even if policy sometimes forgets it, and economy treats them selectively. One must not be uncritically awed by the impressive achievements such as the magnificent Pudong skyline in Shanghai or by the 38,000 kilometers of high-speed railway, as one also needs to know that public healthcare expenditure represents only about 2 percent of China's GDP, and the guaranteed monthly income, *dibao*, amounts to the modest RMB 600, which can buy not much more than a bowl of noodles a day. One can marvel at the architectural perfection of the Zhuhai opera house, whose beauty may rival the one in Sydney, but one cannot be indifferent to the fact that on many occasions peasants are removed from their fields through corrupt lawsuits where land is taken over to build mega-housing projects of doubtful appeal. One cannot help but admire the reach and dynamic growth of the *Weibo* social media platform and *WeChat* mega-app, each used by hundreds of millions, but one cannot help but complain that *BBC News* online service is blocked by *Great Firewall*, which is very technologically advanced, by the way. Hence, the big picture is very complex.

What will be pivotal for the future is to what extent and how quickly changes will take place as regards the satisfaction of the changing needs of the population. The same is ever increasing in countries working their way up and ever smaller in rich countries which, with exceptions, welcome immigrants. In China, the population will soon cease to grow though it will continue to age.

According to UN projections, China's population will start to decline after 2030. Meanwhile, such a turning point will happen for India a generation later, after 2060. It is of significance in this context that India—unlike China and other countries with a quickly aging population—can leverage its demographic dividend in the form of relatively young population, which is a contributing factor for dynamic economy. While median age in the former country is around twenty-eight years, in the latter, it is over thirty-seven (the global average being thirty years).[2] Hence, in this respect, China's situation is already unfavorable and it will continue to deteriorate.

The society's condition and the well-being of the people, especially the financial circumstances of their households and the assessment of individual economic situation are determined neither by the economy size nor by the nation's population. That "we are the largest country" or "we are more numerous than you" counts for something—more in political than in psychological terms—but welfare and the subjective sense thereof is not improving much in China just due to the fact that the Chinese are still the most numerous in the world[3] and that they produce the most at PPP. Likewise, the fact that, say, Indonesians are seven times as numerous as Poles and that in total they produce almost three times as much is little cause for rejoicing for the former if their country's GDP per capita represents only 42 percent of the same category in the latter, where, for this reason, among others, the average lifespan is nearly five years longer. In China, one lives, on average, only two years shorter than in the United States (seventy-seven compared to seventy-nine years), enjoying an average income that is rising very fast but still represents only 30 percent of the American income, which stood at USD 64.700 per

Table 9.1 Population Growth Forecasts, 2020–2060

	Year		
Country	*2020*	*2060*	*Growth/Fall in Percent*
China	1439	1333	–7.4
India	1380	1651	19.6
United States	331	391	18.1
Russia	146	133	–8.9
Japan	126	98	–22.2
World	7795	10151	30.2

Source: UN 2019.

Table 9.2 Human Development and Inequality Adjusted Human Development Indices

Country	*HDI rank*	*HDI*	*IHDI*	*Overall Loss (percent)*	*Difference from HDI Rank*
Norway	1	0.954	0.889	6.8	0
USA	15	0.920	0.797	13.4	–13
Japan	19	0.915	0.882	3.6	15
Russia	49	0.824	0.743	9.9	1
China	85	0.758	0.636	16.1	4
India	129	0.647	0.477	26.3	1
World	–	0.731	0.584	20.2	–

Source: UNDP 2019, 308–11.

capita in 2019. These are the reasons why one needs to draw on more adequate information than the simple measure of income per capita. Categories describing the human capital level are highly useful from this perspective.

In terms of HDI, the United States ranks fifteenth, between New Zealand and United Kingdom, and Belgium and Japan,[4] and China, eighty-fifth, between North Macedonia and Peru, and Ecuador and Azerbaijan.[5] Norway tops the list (HDI of 0.954), and Niger is at the bottom (HDI 0.377). Taking account of income distribution inequalities—very high both in the United States and in China, with Gini index of 41.5 and 38.6 respectively—the United States goes down thirteen spots, to twenty-eighth place, and China moves up by four, to eighty-first place,[6] so the distance between them is slightly shorter than in income differences.

Another thing that matters is the dynamic of change and the shifts on the world map reflecting differences in the level and quality of human capital. In just three decades, since 1990, the average HDI for the world as a whole has risen from 0.598 to 0.731, whereas in the United States it has gone up from 0.860 to 0.920, and in China from 0.501 to 0.758. Hence, thirty years ago, China was below the global average, and now it is already above. While the quality of human capital measured this way has been rising globally by 0.72 percent a year, the pace of its growth in the United States was three times as slow (0.24 percent), and in China, twice as fast (1.48 percent). It is understood, of course, that it is easier to work your way up to higher thresholds when you start from a low level. Now it is getting ever more difficult.

NOT ONLY CAPITALISM, ALSO CHINISM

Branko Milanović in his interesting book titled "Capitalism, Alone: The Future of the System That Rules the World" argues that, though following the fall of the Soviet-style state socialism (most often referred to in the literature as communism[7]) the history by no means came to an end, capitalism triumphantly and universally took hold over the world (Milanović 2019). He believes that the future must follow its path, as there is no alternative to the victorious capitalism. One could reduce the matter to definitions, but it is much more complicated. Especially that the author often puts different categories of political and economic systems under the umbrella term of "capitalism," distinguishing between its two fundamental types: meritocratic liberal capitalism headed by the United States and political capitalism headed by China. Therefore, even though the book title speaks of capitalism alone, in the capitalist reality suggested by the author we would deal with more than just one its identity.

Perhaps this is the case, but the problem is that rather than two varieties as part of one system, we can see a systemic multiplicity. It is not the same case as that of, say, gorilla and orang-utan, two apes belonging to the same family of creatures, but one more similar to that of monkey and a lemur; very similar on the exterior but different deep down. One can hardly squeeze in such vastly diversified present and future time into one systemic category, as there are many of them. We still have several worlds, and the point is to decide which of them deserves to be dubbed the first one, where the second one is and what is going on with the third one, and perhaps with yet a couple more others.

We must agree that there is a need to distinguish between liberal capitalism that evolved in the West over a long historical process, and state capitalism that originated from a shorter historical process in many postcolonial countries—the erstwhile Third World—and some countries of the post-socialist transition. In the first group of state-capitalist countries, classical example would be economy such as Egypt, in the second such as Russia.[8]

China differs in terms of quality and it would be too far-fetched to classify it according to that model. This is neither a case of communism, as some would still have it (Fun and Zheng 2020), nor of capitalism, even one adorned with this adjective or another, but that of a different quality. It is a political/social/economic system in its own right that I refer to as Chinism (Kolodko 2018, 2020a). It is no *Beijing Consensus* laden with statism and centralized bureaucracy, which some attempted to hail for a time as the antithesis for the neoliberal *Washington Consensus* (Halper 2010). Though one can see some analogies between those concepts, there are definitely more significant differences (Lin 2013). Neither is it a simple period of transition from centrally planned economy to market economy, though in the form of state capitalism (Lardy 2014).

Francis Fukuyama believes—now that he can see with his naked eye that history is still going on[9]—that China since the takeover of power by Xi Jinping's team in 2012 has been moving from the authoritarian to the totalitarian system. While this is highly debatable, if not wrong, Fukuyama is right that in reality the centralization of power and constraining already very limited democracy can be stopped and reversed only by internal forces. The more so because

> unfortunately, over the past three and a half years, the United States has been doing everything it can to weaken itself. It has elected a leader who revels in demonizing his domestic opponents far more than his foreign rivals, who has blithely thrown away the moral high ground that used to be the foundation of American global power, and who has governed the country with such incompetence during the largest crisis of the past three generations that it is no longer taken seriously by either friends or enemies. (Fukuyama 2020)

It is therefore necessary to agree with his conclusion, and more precisely with its first part: "Before we can think about changing China, we need to change the United States and try to restore its position as a global beacon of liberal democratic values around the world" (Fukuyama 2020).

However, there is no way to agree with the second part of the conclusions, because of the failure of neoliberalism and the fiasco of liberal democracy during the presidency of Donald Trump, imagining the future of the United States as a world leader in democracy is a wishful thinking. This opportunity has been missed. It probably was already gone even several years earlier. At that time, I argued with Zbigniew Brzezinski, who in 2007 wrote about the "second chance" of taking global leadership (the first followed the end of the Cold War and the collapse of the Soviet Union) (Brzezinski 2007). That chance was to beat the Republican candidate for the White House and, consequently, change the American domestic and foreign policies. Although this happened because Barack Obama won, the United States was no longer able to restore its hegemonic and leadership position. As I wrote at the time, I think so today: to aspire to global leadership, one must take care of the world, not of one's own interests, often at the expense of the rest of this world (Kolodko 2011a). Undoubtedly, then and now, the possibility of such global re-expansion of the United States has been blocked by the rising China. This fact must not only to be acknowledged, but we have to go further—accept the reality, look for pragmatic compromises and create a positive synergy, not naïvely to dream of lone superpower.

Chinism, sui generis, is a syncretic economic system based on multiple forms of ownership of means of production, with a strong macroeconomic policy and limited government control with respect to microeconomic management. Deregulation is subordinated to maintaining enterprises' activities on the course that is in line with the social and political goals set by the ruling party.[10] Widely used, flexible but generally far-reaching economic interventionism uses both indicative planning addressing the business sphere and command planning with respect to some state-owned enterprises and infrastructure. The country's policy for the government, local authorities and the central bank alike also makes use of classical instruments of market interventionism. The pricing system is essentially decentralized, which, despite not fully hardened budget constraints with respect to public enterprises, guarantees maintaining a dynamic money market equilibrium.

At the same time, Chinism has helped eliminate the shortage syndrome and effectively keep price inflation in check. This is a feat none of the former state socialism economies, neither the Soviet Union nor any of CEE economies, was able to accomplish, which was the main reason behind their economic and, consequently, political demise (Kolodko and Rutkowski 1991; Csaba 1996).

Such hybrid economic system comes hand in hand with an authoritarian, one-party state with centralized power essentially based on meritocracy. The policy implemented by the state is competent and responsible. At the same time, it is oriented to fulfilling long-term strategic goals, to which medium-term and immediate goals are subordinated.[11] The authorities use traditional and modern social impact methods, for example, they resort to controlling the society's compliance with behaviors promoted by the general direction of development set by the party and by legislative and executive power. In exerting social influence, such diverse measures are used as references to Confucian philosophy and quasi-religion, on the one hand, and modern electronic surveillance invigilation, on the other. Digitization of social communication is increasingly used for controlling the public dialogue, inclusive of influencing the content shared on social media.

Chinism does not stand for turning back from the path of market reforms and returning to the omnipotence of the state sector in the economy (Lardy 2019); this is an overly simplified image of a highly complex reality. The state plays a major role—most of all as a regulator and also as the owner of some means of production—but it does not crowd out nor replaces the market but rather corrects and supports it and creates a synergy with its forces (Huang 2017). One should not overestimate isolated events nor hastily generalize individual observations, but the fact that in 2008 the prestigious post of chief economist and senior vice president of Development Economics at the World Bank was assigned to the eminent Chinese economist, Justin Yifu Lin, was meaningful. This was not an empty gesture directed at China in recognition of the country's achievements from those who in fact decided it—the US authorities in consultation with Japan, the United Kingdom, Germany and France. It was a sign, especially to economically backward countries, that valuable conclusions can be drawn from China's experience in the development policy and it is worth adopting such good practices elsewhere. Lin's term of office, 2008–2012, did not revolutionize Washington's technocratic way of thinking or World Bank's activities, but it undoubtedly contributed to this organization's further departure from neoliberal orthodoxy.

RELATIVE APPEAL OF CHINISM

Outside the Middle Country, the appeal of Chinism is limited. Certainly, it will not be transposed to countries of liberal capitalism, but, in turn, it can be—and already is—an inspiring offer, or at least an option worth contemplating for many countries of the former Third World. Of course, this is not an option for countries whose naive leaders believe that their strong political power and a large state sector in the economy are enough to repeat China's boom. Chinism, deeply rooted in historically embedded culture, is much more than that.

So, countries that show certain similarities with the characteristics of Chinism—with all individual caveats—include Brunei, Cambodia, Laos, Myanmar, Singapore, and Vietnam in South East Asia; Azerbaijan, Kazakhstan, Tajikistan, Turkmenistan, and Uzbekistan in Central Asia; Iran, Oman, and United Arab Emirates in the Middle East; Algeria, Eritrea, Namibia, Sudan, and Tanzania in Africa; and Nicaragua in Latin America. In addition, a number of other countries have some similarities, in particular on the economic side a large, centrally controlled state sector and on the political side strong authoritarian government. However, these attributes are not sufficient to qualify them in the same group as the aforementioned countries.

Of course, between China's system and policies, and the relevant features of those countries, there are a number of differences, similar, as they do exist within the same family of "free market and liberal democracy" countries. It is enough to compare the United States with Latin American states such as Mexico, Brazil, Argentina, or Chile; or Great Britain with East Central European countries such as Czech Republic, Croatia, Latvia, or Slovenia; or Japan with Far East countries such as Indonesia, East Timor, the Philippines, or Malaysia. With the criteria of taxonomy outlined in thick lines, they can all be included in the category of market economies and democratic states, but when we look closer at their characteristics, there are many differences between them.

However, none of the countries similar to Chinism or inspired by it in economic reforms and development policy corresponds fully with it. While in each of them the market mechanism and government regulation overlap and intertwine, and private and state ownership coexist in various proportions, in many of them it is quite difficult to see the meritocracy, so symptomatic for Chinism. Everywhere there are authoritarian governments—mono-party or quasi-multiparty, with elections from time to time, but all the time with the same ruling party—reigning with a large degree of centralization, from limited in Singapore to extreme in Eritrea.

What is particularly interesting, while some of these countries—like Cambodia—are pro-Chinese, certain others—like Singapore—are pro-Western, especially pro-American. While some, such as Algeria and Nicaragua, are distancing themselves from the West and approaching China, others, like Myanmar or Vietnam, are politically distancing themselves from China and approaching the United States. Indeed, one can have certain characteristics of Chinism and at the same time be in political opposition to China.

Therefore, this is a seemingly highly diverse group of countries, but when one looks deeper into their systemic features, one can see many similarities vis-à-vis important aspects of China's economy; several indicators of Chinism appear in the economic systems of these countries. Particular attention should be paid to the large share of state ownership, including monopoly in the strategic industries (in this case, "strategic" implies much more than in Western market economies), central planning, control of the exchange rate regime and central bank reporting to the government. There are also certain similarities with regard to economic policy methods, especially state intervention as a mean of industrial and trade policies, protectionism of vital sectors, state subsidies for export-oriented firms, and government influence on major inbound and outbound foreign direct investments. In the case of sectors at a higher level of technological advancement, there is often protection and state financial support to increase the international competitiveness of companies.

Countries of liberal democracy, in the face of the crisis thereof, must look for ways to protect themselves against the wave of new nationalism (Economist 2016) and the crisis-generating potential of neoliberalism (Galbraith 2018), but they will surely not follow the Chinese model. This may be done, though to a very diverse extent, by emancipating economies and societies, that is, those thrown by neoliberalism into the category of so-called emerging markets. The heart of the matter is that two significant processes overlap in the same time: a huge economic success of Chinism on the one hand, and a structural crisis of liberal capitalism on the other.

Countries which look for a lighthouse, on this chaotic ocean of global economy, can be more quickly reached by the light from Beijing than from Washington, more clearly from the Pearl River Delta and Guangzhou than from New York and Manhattan. This is also supported by the strong activity of Chinese foreign policy. Beijing has more diplomatic posts scattered around the world than the United States. Its political impact cannot be underestimated but at the same time one should not fear it will outdo the West, including the Anglo-American influence, when it comes to the so-called soft power. It is a good thing that in numerous countries more than a hundred Confucius institutes were launched, which promote China and Chinese values. It is no threat, on the contrary; a bit more of us will understand Mandarin, which will also contribute to expanding the international exchange in the sphere of education, science, culture and sports. The next culminating event in the soft power clash will be the twenty-fourth Winter Olympic Games in Beijing in 2022, especially after the 2020 Summer Olympics in Tokyo were canceled.

This external expansion—irrespective of its strictly economic goals, mainly to export major surpluses in the infrastructure construction sector, develop outlets for ever more competitive industries and get access to deposits of raw materials and inputs—is pursued on a spectacular scale by means of the Belt and Road Initiative (BRI) (Maçães 2018), often referred to as the new Silk Road. Its principal purpose is not to conquer other countries by making them economically dependent—though this, too, can happen in cases of reckless policy at the recipient country so caution should be exercised—but to maintain an internal economic dynamic. For China, despite the enormous size of the country, this cannot be achieved without having recourse to external factors, without further tapping into globalization for quick growth in domestic production and consumption. Over the last couple of decades, nobody has leveraged globalization so well for its own growth as China has. No wonder that it wishes to continue to do so. The Chinese are better positioned to do that as it seems that, unlike people of the West who, on their visits to China tell the locals how the world should be organized, the Chinese, while traveling, look around for solutions that may prove useful also to them. Probably China has learnt more from the West over the last decades than the West has from China, though quite a lot of things could be learnt there, too.

BRI—and the attendant policy instrumentation and system institutionalization, as exemplified by the relatively easily accessible loans from state-owned Eximbank or the establishing of a multinational investment bank, Asian Infrastructure Investment Bank (AIIB)—warrants a broader perspective. It is not a threat to the West, and not to Western Europe, either, considering the part of BRI known as 16+1, and 17+1[12] since Greece followed in the footsteps of post-socialist CEE economies in 2019.[13] Though much hope was pinned on 16+1, its first seven years have proved rather lean.

Elsewhere, the swift inflow of Chinese infrastructure and manufacturing investments, and trade cooperation, as well as staff training and healthcare offering may result in additional development. Let us look at a broader picture; the faster this growth bears fruit, the greater will be the benefits reaped directly in the countries to which investments and economic aid are addressed. The lower, too, will be the pressure to migrate from poor countries of Asia and Africa to Europe, and the smaller will be the influx of refugees and economic migrants, the waves of which the Europeans have a tough time handling.

BATTLE FOR TOMORROW, OR THE IMPERATIVE OF INCLUSIVE GLOBALIZATION

Ironically, it is the coronavirus-induced impossibility to maintain live face-to-face contacts that brings to the fore the strong and unbridled human desire to travel and absorb other cultures, work together in the field of education and scientific research, exchange and sports rivalry. We want to be together, not apart. These factors, not less than the classical links as part of production, supply and sales chains and global trade makes globalization—understood as the integration of capital and goods markets following liberalization—irreversible. It is even more surprising that the calling into question came from the least expected direction. The opinion-leading liberal weekly *The Economist* comes out with a screaming cover title: "Goodbye globalization" advising its readers: "Wave goodbye to the greatest era of globalization—and worry about what is going to take its place" (Economist 2020b). It can be surmised that its diagnosis is not only due to the pandemic's devastating consequences for liberalization and world economy integration but also that the magazine has understood that the existing form of extractive globalization stands no chance anymore, while it doubts the success of its inclusive version.

It is true that the pandemic—with its psychological and political side effects such as growing xenophobia and mutual hostility—is highlighting the symptoms of protectionism and naive mercantilism that could already be felt before. The neoliberalism-induced financial and economic crisis of 2008 led to a wave of new nationalism. For neoliberalism, intended to help very few get rich at the expense of the majority, the public enemy was the government as the regulator and income redistribution policy-maker, whereas for populism and new nationalism, this role is reserved for globalization. This clash both weakens the capacity—already an impaired one—to focus policymaking on the multinational scale, and is conducive to throwing political, social and economic relations into anarchy.

Adding to the crisis of mishandled economy liberalization—it being improperly deregulated from the point of view of social cohesion and economic equilibrium—is the crisis of liberal democracy.[14] There are those who believe that liberalism has already collapsed (Deneen 2018). This crisis is taking different, sometimes surprising forms—one in the United States following the election of President Donald Trump, another one in Poland ruled by Law and Justice Party; yet another one in Australia with its nationalist government of Prime Minister Scott Morrison, and a different one in Brazil with the populist right-wing president Jair Bolsonaro. In every case, it harms the supranational social cohesion and makes it difficult for globalization to stay on reasonable course.

This course must be based on the nonorthodox economic thought, of particular importance being new structural economics (Lin 2012b), economics for the common good (Tirole 2017) and new pragmatism—a sort of interface between descriptive and prescriptive economics indicating the ways to integrate economic, social, and environmental development into an economy of moderation (Kolodko 2014a). The belief that, though hard, it is possible to create a good economy is voiced by economists of various contemporary theoretical schools (Galbraith 2014, 2013; Rodrik 2015; Stiglitz 2019).

China—this greatest beneficiary of globalization—fully grasps that, which is why (though above all, because it has its own interests at heart), it is its great advocate. It repeats the phrase *win-win* ad nauseam, emphasizing that globalization must be advantageous for all parties involved. It is right though some are sneering that behind this *win-win* lies a desire for a 2:0 win. To save globalization, to make it truly irreversible, it must become inclusive. Letting it continue in its neoliberal variety preferred by interest groups and selfish economic and political lobbies, coinciding with adverse megatrends in natural environment changes, global warming, uncontrollable large migrations and the Covid-19 pandemic, which has led to what I call a Yet Greater Crisis, YGC (Kolodko 2011a, 2020b), is not an option.

Not only an inclusive globalization, but also no globalization whatsoever can be continued without the necessary degree of harmony between the world's two largest economies—that of China and the United States (Kissinger 2011). When it already seemed that we were on the right track in this respect—especially thanks to the efforts of President Barack Obama and President Xi Jinping, yielding a number of bilateral and multilateral agreements of global implications, as exemplified by the fundamental 2015 Paris Agreement on climate change mitigation—there came President Donald Trump, a sworn enemy of globalization who fails to understand its essence. The hope for development of *pro publico mundiale bono* cooperation and friendly rivalry as part of the so-called G-2—or Chimerica—was replaced with Cold War 2.0. In the heat of the pandemic psychosis, both in Washington and Beijing there is talk of possible hot war that may be provoked by a Taiwan crisis. When US hawks make allegations that China is preparing to join the island to the motherland by force, which needs to be prevented through military measures, even if it means unleashing a war, Chinese analysts from a military think tank speculate that it is the Americans who are instigating radicals in Taipei to declare independence (Economist 2020c). The reason why it is dangerous is that in addition to Donald Trump's extreme Sinophobia, republicans' democratic opponents are not fully devoid of the same. It will take some time before better pragmatism-driven relations can be reestablished.

An interesting perspective, one that systematizes the analyses and provides a methodology to facilitate the discussion of China's foreign relations is suggested by Kerry Brown. In his inspiring study "What Does China Want? China's World" he divides China's global surrounding into four zones. The first one is the United States, the second, the rest of Asia (including Russia), the third, the EU and the fourth, other countries of the world (Brown 2017). The China–US relations are paramount for the functioning of the global economy and politics; with or without globalization. Another thing of strategic importance is the behavior of the European Union, which President Trump would like to win over to his side in the US–China face-off. He is failing at that and one should hope that nobody will succeed in turning the EU and China against each other as that would harm them both and the whole global economy alike.

Hard times call for prudence and calm rather than thoughtlessness and overexcitement. Some Western politicians, failing to comprehend the objective imperative of pragmatic co-existence with China, have radically turned their backs to it. This can be felt much stronger in the United States than in the EU. Now, in the face of their own powerlessness, they are losing common sense. While in politics one cannot entirely avoid lunatics and fools who need to be restrained and eliminated from public life, some statements by top-echelon politicians and influential government advisers are in the highest degree alarming. These are people we expect expertise and responsibility from, and if they are guided by cynicism, so common in politics, this should be exposed and opposed to in a debate. If they are losing their heads due to their impotence, things start to get out of hand.

When an expert of the stature of Peter Navarro, an economic adviser to whom President Trump lends an ear, says China

> inflicted tremendous damage (. . .) We're up to close to $10 trillion we've had to appropriate to fight this battle (. . .) A bill has to come due for China (. . .) it's a question of holding China accountable, the Chinese Communist Party accountable. (CNBC 2020)

it is already dangerous. Could it be *Yellow Peril 2.0*? Maybe it would be more legitimate for China to claim from the West, especially from the British, a compensation for giant losses caused knowingly by the intentionally waged Opium Wars in mid-nineteenth century where half-colonized Chinese population was subjected to planned debilitation by being forced to buy poison cultivated by poor peasants in fully colonized India? Let us just wait for somebody to come up with such a demand. Maybe Central and Eastern Europe will demand to be paid back for the losses brought on by the Washington-championed "Consensus" at the time of post-socialist transition? Moreover, while we are at it, the countries of Western Africa may demand retribution for the irreparable damage sustained in the past because of devastating slavery, which was, in turn, one of the forms of original accumulation of wealth in North America. Americans' present-day wealth is also built on blood and sweat of millions of African slaves, which some wish to easily forget but others should never forgive.

When a technocrat of Margrethe Vestager's class—seemingly one of the most competent European Commissioners—warns against the threat of takeover of European companies hit by the Covid-19 pandemic, this must make you wonder and worry. If a Chinese investor knocks to the door of entrepreneurs who are not coping well with the crisis, even with generous public aid from governments and European Commission, one needs to negotiate with him and strike a deal rather than shut the door in his face. Even if the Chinese take full control of some companies and penetrate, to a wider extent, industries of interest to them, still, this will be an inflow of fresh capital, which is in short supply amid the crisis. This will often involve a transfer of high technologies, which are ever more abundant in China, and access on an ever-larger scale to the Chinese market and to third markets. Actually, most of such investments will be oriented to production for exports. When Danish or German capital flows into Slovakia or Poland, these are desirable direct foreign investments, and when Chinese capital flows into Spain or Sweden, this is a "takeover of European firms"?

A harmonized global order requires a strong and united European integration (Shambaugh 2016), but unfortunately it is being weakened due to the financial and migration crisis and the growing wave of new nationalism and devolutionary tendencies. Brexit is further undermining the EU, reducing its economy by ca. 15 percent. Unfortunately, the EU is becoming weaker at the time when it should gain strength to counterbalance China's growing influence. At the same time, the EU is China's leading cooperation partner and strategic rival; this is no contradiction but a sort of dialectic.

Against such backdrop, one should add another complication to this already complex equation: the triangle formed by China—Russia—the EU, notably Germany. The latter wants a strong, more deeply integrated European Union. It also wants good, pragmatic relations with both Russia and China. Now suitable Russian–German relations are not being sought by Kaiser and his cousin, tsar, but by a chancellor and a president who speaks its language. To both China is a vast market outlet; to Germany, for high-tech industrial products, to Russia, for raw materials, of which its land sprawling over eleven time zones has greater underground deposits than any other country.

Geopolitical games played between those three have a major impact on the geoeconomic situation.

China cares about developing cooperation with other countries and regions, at the same time engaging them further in the globalization process. While the United States has over 200 military installations abroad in 120 countries, China has one—a small naval base in the Horn of Africa, in Djibouti—but in contrast, is the largest trade partner for 130 countries. The sheer size of its economy makes it necessary to institutionalize foreign policy in the form of multilateral contacts. China must reach agreements at the bilateral level with countries like India or Russia but not with Tanzania or Argentina. This is why numerous forums have been created for communication and discussion, and sometimes for engaging in joint projects. Contacts with Africa are dealt with as part of Forum on China–Africa Cooperation (FOCAC), of which all of the continent's countries are members except Eswatini, the only country in Africa to still officially recognize Taiwan. To foster cooperation with the South America region, Forum of China and Economic Community of Latin American and Caribbean States (Foro China–CELAC)[15] was established. The organization intended to strengthen contacts with immediate neighbors are China–South Asia Cooperation Forum (CSACF) and China–Central Asia Cooperation Forum (CCACF). There are more such institutions, because China does not lose sight of any world region—including Oceania, the Arctic and the Antarctic. The functioning of those structures certainly brings multilateral benefits, and adds the "Chinese characteristics" to globalization.

Carrying out numerous projects requires finance. If their own funds are not enough, emancipating economies resort to foreign loans. China once used them, too, but at some point it became a lender, especially for developing economies, and now it is the largest creditor in the world. Loans granted by China, nearly none in 2000, in 2020 exceed the sum total of loans extended by the World Bank and the International Monetary Fund. At nearly 400 billion US dollars, they are twice as high as the official public debt of developing economies to the Paris Club countries. These amounts and relations between them are changing due to the pandemic-induced crisis because, on the one hand, both rich countries and China write off some of the irrecoverable debts of the so-called Highly Indebted Poor Countries[16] (HIPC), and, on the other, they extend new loans to those in need. The ongoing shifts in that area will strengthen China's position, especially that the White House's irresponsible policy discourages it from financing the US public debt. Part of the surplus that could have been placed in bonds of the wealthy United States will be invested in securities of economies working their way up. In the long run, it is a favorable structural change as it will boost the development of countries lagging behind, while—perhaps—partly motivating the

United States to crack down on living beyond its means, which is financed with continuous borrowing.

Some believe that in the coming decades the main—not only economic—clash will be in the field of artificial intelligence, AI (Lee 2018). In recent years, China has made enormous headway in this sphere, using scientific and technological breakthroughs in electronic engineering and digitization, as well as its unique position of having abundant Big Data. The bigger the active population is the larger the amount of data that helps build AI applications. In this specific respect, only India can rival China. Meanwhile, the latter has still a lot to learn, and needs to create a more open innovation system (Medvedev, Piatkowski, Yusuf 2020).

Considering the whole context—including the hardware and software quality, and especially highly qualified professionals—the main competitive clash will, again, pit the United States against China. The ensuing economic tensions will become politicized, which can already be felt. It is beyond question that one of the reasons for the trade war and the new Cold War initiated by Americans is this very fear of losing the AI supremacy. We are faced with two choices here: between a rivalry, that upsets the equilibrium and dynamic, or cooperation and looking for synergies. So far, none of the parties seems willing to take the latter path.

Since globalization can no longer be stopped—what is linked with the development and expansion of China—there will be an incessant debate on what is good and bad for the world. Yes, there are good and bad economies (Sedlacek 2011), there are systems that are more and less effective in terms of meeting their objectives, there are progressive and backward ideologies and political systems that follow them. It is all the more important to learn as much as possible from one another and draw on the experience of others in a creative way. Anti-examples are also useful; if only to know what not to do. China has learnt a lot from others, while showing a unique capacity for approaching its problems from a pragmatic standpoint rather than an ideological one—the way it used to do. Nevertheless, it still needs to learn a lot. One should hope that it would be willing and able to.

One of the most interesting comparative analyses of history was suggested by the British historian Ian Morris. He developed an original Social Development Index, which takes particular account of the energy capture, a given social culture's capacity for organization, measured with the size of its largest urban areas, war-making capacity and the advancement of information technology, determined by the speed and extent of the spread of the written word and telecommunications (Morris 2010). Using those metrics, he reaches the conclusion that the West will keep dominating only for a couple of next generations after which, in the first decade of the twenty-second century, the world will be dominated by the East, the most important part being, of course, the Middle Country—China. Well, time will tell.

Long, long time ago—in the Mediterranean world that knew nothing of the Chinese civilization, though already back then smooth silk would be brought from there (Uhlig 1986)—all roads led to Rome; *omnes viae Romam ducunt*. Is it now the time of *omnes viae Beijing ducunt*?[17]

NOTES

1. Specifically, in WEF competitiveness ranking, China ranks higher than Italy, Estonia, Czech Republic, Portugal, Slovenia, Poland, Malta, Lithuania, Latvia, Slovakia, Cyprus, Hungary, Bulgaria, Romania, Greece, and Croatia, whose sixty-third place puts it between the Philippines and Costa Rica (WEF 2019).

2. The population of China is quickly aging, which is, by the way, one more aspect of their economic success. Life expectancy at birth is seventy-seven years for China. For comparison's sake, in Japan it is eight years longer, and in India, eight years shorter—sixty-nine years (Macrotrends 2020).

3. The UN estimates that India will become the most populous country in the world in the beginning of the fourth decade of this century. In 2035, it will have a population of 1.504 billion, while China will be inhabited by 1.464 billion people (UN 2019).

4. In the ranking, Belgium and Japan sandwich Lichtenstein, which I ignore in those comparisons.

5. The ranking includes Hong Kong, which, with a HDI of 0.939 ranks fourth *ex equo* with Germany. Poland, with the index of 0.872, comes thirty-second, between Greece and Lithuania.

6. United Nations Development Programme estimates for 2018 (UNDP 2019).

7. In the West, already back in the period preceding the turning point of 1989, the political and economic system dominating the Soviet Union and Central and Eastern Europe was referred to as communism, while in the part of the world where the system was spreading, the term "socialism" was used to mean the same. Later, in the period of systemic transition, also over there one could most often hear the term "communism" with reference to the period between 1945 and 1989. One could, therefore, sum up saying that it is a matter of terminology, but it is not true as significant substantive differences and ideological disputes lie behind the definition ambiguity (Walicki 1995; Kolodko 2000; Nuti 2018).

8. Let us leave out of this taxonomy the particular cases that need to be assigned their own pigeonhole. Cuba can be classified as state socialism, although following recent gradual market-oriented reforms, it acquires the characteristics of Chinism. A type of its own is North Korea with its unique *Juche* system and ideology (Lankov 2016). We can be sure that none of those models will have any followers in the future. On the contrary; these countries' greatest opportunity for growth lies in following the hybrid system of China. As a side note, when I crossed the border between North Korea and "communist" China on the bridge over Yalu River, I could not resist the

impression that I was entering a liberal country where freedom reigns; everything is relative.

9. "What we may be witnessing is not just the end of the Cold War, or the passing of a particular period of postwar history, but the end of history as such: that is, the end point of mankind's ideological evolution and the universalization of Western liberal democracy as the final form of human government" (Fukuyama 1989).

10. The Communist Party of China. It would be only right to add "the so called" as for a long time now it has been communist in name only, not in essence. This designation is a historic legacy of the bygone days. Now the ruling party advocates implementing and using mechanisms representing quite the reverse of the communist ideals, for example private ownership of means of production and capitalist gain, and situations that contradict them such as unemployment and major income inequalities.

11. The lifting of the two-term presidential limit in China, so unsettling to the West, is generally seen to herald Xi Jinping's continued holding of that office and probably that of the chairman of the party, too, once his second term comes to an end in 2022. This act can be read as a clear message that the policy line associated with him will be firmly pursued in the long term. The West equates this with a yet greater dose of authoritarianism and further restrictions of what already is a surrogate democracy. When the UK prime minister Tony Blair or German chancellor Angela Merkel have their term extended beyond two terms, it is democracy; when the term of China's leader Xi Jinping is extended, it is the assault on democracy (even if there is none over there).

12. China has put seventeen countries in one basket for obvious geographic—and, to be more precise, geoeconomic and geopolitical reasons—but also taking account of the difference of scale. It would suffice to realize that the sum total of GDPs of those 17 CEE economies represents merely ca. 14 percent of China's GDP (ca. 16 percent at PPP).

13. The sixteen CEE countries invited by Beijing in 2012 to join BRI are: Albania, Bosnia and Herzegovina, Bulgaria, Croatia, Czech Republic, Estonia, Hungary, Latvia, Lithuania, Montenegro, North Macedonia, Poland, Romania, Serbia, Slovakia, and Slovenia. This group does not include Belarus, Moldova, and Ukraine. It does not feature Kosovo either, whose independence China has not recognized to date and neither have Chinese maps as they still show Kosovo as a part of Serbia.

14. Some authors, wrongly not distinguishing between neoliberalism and liberal democracy, advocate the view about the fall of the latter in Central and Eastern Europe. In fact, illiberalism or illiberal democracy is emerging in some countries of the region—especially in Hungary and Poland—because of the failure of neoliberalism (Krastev and Holmes 2019). The action causes a reaction; it is not the aversion to liberal democracy that stimulates populism and nationalism, and ultimately illiberalism, but the defeat of neoliberalism.

15. The Forum does not include the region's countries, which maintain diplomatic relations with Taiwan: Belize, Guatemala, Haiti, Honduras, Nicaragua, Paraguay, Saint Kitts and Nevis, and Saint Lucia.

16. The Wold Bank classifies thirty-nine economies as HIPC, as many as thirty-three of which in Sub-Saharan Africa: Benin, Burkina Faso, Burundi, Chad,

Democratic Republic of the Congo, Eritrea, Ethiopia, Gambia, Ghana, Guinea, Guinea-Bissau, Cameroon, Comoros, the Congo, Ivory Coast, Liberia, Madagascar, Malawi, Mali, Mauretania, Mozambique, Niger, Senegal, Sierra Leone, Rwanda, Central African Republic, Somalia, Sudan, Tanzania, Togo, Uganda, São Tomé and Príncipe, and Zambia; one in Asia, Afghanistan, and five in South and Central America and in the Caribbean—Bolivia, Guyana, Haiti, Honduras, and Nicaragua (World Bank 2020a).

17. Published by the University of California Press in: *Communist and Post-Communist Studies*, 2020, No. 4: 259–279.

Part III

PRAGMATISM AS A KEY FACTOR FOR SOCIOECONOMIC PROGRESS

Chapter 10

The Great Chinese Transformation

From the Third to the First World

THREE WORLDS IN ONE

The idea of the so-called Third World was never clear. In the decades preceding the great post-socialist transition boosted by Poland's political breakthrough of 1989, it was most often assumed, without going into the intricacies of terminology and definition, that the first world is the highly developed capitalism headed by the United States, the second world is state socialism with the Soviet Union at the helm, and the Third World is all the rest—most often poor and backward countries, in many cases, especially in Africa—ones still shaking off the legacy of colonialism. One would also often refer to this group of countries as developing countries, though in many cases development was not one of their characteristics. In such a triple division, the Third World was characterized by low output and living standards, and by a large population and a quick growth thereof. Even back then one already had to wonder to which world China belonged. Certainly not to the first one, from which it was separated by an unbridgeable gap, but to the second or third one.

China did not wish to be classified as the "second world" as it would not accept the "with the Soviet Union at the helm" formula, while being unable to put itself at its helm. Maybe in the very beginning of the People's Republic of China's existence, in early 1950s, it had accepted Soviet political predominance but later this changed. Curiously, the Chinese leader Mao Zedong (1893–1976), in the final years of his rule put the USSR in the same group as the United States. In 1974 he said,

> In my view, the United States and the Soviet Union belong to the first world. The in-between Japan, Europe and Canada belong to the second world. The

> third world is very populous. Except Japan, Asia belongs to the third world. So does the whole of Africa and Latin America. (Mao 1974)[1]

Of course the "third world" defined this way should have had China at its helm to be able to stand up to the other two worlds and follow its own, only legitimate way toward a better future.

At that time China was already the world's most populated country, inhabited by 22.5 percent of global population, but it was also one of the poorest countries with a very backward agriculture producing as little as 2.8 percent of the global output. To realize how extreme the poverty was there, it is enough to be aware that, according to today's poverty measure (USD 3.20 per person a day at purchasing power parity, PPP), in the initial years of the PRC more than 99 percent of the society suffered from it! This was truly a country of paupers. Now the poor people represent less than 1 percent.[2] Poverty is a relative term. Its definitions and scales vary. The ambitious Chinese plan to eliminate poverty altogether in 2020 would mean a situation where the economy and social policy provide everyone with a net annual income above RMB 2,300, an equivalent of ca. USD 324 at the market exchange rate, and of ca. USD 684 at purchasing power parity. Unfortunately, the perturbation brought by the Covid-19 outbreak will doubtless delay this historic achievement.

There is a saying I once heard in Africa: if you want to go fast, go alone, if you want to go far, go together. China is showing to all humankind—both the rich and, more importantly, the poor—that one can both go fast and far. In just a lifetime of two generations—between 1979 and 2020, when the population figure has risen by ca. 45 percent, from 970 million to 1.4 billion—China has increased its output measured with gross domestic product (GDP), the unprecedented 40 times. It is hard to believe but these are the facts.[3] Considering the purchasing power and its changes, GDP has grown from ca. USD 690 billion to nearly 27 trillion. According to the same PPP measure, GDP per capita has risen nearly twenty-seven times in this period, exceeding the world average by 6–7 percent.

As is always the case with such comparisons, we are dealing with a whole lot of methodological issues as there is more than one way to calculate and more than one comparative measure. According to other estimates, China's GDP per capita has risen from just USD 1,600 in 1978 to almost 16,000 in 2019, or exactly ten times. In both cases, these are values calculated at constant prices for 2018 but subject to different assumptions and appraisals of changes to the purchasing power, hence the significant differences. The author of those alternative estimates, The Conference Board, in particular, believes that the official Chinese data seriously underestimate the historical base or point of reference—income in 1978 (CB 2020).

Table 10.1 The Value and Dynamics of GDP of China, United States, and Poland in 1978–2019 (purchasing power parity)

	Total GDP (in billions of 2018 US$)					
	Official data			Alternative estimation		
Country	*1978*	*2019*	*Quotient 2019/1978*	*1978*	*2019*	*Quotient 2019/1978*
China	691	26952	39.0×	1516	21956	14.5×
United States	7251	20993	2.9×	–	–	–
Poland	476	1257	2.6×	–	–	–
	Per capita GDP (in 2018 US$)					
China	723	19387	26.8×	1586	15973	10.1×
United States	32574	63126	1.9×	–	–	–
Poland	13631	32775	2.4×	–	–	-

Source: The Conference Board Total Economy Database (CB 2020) and own calculations.

Speaking of which, it is hard to miss the identical GDP level per capita in the United States in 1978 and in Poland in 2019. If the differences in the level of development and living standards only boiled down to that, the countries would not be so far apart. After all, what are four decades on the long path of history?

According to the World Bank's classification, developed high-income countries are economies with a GNI per capita of USD 12,375. This time it is not GDP but Gross National Income, though the two categories are not far apart. For China, GNI is lower than GDP by around 6 percent and in 2019–2020 it could be estimated at ca. USD 10,200. Hence, the high-income country status is not far away; all it takes to reach it is a ca. 20 percent growth. Once the shock related to the Covid-19 pandemic has been successfully dealt with, this should take three, maybe four years.[4] And that is how, in merely half a century, between 1974—when Mao rightly saw China in the Third World—and 2024, the country will have moved its economy to the first world. Although it is far more complicated, because quantity is not all that counts. Sometimes it even counts less than quality.

LONG, LONG TIME AGO . . .

The Chinese path to the "first world" has a rich and complex history. On a short timeline, it is usually traced back to its opening to globalization and the attendant liberal economic reforms of Mao's successor, Xiaoping (1904–1997). His famous quip: "It doesn't matter if a cat is black or white, as long as it catches mice" is truly the quintessence of pragmatism that has informed Chinese market reforms of the past four decades.

A yet shorter timeline starts with the change of narrative during the rule of Xi Jinping, the party's current leader since the end of 2012, and the president of the PRC since the spring of 2013. Deng advised humility and mostly inward orientation, saying in 1990 "hide your strength and bide your time," whereas Xi believes that this time has already come, and he is promoting the "Chinese dream" (Xi 2014) as well as economic and political external expansion. China is moving from the "peaceful growth" to an "assertive growth," as declared in the documents from the nineteenth National Congress of the Communist Party of China. Xi said, "The path, the theory, the system, and the culture of socialism with Chinese characteristics have kept developing, blazing a new trial for other developing countries and nations to achieve modernization. It offers a new option for other countries and nations who want to speed up their development while preserving independence; and it offers Chinese wisdom and a Chinese approach to solving the problems facing mankind" (China Daily 2017, 8) and quite unequivocally: "It is time for us to take centre stage in the world and to make a greater contribution to humankind" (Financial Times 2017).

On a very long timeline of the past, the situation varied; at times China was closer to more developed countries and economies, occasionally even leading the world, some other times the distance was growing and sometimes it was even lagging far behind. Leaving aside ancient times—the highly developed civilization of Confucius era (551–479 BCE)—these days there are frequent mentions of great sea voyages of admiral Zheng He (1371–1433), who reached Arabia and eastern coasts of Africa 600 years ago. Rather than by an expansion akin to the one brought by Columbus's voyages to America, these escapades were followed by an utter retreat, which has been never fully explained. Most probably it was necessitated by the need to focus on the heavy load of internal problems, not by a weird phobia of the then emperor of the Middle Kingdom. Today China has a presence in these regions again and there is no indication of its intention to withdraw, quite the contrary. There are those in global politics that would be happy should China's mounting internal problems cause it to take in the sails also this time. That will not happen as this time China is unfurling them to better overcome the difficulties experienced back home by penetrating other parts of the world.

In the late sixteenth and early seventeenth century some of the illustrious European minds had high regard for Chinese achievements, treating them as a sign of higher level of development. Gottfried Leibniz (1646–1716), German philosopher and mathematician believed that in the field of exact science the West was at the leading edge, while the Chinese surpassed Europeans in "practical philosophy," in the way it organized the society where "laws are beautifully directed toward the greatest tranquillity and order" (Obbema 2015, 18). Leibniz, learning about China from Catholic missionaries returning from there, and living in a Germany ravaged by the Thirty Years' War (1618–1648), wished Chinese missionaries would arrive in Europe and dreamed of a new global culture combining the best of China and Europe. Some 300 years have passed; missionaries—now civilian rather than Jesuit ones—imbued with all kind of ideas travel both ways with unprecedented frequency, and yet this longed—for global culture is still far ahead.

Half a century later, Voltaire (1694–1778), a great philosopher and writer of the Enlightenment, wrote of China with esteem. He was certainly inclined to do so by the background of crisis and chaos prevailing in the pre-revolutionary France. When in 1764 he observed: "Their empire is the best that the world has ever seen" (Obbema 2015, 18), he presumably met with similarly critical reactions to those experienced by today's apologists of the complex Chinese reality. Voltaire even created poems about the Qianlong Emperor (1711–1799), whom he perceived as a Platonic philosopher-king.[5] By contrast, his contemporary, Montesquieu (1689–1755), treated China as a "despotic state, whose principle is fear" (Obbema 2015, 19). Some Sinosceptics would concur with him also today.

Hard as it is to believe, 200 years ago China produced ca. 32 percent of the global output. It will be easier to understand, however, when we realize that back then the country was inhabited by more people than now in relative terms; ca. 38 percent of the entire world's population. There were more than three times as much of Chinese people as Europeans; 381 and 122 million respectively. Then there came a period of slowdown and regression. While first Europe, and then North America were gathering momentum as a result of subsequent industrial revolutions, China—not without help from some empires of Western Europe—descended into stagnation. In the late nineteenth and early twentieth century it was a semi-colonized economy. That "century of national humiliation" is often recalled today. It is known to all primary school pupils, making them even prouder of their homeland's contemporary achievements and avid for something worthy of being the Chinese dream of twenty-first century.

History never repeats itself to the letter, but sometimes the contemporaries cannot help but be reminded of the past. The Chinese were once already the object of fear, or to be more exact, that of scaremongering, amid a surge of xenophobia. The end of nineteenth century in both North America and Europe went down in history as the inglorious time of "Yellow Peril." It was essentially an anti-Asian racism where fear of migrants from the region was deliberately instilled in the local population, and disgraceful racist practices were resorted to, at times, on the grounds of the obvious superiority of the American and European civilization. In the United States in 1882, the *Chinese Exclusion Act* was enacted, which was repealed in 1943, and the Senate was kind enough to apologize for it only in 2011. Had it not done it back then, this certainly would not have happened now, with a Republican majority. Whereas in Europe in the late nineteenth century the German kaiser Wilhelm II would fuel the hatred toward the Chinese with the threatening vision of their invading hordes. It was to that end that he sent to his distant cousin, the tsar of Russia Alexander III, a drawing depicting a Chinese dragon trampling over the Christian Europe. The multiple copies of the image had a vast success as contemporarily do some chauvinistic and racist memes.

The inability to go with the creative and pro-development flow of nineteenth-century industrial revolutions, as well as the social and military shocks of the first half of the twentieth century caused China to be incapable, for a couple of generations, of overcoming a systemic—economic and political—collapse. China's GDP in mid-twentieth century, when the People's Republic of China was founded, with the Communist Party of China at its helm, represented no more than a meager 2 percent of the global output. This fall—as a fall it was—in the form of a drastic downward slide in just 130 years from a situation where the country produced one-third of the global output to producing merely its one-fiftieth, coupled with the immense population it affected, was an unprecedented process.

FROM EVER MORE TO EVER BETTER

Now, at purchasing power parity, China's GDP is back to ca. 20 percent of the world's output. Over time, the figure will keep growing; one day reaching again over 30 percent, like two centuries ago. This has its obvious determinants and less obvious implications. It is the Chinese political and economic system that has enabled such progress, especially in the period of opening and reforms post-1978 (Economy 2018). However, it comes at a huge cost and yields negative consequences the GDP value alone fails to show. Particularly acute are the ecological costs in the form of environmental devastation and the immense scale of income inequalities. These two areas—in addition to the need for economic equilibrium especially with respect to finance and trade—represent the greatest challenges faced by the economic policy in the coming decades. Improving the environmental situation and reducing income and wealth differences are issues of more importance than constantly maximizing the rate of the traditionally defined economic growth.

Naturally, the latter cannot be disregarded. After all, it is the value of goods produced and services supplied that provides the material foundations of life and determines the well-being. Moreover, maintaining a relative balance on the labor market requires, as can be estimated, at least a 5 percent GDP growth rate. The economy needs to absorb each year over a dozen million employees migrating to industry and services located in urban areas. This is one of the conditions for keeping social peace, much more important than catching up with and outpacing others. After all, the reason why China has the policy of fast economic growth in place is not to be able to outdo Japan and the United States in terms of output, but to better satisfy the needs of its numerous population.

China has picked up speed. Its economic dynamic greatly exceeds that of highly developed countries, constantly reducing the gap.[6] What also matters in the context of geopolitics is that in the second decade of the twenty-first century India's economy is growing almost just as fast. In the previous thirty years it was not the case, which is of significance for discussions comparing different political and economic models; in 1980–2009 India's total GDP rose ca. 7.2-fold, and in China, as much as ca. 26.7-fold. In that time, India, which until 1992 had a higher income per capita, was left far behind by China. In turn, while total GDP in China in the decade of 2010–2019 slightly more than doubled, in India it almost doubled. Consequently, now a Chinese person's average income is nearly two and a half times as high as that of an Indian person.

Though we are already living in a beyond-GDP reality (Kolodko 2014a; Stiglitz, Fitoussi and Durand 2018; Kozminski, Noga, Piotrowska and Zagorski 2020), let us dwell a while longer on the GDP analysis. It is important because also in this field a lot will change due to the confusion caused by the Covid-19 pandemic. According to the spring estimates of the International Monetary Fund (WEO 2020a), economic growth was supposed to continue in 2020 in those former Third World's largest two economies, though on a much lesser scale as a result of the lockdown of part of the economy, intended to prevent the spreading of the contagion, and the disruption of the transnational supply and production chains (Kolodko 2020c). In its World Economic Outlook for autumn, IMF forecasted for China GDP growth of 1.9 percent and for India a recession of 10.3 percent in 2020 and an exponential growth of respectively 8.2 and 8.8 percent in 2021 (WEO 2020b).[7] For highly developed countries a major downturn in output was expected.

Should such scenarios materialize, China's GDP at PPP will increase from ca. 128 percent of the US level in 2019 to ca. 143 percent in 2021 or—reversing the perspective—the US income will decrease from 78 to 70 percent of that of China. This is indisputably not the effect desired by the president of the United States Donald Trump, whose policy is intentionally designed to relatively weaken the Chinese economy and *Make America Great Again!* in

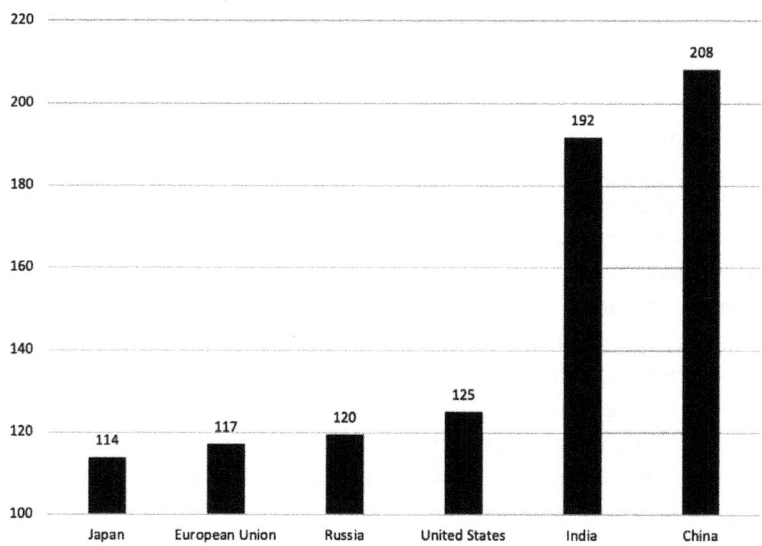

Figure 10.1 China and Big-5: Gross Domestic Product (2009 = 100). *Source*: Own calculations based on the data of International Monetary Fund (WEO 2019).

Table 10.2 Forecasts of Recession and Growth in 2020–2021 (fall/growth of GDP in percent)

Country	*2020*	*2021*	*2021 (2019 = 100)*
China	1.9	8.2	110.3
India	–10.3	8.8	97.6
Japan	–5.3	2.3	96.9
Russia	–4.1	2.8	98.6
United States	–4.3	3.1	98.7
World	–4.4	5.2	100.6

Source: WEO 2020b.

this context. Therefore, the scale of shifts taking place on the global scene is gigantic. Let me just point out that the China's national income estimated this way is only counterbalanced by the sum total of income of the United States, Japan, and Russia.

China's total national income (PPP-weighted GDP) is more than one-fourth higher than that of the United States, whereas at the current exchange rate it is still much, nearly one-third, lower. In 2019 these figures stood at ca. USD 21 trillion and 14.4 trillion. A better and more informative category is income at purchasing power parity as this figure tells us how much it is actually worth, or, more precisely, what comparable value of goods and services it can be converted into, considering the international price differences. If we were to stick in our analyses to income calculated at the market exchange rate, adopting the simplifying assumption that these countries will maintain

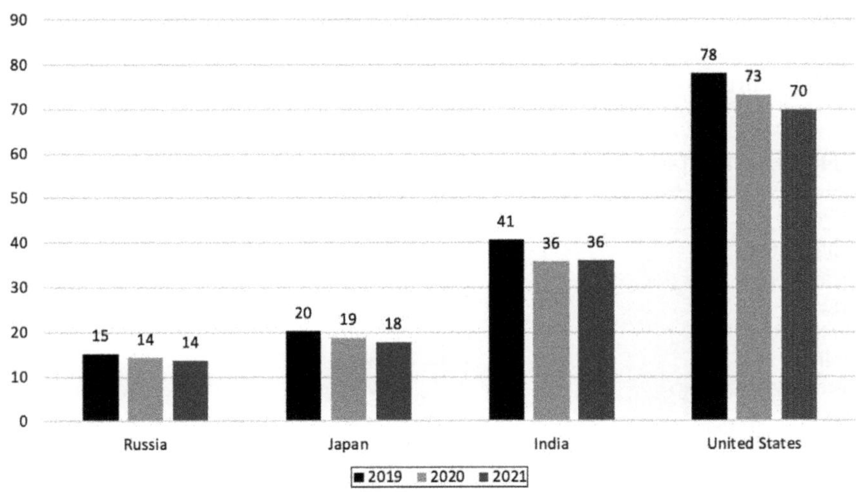

Figure 10.2 China versus Big-4 GDP of Selected Countries in Percent of China's GDP (purchasing power parity). *Source*: International Monetary Fund (WEO 2020b) data.

post-2020 the average GDP growth rate at the level achieved in the year preceding the Covid-19 pandemic, meaning 2.3 and 6.1 percent, respectively, then China's GDP, reaching USD 26 trillion (at constant prices for 2019), will exceed the United States' level in 2030.

What also, and sometimes especially, matters in the global economic cooperation and rivalry for political supremacy is how China's output impacts other countries. It was not until 1995 that China made it to the very end of the list of top fifteen global exporters and, just after eighteen years, in 2013, it took the lead which it will continue to hold in the foreseeable future.[8] China's total international trade amounted to USD 4.6 trillion in 2019, with exports up by 0.5 percent and imports down by 2.8 percent compared to the preceding year.

Let us also note that the relatively very high exports to Hong Kong are nearly entirely re-exported by the same. Therefore, the actual exportation of goods to respective foreign markets is higher than revealed by the data quoted here. In the last year before the pandemic that shook the world economy, including the international trade, China had a positive balance of USD 421.5 billion, higher than in the preceding year, despite the sanctions resulting from the trade war waged by the United States. China remains the United States' largest trade partner as, regardless of the protectionist restrictions imposed by President Trump's administration, it is the recipient of goods worth over half a trillion dollars, that is ca. one-fifth of total US exports. Another thing that matters in the global rivalry is the state's financial reserves, in which respect China, again, with foreign currency reserves worth the equivalent of ca. USD 3.1 trillion, ranks first worldwide.[9] These reserves were ca. USD 750 billion higher in 2014, but in the following five years they were sensibly used by financial policy to stabilize the economy and stimulate the output growth. It is worth pointing out here that Beijing holds a third of reserves in US securities, binding these two economies even

Table 10.3 Top Ten Countries of Chinese Exports in 2019

Country	*In bln USD*	*In percent*
United States	418.6	16.8
Hong Kong	279.6	11.2
Japan	143.2	5.7
South Korea	111.0	4.4
Vietnam	98.0	3.9
Germany	79.7	3.2
India	74.9	3.0
Netherlands	73.9	3.0
United Kingdom	62.3	2.5
Taiwan	55.1	2.2

Source: International Trade Centre based on General Customs Administration of China Statistics (Trade Map 2020) and own calculations.

further. Two-thirds are distributed among other reserve currencies, euro having the greatest share, followed by yen, Hong Kong dollar,[10] British pound sterling, Korean won, Australian and Canadian dollars, and Swiss franc. Approximately USD 100 billion is held in gold. It is the China central bank's large-scale purchases of the latter in recent years that have led to a major increase in the prices of this precious metal. On the other hand, only ca. 2 percent of the global currency reserves are held in the Chinese currency. It can be estimated that other countries' central banks have accumulated in RMB no more than the equivalent of a quarter of a trillion of dollars. That is the current status but it will change and RMB's share of global currency reserves will systematically, though slowly, rise. Undoubtedly, at first at the expense of US dollar, which will also have its political implications. Furthermore, China, provoked by the US hostility and aggressive trade policy that hinders economic development, is consistently setting up a parallel financial system, which will help go around USD-based payment mechanisms (Economist 2020d). Currently, the way the international financial clearing system works means that a vast number of international trade transactions cannot be concluded bypassing USD. This enables the United States to impose severe sanctions on others or blackmail them with a threat of sanctions, which is being experienced by Iran these days and which threatens to befall its trade partners.

Sometimes hostile emotions virtually lead to loss of reason. This is what can be said of prominent representatives of the US political establishment formulating accusations against China and demanding financial compensation for the losses sustained by the US economy because of the Covid-19 pandemic. The media have reported on the fantastic idea popularized by sources within the administration that "the White House is thinking of cancelling part of USD 1.1 trillion debt to China to 'punish' the country for the pandemic" (Economist 2020b). "Congressional Republicans such as Sen. Lindsey O. Graham (S.C.) have increasingly demanded the United States 'make China pay big time' over the damage" (Washington Post 2020). Senator Marsha Blackburn went even further, reaching the absurd, as she "floated waiving interest payments to China for any holdings of U.S. debt, because 'they have cost our economy already $6 trillion and we could end up being an additional $5 trillion hit'" (Washington Post 2020). Such public declarations by major-league politicians are the grist to the mill of xenophobia as if there was not enough of it already. During the electoral campaign, striving for re-election of President Trump, his henchmen are paying for media ads insinuating that "China is killing our jobs and now, killing our people" (Washington Post 2020). Chinese state-owned media were quick to respond, fanning the nationalist emotions with invectives against Mike Pompeo, the US secretary of state, calling him "evil," "insane," and a "common enemy of mankind" (Washington Post 2020).

A fascinating though often nasty clash between geoeconomics and geopolitics is underway. Both these mega-processes are interconnected, but—assuming that we manage to avoid the ruinous hot war, which assumption I consistently make—in the world of tomorrow, economic processes will be undoubtedly of crucial importance. Power relations will be determined by how these unfold rather than by subjective desires and ambitions of politicians for whom power and influence are everything, and solving social and economic problems only serves as an instrument of their dominance. From this standpoint, China's relative position in the global arena will continue to grow stronger for many years to come as its economy will grow in both absolute and relative terms, though no longer at the rate it did until recently.

CONCLUSIONS

China not only does not fall under the rule of "communism" (Sun and Zhang 2020), but thanks to its unique features continues to grow at an above-average pace. Following the victorious, several decadelong war on poverty, it is in for another war, this time one to protect natural environment. In addition, this one can be won over time, and this will prove the *conditio* sine qua non of the Chinese specific political and economic system—so-called Chinism (Kolodko 2018)—a being accepted by next generations. Earlier on, China and especially its leaders were unwilling to sacrifice maximizing the traditionally defined (in the narrow quantitative terms) economic growth rate. Now—on the eve of being promoted to the group of high-income countries—it must sacrifice the same at the altar of development that is triply sustainable: economically, socially, and environmentally. If it manages to do that, it will peacefully win another era on the never-ending path of development.[11]

NOTES

1. It would be interesting to know where Chairman Mao saw the place of Central and Eastern European countries in his classification. Probably not in "Europe" but rather by the Soviet Union's side, so in the "first world."

2. According to the World Bank's estimates, during the four decades of China's market reforms and opening to the world, over 850 million people got out of poverty in China. However, as many as 373 million people are still living on less than USD 5.50 a day over there, which is below the poverty line set for upper-middle income economies, a category to which China belongs (World Bank 2020b).

3. At constant prices for 2010, China's real GDP rose from nearly 290 billion dollars in 1978 to ca. 11.5 trillion in 2019. Cf "World Bank national account data, and

OECD National Accounts data files" (https://data.worldbank.org/indicator/NY.GDP.MKTP.KD?locations=CN; retrieved 11.05.2020).

4. This may happen but does not have to. Some think that the post-pandemic world will prove much worse for China, which will slow down its growth and greatly lengthen its path to catching up with richer economies. According to those opinions, the West may isolate itself more, blocking the influx of Chinese capital, slow down the knowledge- and technology-sharing and introduce further trade restrictions. The decline in mutual trust will also affect the West–East relations.

5. In our day and age, the lack of such poems can be hardly made up for to the president of the PRC by paeans in his honour written in prose in a dozen or so of Chinese institutes established "to study and interpret Xi Jinping Thought on Socialism with Chinese Characteristics for a New Era." This smacks of cult of personality, which the Chinese leader does not need.

6. It is worth comparing, subject to all relevant methodological reservations, the economic dynamic of China with the country of the most successful post-socialist transition, Poland (Piatkowski 2018; Kolodko 2020a). Well, Poland's GDP approximately tripled in the three decades between 1990 and 2019, whereas that of China increased as much as fifteen times. Per capita, for Poland this is still more or less three times as much, because the population has slightly decreased, while for China, as we know, the real income per capita has grown approximately twelve times.

7. At the same time, the European Commission forecasted China's GDP growth in 2020–2021 at 1.0 and 7.8 percent (EU 2020).

8. With the incredible frictions caused by the Covid-19 pandemic and the often chaotic economic policy reactions, it is rather a question of unforeseeable future.

9. It is also worth noting that both Hong Kong and Taiwan have reserves that in both cases greatly exceed USD 400 billion. Hence, looking at the so-called Greater China, its currency reserves go up to ca. USD 4 trillion.

10. Hong Kong dollar, HKD, is de facto pegged to the US dollar under the currency board regime, so from the macroeconomic perspective both currencies can be treated similarly.

11. Published in *Acta Oeconomica*, 2020, Special Issue: 71–83.

Chapter 11

Income, Fiscal Transfer, and Conflicts of Economic Interests

The efficiency of any public finance system—tax collection, transfers, and expenditures—must always be assessed in terms of the two fundamental functions that the system must perform. On the one hand, it is intended to foster social cohesion, which manifests itself in a sense of social justice, wide access to public services, acceptance of economically justified inequalities in the distribution of income and wealth, integration of various sociocultural groups, and mutual trust between the state and economic operators, both households and entrepreneurs. On the other hand, the system must foster capital formation, that is, saving and investing, without which there is no development. It is not only about physical capital, including infrastructure, and financial capital, but also about human and social capital.

There is no ideal situation in this respect anywhere in the world; after all, there are systems that are closer to it than what we have managed to shape in Poland so far. Improving the existing system (there are worse) is a permanent process. No wonder, then, that from time to time its various threads come to the fore. The same is true nowadays and that is why it is worth to pay special attention to some of them.

DISPUTE OVER THE 30-FOLD LIMIT

The functioning of the pension scheme is extremely complicated, because apart from a typically conflicting situation that we have to deal with in the system of public finances (the stream of taxes paid and transfers received and public goods is different for individual entities and social groups), there is also the redistribution in time. So, not only does someone else pay contributions/taxes and someone else receives benefits, but there is also a shift of transfers by at least one generation.

It is worth recalling the basic arguments that prompted the legislator to introduce a limitation in the payment of contributions. The 30-fold limit was introduced together with the pension scheme reform in 1998. It means that *The annual calculation basis for retirement pension and social security insurance contributions* in a given calendar year may not be higher than the amount corresponding to the 30-fold amount of the forecasted average monthly salary in the national economy for a given calendar year (ZUS 2018).

By introducing such a limit, it was decided to opt for a defined contribution system where the future benefit is based on the number of contributions paid throughout working life. In this respect, Poland has followed most of the member countries of the Organization for Economic Co-operation and Development (OECD), where the defined contribution model became common, which has a number of advantages over the defined benefit system, where the amount of a pension depends on factors other than the sum of benefits paid. These may include seniority, last salary, or the nature of the profession.

The advantages of such a system are as follows:

- A specific justice understood as: you get what you paid in.
- Limiting the grey market, because only when being officially employed and paying contributions you save in the pension scheme.
- Promoting longer working lives after reaching the retirement age, because the longer you work and pay contributions, the higher the future benefit.
- Some protection against demographic change, as extending life expectancy automatically reduces the current benefits that result from the quotient of accumulated contributions and the projected number of months of life that remain after retirement.

After all, one should remember about the limitations of the defined contribution model:

The pay-as-you-go financing of the system causes tensions when the next generation of employees is significantly less numerous than the previous generation, because the relatively large benefit stream resulting from the number of employees in the previous generation, and thus the value of the paid contributions, will have to be financed by a much smaller number of economically active employees in the future.

By its very nature, the defined contribution system does not include a redistribution mechanism, i.e. income inequalities among employees automatically translate into the income structure of future pensioners.

The room for maneuver in manipulating basic parameters such as retirement age or current contributions only changes the structure of financial flows over time, but the degree of system balance does not change. Higher contributions paid today increase the income of the Social Insurance Fund (FUS), but at the same time determine higher benefits in the future.

The same applies to the case of increasing the retirement age. The current situation is getting better, because we work longer and pay contributions, while fewer people receive benefits. However, this means much higher expenditure in the next period. More deposited contributions—due to a longer period of professional activity—automatically translate into higher benefits, which are additionally increased as the retirement age is raised. This reduces the number of months of life left after retirement.

Being aware of these features of the defined contribution scheme, two important solutions have been adopted to limit its disadvantages:

- The institution of a minimum pension has been established, to which those who have worked a certain number of years (twenty-five for men and twenty for women) are entitled, even if the quotient of accumulated contributions/the number of months in retirement gives a smaller amount than the administratively established minimum pension (Chłoń-Domińczak and Strzałecki 2013).
- A mechanism of a 30-fold limit has been introduced.

The multiplier of thirty was set quite arbitrarily—it might as well have been twenty-five or forty, although the authors of this proposal took into account the consequences of its amount for both the state of public finances and the inequality in the distribution of income of different types of households. Contributions are, therefore, not so much state income, but a loan granted by the contributors, which has to be returned when the employee becomes a pensioner. While forcing such a solution, it was argued that high salaries should not be charged with contributions in order not to pay very high pensions afterward.

The defined contribution system is capital-based (I get as much as I paid in), but it is financed on a pay-as-you-go basis, based on intergenerational solidarity. It is the current working and earning generations that contribute to the pensions currently paid out, which are obtained by those who once maintained the previous generation of pensioners in a similar way. So, if we were to increase the amount of contributions paid today and there were fewer workers than pensioners in the future—and this is what will happen as a result of the inevitable demographic processes—we would be giving our children and grandchildren a difficult future; the few working would have to finance numerous and, in the growing number of cases, high, sometimes very high, pensions.

Thus, while a departure from the 30-fold criterion would improve the public finance balance in the short term, additional tensions in the state finances would arise in the long term. Yet, we already have plenty of them. All these economic arguments were certainly taken into account in the government's decision to withdraw from the idea of abolishing the 30-fold limit, but essentially, it was done for political reasons. Tensions within the ruling party caused the government to doubt that there were chances of passing the already submitted bill in the Sejm. In total, it is good that this change has been abandoned, because the elimination of the existing rules would not only have positive effects but also many negative effects. Moreover, such important adjustments to the social security system should not be made in a hurry just because next year's budget already lacks several billion zlotys.

There were two objectives for the cancellation of the upper limit, beyond which contributions would not be deducted from remuneration. First, it was about additional revenues to the public finance system. If the total remuneration, regardless of its amount, is subject to contributions, the FUS records higher income from contributions paid by the employee and the employer; it is estimated that this would be about PLN 7.2 billion in 2020. Thus, the subsidy from the state budget to the structurally in deficit FUS automatically decreases. This operation has a positive effect on the balance of the state budget through lower expenditures rather than higher revenues. The revenues of central, local government and National Health Fund (NFZ) budgets are even decreasing, as social security contributions are deductible from income, so the contribution of all salaries reduces the basis for calculating the personal income tax and the health insurance contribution. It can be estimated that the state budget would gain about PLN 5 billion net in 2020, which is a combination of a lower subsidy to the FUS and lower revenues from the personal income tax (PIT).

Secondly, the 30-fold limit means that the Social Insurance Institution (ZUS) does not have to pay very high pensions to people who previously earned a lot. Currently, about 370,000 employees have income above this determined level. If they were to pay monthly social security contributions from their sometimes very high, income, over time they would also receive very high pension benefits, sometimes even several dozen times higher than the lowest benefits, with all the consequences both for the revenue side of the public finance system and for the increase in the scale of income inequality in society. While such situations can be tolerated in the case of private funded pension schemes, where too great an imbalance can be addressed by an appropriate personal income taxation system, they are more difficult to be accepted in relation to state schemes.

However, it should be remembered that the 30-fold level makes the tax and contribution system regressive. If the salary exceeds thirty times the average salary during the year, the monthly disposable income increases because the person no longer pays social security contributions. These contributions were deducted from taxable income, so now—when they no longer are—the progressive PIT burden increases. As a result, we have a system in which there is a range in which the more you earn, the lower the relative burden of the received salary. After exceeding the 30-fold limit (in 2019 it was PLN 142,950), contributions are no longer paid from the remuneration, and the remuneration is only subject to PIT.

Therefore, we have created a tax and contribution system that favors those who earn better. They are less taxed because they can choose self-employment with fixed nominal contributions paid to the ZUS and linear PIT, and when they are employed, they benefit from the 30-fold limit.

For earnings exceeding the 30-fold limit, the scale of personal income tax and contributions is decreasing and it is increasing again only in the case of much higher earnings, where progressive PIT is becoming more and more important, that is, cumulative income exceeds the highest tax threshold.

The entire fiscal system is regressive when we take into account indirect taxes, which burden the lower-income population to a greater extent, who spend on an ongoing basis a relatively large part of their disposable income (sometimes even the whole of it, because they are unable to save anything), each time paying the value-added tax (VAT) or excise duty, integral to the expenditure. Studies taking into account the propensity to consume of various income groups confirm that the tax system in Poland is regressive. The scale of the relative burden with contributions and taxes—PIT and VAT—drops sharply, in particular, among self-employed people (Tomkiewicz 2016).

The cancelation of the contribution payment limit seems sensible at first sight, because it increases public revenues and reduces the regressivity of the tax system. However, a comprehensive look, with a longer time perspective

Table 11.1 Salaries of Employees under Employment Contract in 2019 (in Polish zlotys)

Annual gross salary	*Annual net salary*	*PIT and contributions in percent of gross salary*
60,000	42,660	28.9
120,000	83,474	30.4
156,000	10,4255	33.2
168,000	113,030	32.7*
180,000	119,970	33.4
240,000	158,370	34.0

* decrease.

Source: Own calculations based on applicable regulations.

of the analysis, shows that the situation is not so obvious. In the end, the state of public finances could deteriorate.

By the way, it is also worth remembering about lower revenues of local governments (it would be about PLN 600 million in 2020) and the NFZ. Additional negative financial consequences for some parts of the public finance system, the size of which is difficult to estimate, would also be:

- Lower income tax revenues from the corporate income tax (CIT), and the cancellation of the contribution payment limit would mean a higher cost for companies, and thus a lower tax base.
- Higher expenditure of public institutions related to wage costs incurred for hiring employees.

A similar problem, that is, short-term benefits and long-term costs, exists in the case of income diversification. If the 30-fold limit is cancelled, income inequalities will fall in the short term, because high incomes would be subject to higher contributions, which would reduce the disposable incomes of people with salaries higher than this 30-fold limit. In the future, though, they would receive significantly higher pensions, which would imply significant inequalities; all the more so because at the same time those who worked part of their lives on the so-called junk contracts, would start to retire.

It is also worth noting that departing from the 30-fold rule would increase personnel costs because of increasing the amounts that employers would have to pay to the ZUS. This applies, in particular, to the costs associated with the employment of high-class, and thus, significantly highly paid specialists. For this reason, well-managed companies would not go bankrupt, but their owners' profits would relatively decrease. It is difficult to determine clearly, what would be the final effect of such a redistribution of income on investment in the entire national economy, since capital would be formed in other places and would be invested elsewhere and by someone else. It is worth examining this aspect of the case further.

PILLARS OF A GOOD SYSTEM

A good contribution and tax system must be based on several assumptions. Above all, it is necessary to take care of a long-term and dynamic socioeconomic balance. Pensions are intended to allow for a decent living with relatively balanced public finances. People cannot be scared that the ZUS will go bankrupt, because it will not go bankrupt. This is legally impossible and politically unacceptable. It is possible, unfortunately, that a scenario will happen in which the majority of public funds will have to go to the pension system instead of education, science, culture, health and environmental protection. This would erode social cohesion and would be damaging to the accumulation of capital, which would slow down the overall pace of development and, consequently, hinder or even prevent the improvement of welfare. Therefore, on the one hand, the structure of public spending should be rationalized—for example, by moderating wasteful armaments spending or verifying poorly addressed social transfers—and, on the other hand, additional revenues should be sought that do not increase the state's liabilities in the future.

The fundamental role of the public finance system is to collect and allocate funds necessary to finance public goods and services and to correct the market distribution of income, which leads to socially unacceptable income and, over time, property inequalities. This is not only an ethical issue, but it is also related to the effectiveness of management, against which excessive income inequalities turn (Fischer 1999; Kolodko 1999; Tanzi, Chu and Gupta 1999). The tax system must be based on indirect taxes, especially the VAT, and the progressive PIT.

In the course of these considerations, several important issues must not be lost from sight. First of all, it is important how many thresholds we have and what are the tax rates, but no less important is to cover the vast majority of income groups with the system. The highest tax threshold is currently exceeded by only about 3 percent of taxpayers, which does not correspond to the actual income distribution. In other words, many of those who de facto earn relatively much money are not covered by the progressive tax. It is here, where additional public revenues should be sought. They should also feed the budgets of local governments, as the growing scale of their tasks requires growing revenues.

Secondly, there must be no illusion that the problem would be solved by the simultaneous cancellation of the 30-fold limit and introduction of a maximum pension. Such a solution is questionable from a legal point of view (the law does not have a retroactive effect; by taking up work and paying contributions, one has acquired the right to a pension based on the contributions paid). In addition, it would create chaos in the system, as different people would receive a benefit calculated in different ways. Income inequalities should be corrected by the progressive PIT and not by various manipulations that spoil the system.

Thirdly, the current income of the pension system must be ensured by making it universal. So, "junk contracts" cannot be tolerated when the employee actually works full time. All salaries should be accompanied by contributions to the ZUS.

Fourthly, there is no economic justification for intentional measures to support entrepreneurship, such as the so-called small ZUS. After all, contributions to the ZUS are not only future pensions but also a share in financing current benefits. There is, therefore, no reason why entrepreneurs should pay less than employees. Above all, it is necessary to be aware that the part of the social insurance contributions paid to the ZUS by the entrepreneur is neither a tribute nor a charity, only a part of the payment for the employed labor force. It is an integral part of the wage, that is, the price of the labor force, whose value in market economy conditions is determined by the cost of its reproduction throughout its life cycle, including the post-productive age.

Finally, fifthly, long-term savings must be supported. From this point of view, Employee Capital Plans (PPK) is a worthy institutional solution because they encourage the formation of an additional stream of long-term savings, which can be the basis for key investments. Of course, it is crucial to ensure effective public oversight and appropriate regulation of private funds managing the collected savings.

One cannot uncritically succumb to the view that the PPK system reduces the current disposable income of employees and employers. Yes, savings by nature constitute unconsumed income, but the PPK is a kind of justifiably enforced additional savings, since households are not willing to put off more of their own. Over time, these funds—with interest, if invested cost-effectively and in a dynamically sustainable economy this is what happens in the long run—will finance consumption, while immediately, in the national economy the willingness to save is increasing and the pool of funds that can be used to finance development is growing.

For years, it has been indicated that the Polish economy suffers from an accumulation rate, which is too low in relation to development needs (EBRD 2004, 2013; Kolodko 2009). The government is also fully aware of this fact (Strategia 2017). Domestic savings and investments, which are almost equal (current and capital account balance is about 0.7 percent in 2019) at the level of about 18 percent of GDP, are much less than those of countries that have recorded a qualitative development leap. This applies to the already more advanced Asian economies (World Bank 1993) and post-socialist transition countries (EBRD 2019). In Poland also the investment rate was already much higher than nowadays, as both the relative level of domestic savings and the inflow of foreign investments were higher.

MULTI-LEMMA OF 30-FOLD LIMIT CANCELLATION EFFECTS

Hence, the problem is highly complicated, because we are looking for a creative compromise between conflicting interests: ourselves as current employees and future pensioners, employees and entrepreneurs, richer and poorer, those paying and receiving contributions, central and local budgets, public debt that is current and burdening future generations, immediate and prospective period.

There is no ideal answer here, because we are looking for a solution not so much to a mathematical equation—already complex enough anyway—but to an economic, social, and political multi-lemma.

The neologism of the "multi-lemma"—as opposed to a simple alternative such as the dilemma of either–or, or the more complicated trilemma, where the choice of two out of three options excludes the third one—is introduced here to emphasize the multidimensionality of the extended space of the selection made. Two trilemmas are particularly well known in economics—the obvious one of Robert Mundell's, which refers to the relationship between the exchange rate, interest rate and production (Vernasca 2014) and the debatable one of Dani Rodrik's, which considers the relationship between democracy, advanced globalization and the sovereignty of states (Rodrik 2011). The multi-lemma discussed here requires taking into account several factors of different force of influence, in different time horizons, with various financial, economic, social, cultural, demographic, and political consequences. Economic policy preferences for the good sides of specific factors determine negative consequences for others.

For example, the simple cancellation of the previously binding 30-fold limit of the average wage as the maximum remuneration for work charged with the obligatory social security contribution to the ZUS has its good points in the form of a certain reduction of income inequalities and a certain improvement in the current state of public finances, but at the cost of an increase in these inequalities and a deterioration in the balance of public finances in the long run. Alongside, the position of local government budgets is deteriorating. The costs of entrepreneurs are also rising.

It is, therefore, necessary to avoid short-termism and selectivity—sometimes biased—in addressing this issue. Only a comprehensive and dynamic approach to the problem can provide a chance to solve it properly, which must be kept in mind when looking for the optimum in this matter. Looking for it, though it cannot be found. The thing is to get as close to it as possible. The contradictions that exist in this multidimensional space between the various effects of actions taken can be presented collectively.

Of course, the above assessments are blurred and, thus, must be debatable. Will the indeed relatively lower incomes of highly paid professionals result, ceteris paribus, in the emigration of some of them and, consequently, in a relative decline in the supply of their services on the domestic labor market? Maybe so, but it does not have to be the case. It depends on a number of other factors, above all, whether, in the context of culture and family, they will want to leave and whether there will be a demand for their employment on better pay terms abroad. Will production costs, and consequently, inflation, actually increase?

Table 11.2 Multi-lemma of the Cancellation of the 30-Fold Limit of the Forecasted Average Monthly Salary in the National Economy as the Basis for Calculating Pension and Security Insurance Contributions

Sphere of effects	*Short term*	*Long term*
Balance of the state public finances	+	–
Local government budgets	–	–
Income of highly paid personnel	–	+
Span of incomes	+	–
Costs of production and providing services	–	n
Inflation	–	n
Supply of highly qualified labor force	n	–
Social cohesion	–	+

+ beneficial change; – unfavorable change; n neutral effect.
Source: Own study.

It depends, because instead of pushing up the overall costs due to the increase in the costs of labor (and trying to pass this on to the increase in the prices of the products and services sold), the profits of businesses may fall. This, in turn, would result in an alternative: lower consumption of capital owners or smaller private investments. Within the framework of this multi-lemma, each answer gives rise to another question.

Therefore, it is worthwhile to discuss the target tax and contribution system seriously—with social concern, but also with technocratic responsibility, with political seriousness, but also with accounting precision. Many issues were successfully solved in Poland during the political transformation, often better than in other countries facing similar challenges (Piatkowski 2018; Kolodko, 2020a), in which a relatively better starting point for a full-blooded transformation three decades ago certainly helped (Kolodko and Rutkowski 1991). Unfortunately, this still cannot be said about the pension scheme. Due to changing social and economic conditions, in particular demographic and financial determinants, such a system cannot be rigid, fixed once and for all. It must be tested in practice and periodically reviewed to ensure that it fulfills its essential functions as well as possible—promoting social cohesion and capital formation. Yet, it cannot be changed too often, and certainly not hastily, under the influence of immediate economic difficulties and an emotional political impulse.[1]

NOTE

1. Coauthor: Jacek Tomkiewicz. Published in: *Business Science Quarterly*, 2020, No. 4: 11–21.

Part IV

ECONOMICS OF SUCCESS VERSUS ECONOMICS OF FAILURE

Chapter 12

Chinese Economy at the Era of Globalization

THE GROWING IMPORTANCE OF ASIA IN THE GLOBAL ECONOMY

China is as much as and, yet, merely the Middle Kingdom. While it may not be the Middle Kingdom of the whole world, then at least of Asia, where the importance of better developed economies and increasingly educated societies is on the rise. Therefore, the question is not whether China alone, but Asia with China at the forefront, is moving to take dominion over the world. Some people think that this is the case, and, even if it is not a deliberate intention of the elites ruling therein, such is the logic of the historical process. Following this interpretation, there are only 90–100 years left before the end of the Western dominance and the takeover of this position by the East. It is supposed to happen at beginning of the twenty-second century (Morris 2010).

The growing strength of Asia is much more than China. The volume of production and size of the population is rapidly increasing. The continent has almost 4 billion 500 million inhabitants in total; that is, about 60 percent of the world population and about 55 percent outside the Middle East, often treated separately for geopolitical reasons.[1] This large population produces 47.3 percent of the gross world product, GWP—slightly more than Europe and North America combined. From a slightly different perspective, it is as many as eight percentage points more than the United States and the EU combined. In the future, both the share of Asian population and production will continue to grow due to both the natural increase and economic growth rate being higher than the global figures. It would be pertinent to realize that once—in actual fact throughout all the centuries of the previous millennium, until around 1820 with its powerful onset of the Western World industrial revolution—Asia kept turning out over 60 percent of the global production.

In 1950, it was less than 20 percent, but two generations were enough to make this index more than double.

China itself 200 years ago—before the industrial revolution gained momentum; first in England and soon after in Western Europe, and before the Middle Kingdom turned its back on the world and kept itself strictly to itself—China turned out almost a third of the world production. Five or six generations of disastrous domestic policy and the unfavorable external circumstances, including the British and Japanese colonial practices, were enough to go dramatically down this scale to below 5 percent half a century ago. No wonder, then, that some authors write about China's return to the international arena because it has already been there.

Now a digression. My perennial efforts to avoid tautology in the form of the term "globalized world" do not seem very productive. It is so often that both in everyday language and in scientific literature this mistake is repeated! The world is global by definition, as is the globe, hence the world cannot become global (or worldwide) and the globe cannot globalize because they have always been such. What undergoes globalization is economy, trade, capital flows, technology transfer and workforce, albeit, with significant constraints resulting from cultural, social, and political reasons, and outside the *strictly* economic sphere—also magnificent things like culture, and nasty things like terrorism. Globalization is a historical and spontaneous process of liberalization and integration following its example, turning hitherto largely isolated in their functioning national economies and local commodity markets into one, great, mutually interconnected and intertwined worldwide market of capital, goods, and workforce (Kolodko 2002a, 2002b). Globalization also has its microeconomic aspect related to the networking of production and exchange by incorporating into the process of production and distribution companies from many countries, still treated as national economies, although the management process is carried out increasingly on a supranational scale.

The Asian continent is highly diverse—culturally, politically, and economically—especially if it is treated literally; in geographical terms and stretched from Turkey and Israel in the west to Japan and Russian Siberia along with Kamchatka and Chukotka in the Far East. Apart from the Asian part of Russia, which is not usually included in the Asian calculations, its four main parts are China and Japan and two regional integration groups—ASEAN in Southeast Asia[2] in which none of the economies predominates, and SAARC in South Asia,[3] which is dominated by India which is a regional population (1.28 billion inhabitants), economic (7.4 percent of world production based on purchasing power parity, PSN) and military (military expenditure 2.5 percent of PPP) superpower.

Of the twelve countries with more than one hundred million inhabitants, as many as seven: China, India, Indonesia (261 million), Pakistan (206),

Bangladesh (159), Japan (126) and the Philippines (105) are located in Asia.[4] We omit here the Eurasian Russia, which is inhabited by 142 million people, of which only a quarter lives in its Asian part. Soon, still during this decade, another country will join them—Vietnam (97 million inhabitants in 2018). It is worth adding that in this group of countries the population is decreasing only in Japan; there are fewer and fewer inhabitants every year, and at the same time they are getting older. The median is as much as 47.3 years, which means that half of the population is above this age. However, the societies of India are young (median 27.9 years) as is Bangladesh (26.7). These are very important comparisons, because aging societies are deprived of the so-called demographic dividend, which affects the supply of labor to the labor market. For this reason, ceteris paribus, one can expect in the future a faster rate of economic growth in India than in China.

Of the twenty economies producing more than 1 percent of the world production, nine—China, India, Japan, Indonesia, Turkey, South Korea, Saudi Arabia, Iran, and Thailand—are located in Asia. Therefore, reflecting on the future role of Asia—its demographic potential and culture, political significance, and above all, economic influences—it must be borne in mind that it is almost the largest region of the world in every respect.

Is it actually so that things have already gone so bad (in the West) and so good (in the East) that Americans have to resort to wicked protectionist practices to save their own skin? Or maybe the Chinese indeed are plotting and using globalization to bring the world under their heel? Is the era of Asia's domination indeed under way with the Euro-Atlantic civilization relegated to a secondary position? Do we already need to learn Chinese first and then English?

NEW SILK ROAD

There is no doubt that both the absolute position of China—the economic one and, consequently, as is the case with a great country, the political and military one—and their influence on what is happening in the world, are growing (Huang 2017). It will remain this way in the foreseeable future because this process cannot be stopped, let alone reversed by peaceful methods—other ones are out of question. All others must acknowledge this, regardless of their own interests and biases. Moreover, certainly, China will not turn away from the world and will not shut itself down in destructive autarky, as it once did.

The size of the country has its advantages, but it is also a curse. Norway or New Zealand, Canada or Australia, Chile or Malaysia, Tunisia or Bulgaria do not have to lose sleep over power, because they are in no danger of becoming one. They are to sustain or create well-being for their citizens and that will suffice. In contrast, China, like the United States and Russia, and to a lesser extent India and Japan or France and Great Britain, as well as Brazil and Nigeria regionally, must demonstrate greatness economically, politically, and militarily. Only countries like Singapore or Costa Rica can afford a pacifistic orientation but by no means China or the United States.

What needs to be done is take a leap into the future and seek reconciliation with others in addition to finding the right place in the ever-shifting world. It should be somewhat easier nowadays since some processes are running in opposite directions than before. On the one hand, China is constantly attracting the production capacities of Western corporations, transferring on that occasion their hi-tech, while placing more and more of its production abroad, this time already having modern manufacturing techniques at its disposal. On the other hand, direct investments from richer countries still go to China, but also to other economies, not only Asian ones, where wages are lower than in China. Their beneficiaries include, among others, India and Pakistan, Vietnam, Cambodia, Bangladesh, and Myanmar. The effects of the ongoing appreciation of the Chinese currency are adding to this process. It is getting stronger, so for wages of, let's say, 3,000 yuan per month, you have to spend about $475, unlike a few years ago, when for half the nominal salary of 1,500 yuan, at the exchange rate of 8.2, 183 dollars was enough. With the increase in staff production costs, which have been recently growing by 20 percent per year, and currency appreciation, China ceases to be as competitive as it once was. The process that previously affected countries like Japan, Singapore, South Korea, Taiwan, and although on a smaller scale, Malaysia and Thailand, is yet again repeated.[5]

What is more, in the United States and other highly developed economies of the West, one can notice that the tendency to outsource and offshore is inhibited. This happens in such cases, where low labor costs play a relatively small role in the total expenditure on the production and sale of a specific product. There are quite striking calculations demonstrating that in the price of a 16KB Apple iPad, which was sold on the US market for 499 dollars in 2010, the cost of Chinese labor amounted to only $8, or 1.6 percent (Kraemer, Linden, and Jason 2011), though perhaps more, because the calculation includes an "unidentified" labor costs category, suggesting that they were incurred outside the United States and outside China. In such situation—and in the face of political pressure to stop the "export of jobs to Communist China"—a producer may come to the conclusion that even if they pay five times more for the same labor, but the merchandise will be *Made in USA* (and with peace of mind about excuses for outsourcing and offshoring), its assembly will take place again near San Francisco and not near Shanghai. The economic calculation of costs will not be overturned, but the political narrative could be "straightened out."

This time the Chinese challenge is not derived from the old attempt to export the revolution—fortunately unsuccessful—but primarily from the export of goods and, what is important, capital. This is accompanied by various related transactions that increase Chinese presence around the world. This can be seen in international statistics, but also with the naked eye when traveling around various parts of the world. However, what is not immediately visible and what is of great significance is the far-reaching effects of numerous infrastructure projects financed in exchange for long-term, strategic contracts for supplying raw materials. This is particularly pronounced in Africa and in Latin America, but still on relatively smaller scale in Central Asia, the Middle East, Eastern Europe, and—what is very important and interesting—in Russian Siberia. In the future, radical changes will take place here, and the great program propagated as the New Silk Road will play a key role in this matter. This is a popular term for a program known by its official name *One Belt, One Road*, OBOR, or recently more often as *Belt and Road Initiative*, BRI. It is a project of significant infrastructural investments that are intended to promote the expansion of trade between China and their foreign partners in the west, south, and north. The program is aimed at cooperation with several dozen countries in Asia, the Middle East, North and East Africa and in Central and Eastern Europe.

What is BRI? How to approach it? Is this a policy or an institution? Or maybe, an organization or structure? I think it is best to talk about it, as the Chinese themselves have proposed, as an initiative. Or as a project. There are always two "i's" behind any projects: ideas and interests. This is the case now, although this time, unlike in the times when Chairman Mao wanted to export the communist revolution, ideas are in the background. Although some argue that China intends to ideologically and politically expand outside, it is clearly not about encouraging others to follow the Chinese path or even impose the Chinese economic and political model, but about economic reasons. Yes, in some regions of the New Silk Road, like in the countries of Central Asia—whereby the way this old Silk Road beautifully thrived and left its imprint centuries ago—the system with Chinese characteristics may seem more tempting than Western liberal democracy, but in Central and Eastern Europe, it hardly inspires anyone.

Chinese politicians and economists emphasize the imperative of continuing globalization and there is nothing strange about it because it benefited them more than anyone else. At the same time, they emphasize the need to change the character of the current course of the globalization process. That is why so much is heard about the "transformation of globalization," which should be inclusive and fairly distribute the fruits of supranational cooperation in all fields: from the economy and the natural environment through security and technology to science and culture. In this context, the instrumental significance of BRI is being highlighted. This initiative is intended to help transform the globalization from its current form, rejected by many, into globalization, which will be socially more useful on a global scale than what the West has proposed. That is why some countries, rather from outside the West, place a lot of hope in it, while others, in the West, voice certain apprehension. The former are curious about what this "globalization with Chinese characteristics" could bring them, the latter probably would prefer not to experience it, and others are watching with interest what will come out of it.

The second "i"—interests, clearly moves to the forefront. Big business, because as regards its size, it is a great project, although its scale is still not fully known, neither in Beijing. It is said that BRI encompasses sixty-five Asian, European, and African countries inhabited by more than 60 percent of the world's population over 38.5 percent of its area. The trade between these countries accounts for 35 percent of the world turnover; their gross product is 30 percent of global production, and household consumption is 24 percent of what the whole of humanity consumes.

THE ONE BELT AND ONE ROAD INITIATIVE AS AN INSTRUMENT OF INCLUSIVE GLOBALIZATION

As the Chinese authorities emphasize, BRI creates great cooperation opportunities in five fields:

- Cultural exchange through the promotion of interpersonal relations and cooperation.
- Policy coordination through planning and supporting large infrastructural development projects.
- Financial integration through strengthening the monetary policy coordination and bilateral financial cooperation.
- Trade and investment through encouraging cross-border investments and cooperation in supply chains.
- Facilities connectivity by creating facilities enabling contacts along the belt and road.

Although the name of the project is the word "way," it is by no means clearly delineated by the authors. There are no official maps showing where this road is supposed to lead, therefore there exist large flexibility in their charting; a specific cartography is being developed. Of course, in the countries that the project intentionally includes, the road must lead through their territory. There are also twelve African ports on the BRI map, of which ten is located outside Egypt, which is the only country from this continent included in the project. That is the point: Who included whom and on what basis was it carried out?

Of course, it was China that included them, although the rules are not entirely clear. This is a fascinating geopolitical and geo-economic game, the goals of which are not clearly defined and the rules are not entirely clear. There are many players; cards have been supposedly handed out, but nobody knows if all of them. And whether the game is played only on the table, or whether some cards are passed under it. Who is risking what and in the name of how high hypothetical win? Political declarations sin through vagueness and, of course, are full of assurances of the goodwill of the initiator, but in many places of Eurasia—and elsewhere—they arouse various reflections, doubts, suspicions, anxiety. The economic goals are still drawn with a thick line and it is impossible to form a concrete opinion about what and why, where and when, for whose money it will be built and how it will be managed. That is how this kind of open-end game is going on.

The invited participants are looking forward to it, hoping that joining a project in this phase will not cost anything, and maybe some, maybe even significant, economic benefits will be brought thereby over time. Reputation is not endangered either, because despite the exacerbating attacks coming from the West toward China, cooperation with it is something obvious. Thus, nobody has refused to participate in the project, even the countries that have not had the best relations with the Middle Kingdom lately, such as Vietnam or the Philippines. It must be strongly emphasized that only China can afford such a huge project, announced and initiated in a way that it specified on its own.

If the United States proposed something similar under the name of, let us say, *Great Americas* and pulled out a map with an area stretching from Alaska to Tierra del Fuego, this plan would be a false start, because certainly some of the Caribbean and Latin American countries, such as Haiti and Venezuela, would not benefit from such dictum. If the EU announced, let us say, a *Euro-African project*, without proper arrangements made ex ante some of the post-colonial countries might not take part in such an enterprise. Only China can afford something whereby Pakistan and India, Poland and Russia, Israel and Syria, Myanmar and Bangladesh, Saudi Arabia and Iran, Nepal and Bhutan would more than willingly and without any pre-conditions join their project.

When looking at the map, the geographical criterion strikes the eye first. Almost all the countries of Asia, all of Central-Eastern Europe have been drawn to the project, and Egypt too, as what kind of road it would be if the Suez Canal was not en route. Almost all of Asia, because for political reasons the two Korean countries and Japan have not been included. It happened to the former because it was not possible to sign up only South Korea while sharp sanctions have been imposed on North Korea, so China have chosen to avoid accusations that they are cooperating with the regime in Pyongyang. The latter one, meaning Japan, was left out because relations with rich Japan are not the best, and it would be necessary to negotiate BRI with it, for which, unfortunately, there is no conducive atmosphere. Finland and Greece are absent from the edge of the map, because they are Western European countries, and on the other side, Papua New Guinea is missing, because it is already "Australia and Oceania." Therefore, due to the specific political correctness and simplicity of including in the map the countries through which the New Silk Road is supposed to run, that is, its land and sea belt—such countries as East Timor or Bahrain, Macedonia and Estonia are featured, although most probably no camels will roam that way, nor a single junk will sail nearby.

China basically did not ask anybody whether they wished to be included in this project. First, they signed up whoever was needed—and, apart from the exceptions mentioned above, they subsequently announced it. However, if someone is not on the list, it does not mean that they are omitted at all, like Greece. Greece is not a member of NATO and the European Union—yet the port of Piraeus, which is largely in the possession of Chinese capital, is marked.[6]

Formally, the Latin American countries have not been invited to BRI, but the hosts refer to them as a "natural extension" and "inalienable participants" of the venture. In other words, China is carrying on as usual, investing more and more in Latin America and encouraging its companies to penetrate those markets, unlike their neighbor from the north, who frankly discourages such movements through Donald Trump's behavior, offending some, especially Mexico and El Salvador. At the same time, when the American president in his typical style says that he said something different than de facto he said—this time at the World Economic Forum in Davos a year later than the Chinese president—Chinese foreign minister WangYi appeared at a meeting of all thirty-three countries belonging to the Commonwealth of Latin America and the Caribbean, CELAC (Spanish *Comunidad de Estados Latino Americanos y Caribeños*) advocates against trade protectionism and offers the region "a strategy of mutual benefits and mutual profits" (Economist 2018).

In fact, nobody knows exactly how much, where, when, and how the Chinese intend to invest in land as well as sea routes when implementing the New Silk Road project. The amount of 4 trillion dollars appears in circulating information, which must impress everyone, even in the most affluent countries, which are a bit further, at the end of the road, in France and Great Britain, because it is more than their GDP. No wonder that in both of these countries celebration surrounded the arrival of a freight train from China which traveled a long way, using the already existing infrastructure, but also signaling the need for its modernization and expansion, which is what the New Silk Road concept is all about. It was similar in Poland, when in June 2016 a freight train arrived from China to receive a welcome on the platform in Warsaw from presidents Andrzej Duda and Xi Jinping who was on an official visit to the banks of the Vistula River. It comes as no surprise either that Western European politicians who visited Beijing in early 2018—in January French president Emmanuel Macron, a month later the British prime minister Theresa May—talked about trade and investments more than about security and international relations. Everyone wishes to be on the receiving end of a 4,000-billion-dollar trickle, even a little bit.

In underdeveloped countries, China contributes a good deal for the infrastructure strengthening human capital—for schools and universities, for health clinics and hospitals. For this purpose, they use a soft loan instrument, which is often partially redeemed and turns into grants. On the implementation of projects, powerful Chinese construction companies are often involved, so it is not surprising that they are becoming global tycoons. When looking at the geopolitical map of the world from this perspective, it is easy to notice that China is particularly active where the West failed. Once, in colonial times, instead of helping, the West conducted exploitation, then, in neocolonial times, when instead of cooperating, it cheated, and recently, in times of globalization, when sometimes instead of creating areas of positive synergy, it marginalized.

Interestingly, they are also active where the Soviet Union failed, especially Russia as its core. This let-down is still casting a long shadow over politics and economy, as well as over culture and mentality in Kazakhstan, Kyrgyzstan, Tajikistan, Turkmenistan and Uzbekistan. Geography and history may have gone their way, but contemporary interests have their own agenda, which is clearly visible in the area of these post-Soviet Central Asian republics. In this very interesting region—and one by no means automatically set to maintain political stability and sustainable development—we have a unique mix, as it is the crossroads of deeply rooted features resulting from Russian, Asian, and Islamic influences, as well as Soviet legacy. Now the impact of the Chinese is added to all of these along with Western influences. The latter is due to, on the one hand, the significance of the region in the fight against international terrorism, whose tentacles reach these lands, and, on the other one, because of the rich energy resources, which are relevant in the global accounts.

By the way, it is worth noting that the geographical location, which economy and politics do not choose, maybe a blessing, as in the case of Switzerland sandwiched between Germany, France, Italy and Austria, or maybe a curse, as experienced by Iraq lying between Iran, Turkey, and Saudi Arabia. It is upon the political skill and ability to implement beneficial national strategies for socioeconomic development to determine whether the post-Soviet Central Asian republics, which occupy a prominent place on the New Silk Road route, will also use this aspect of their position to their own advantage or whether others will take advantage of them. If someone is located in the zone where China and the United States or the European Union and Russia are vying for influence, there is a lot to lose just as quite a lot to win on that. For this to happen, however, in the first place one cannot allow themselves to be antagonized either with one another or in the relations with these great global players.

GLOBAL EXPANSION OF CHINA

Although, obviously, Chinese activity contributes to poverty reduction and supports socioeconomic development, also for this reason China is suspected and even accused of bad intentions, ideological indoctrination and of political corruption. If that was the case, even partially, it would not change the fact that such a strategy helps other economies being at a lower level of advancement in their struggle for emancipation. In addition, if it threatens the balance of influences, then instead of unproductive criticism of Chinese expansion, it is better to increase one's own support from the rich West, and pragmatically reorient the ways and directions of international organizations remaining under the prevailing influence of the West.

There is nothing ill advised—actually quite the opposite—if alongside the export of capital and goods, China also "exports" some of its good skills from the sphere of soft infrastructure. These are precisely the good practices that we are so keen to talk about in the management science (Cieślik 2016). As in China itself, even the fastest trains cannot run without proper traffic regulations, or personnel that are more educated do not automatically ensure socioeconomic progress, so even more so it cannot be successful in the economies being backward compared to China. Therefore, they can and should learn from them. Knowledge and skills is currently a particularly valuable "commodity." I put this word in quotation marks on purpose, because it is not literally about a commodity, meaning a product of human labor intended for market exchange, because in this case, it is often a matter of nonfinancial transfers.

By using scholarships, tens of thousands of foreign students reside in China, obtaining knowledge in the fields that are preferred from the point of view of China's external expansion. When I lectured at the University of Beijing for a group of forty foreign scholarship holders, they all came from "developing" countries, among which the most developed ones being Turkey and Kazakhstan. Almost all of them—with exceptions of a Polynesian from Tonga and a Caribbean man from the Bahamas—were citizens of countries that have found themselves on the New Silk Road or, lying in Africa, for similar reasons remain in the sphere of the Middle Kingdom's interest. There are no coincidences here.

China also uses its presence and growing activity in international organizations, especially the World Bank, WB, the International Monetary Fund and the Asian Development Bank, ADB, to influence institutional solutions, directions and instrumentation of development policy in the countries to which these organizations channel their financial assistance and expert advice. By no means did they prevail, especially in WB and IMF, over Western influences, but increasingly often in the economies undergoing emancipation one can observe Chinese experts sent there by this or that international organization and increasingly often one can sense the "Chinese spirit."

In the wake of all of these follows a diplomatic offensive. Currently, Beijing hosts 166 embassies and has as many of its own ones worldwide. The United States has one more, 167. Soon, however, they will be overtaken in this regard, as soon as another country that has so far recognized Taiwan as the representation of China changes their mind. A remnant of the Cold War, the first one, there are still twenty embassies of Taiwan: as befits an island, six in the island Pacific countries and five in the Caribbean, five in Central America and one in South America, two in small African countries and in the Vatican. In time—when the reintegration of the People's Republic of China and Taiwan will take place (because it shall happen)—it will be China that has the most numerous diplomatic representation in the world. Currently, taking into account not only embassies but also all diplomatic posts, China has 268 of them, and the United States have 273. For comparison, it should be mentioned that in the case of Russia, the figure is 242 posts, and France 266.

China is the largest or the second largest trading partner for around eighty countries. Therefore, it is no wonder that what is happening there largely determines what is happening elsewhere in the global economy. When it comes to Chinese exports amounting to USD 2.2 trillion the addressee number one is the United States (18.2 percent), followed by (without taking into account Hong Kong where the PRC sells 13.8 of exported goods) Japan (6.1 percent), South Korea (4.5 percent) and not much less to Germany. As for imports—about $425 billion less—the number one is South Korea (10.0 percent), followed immediately by Japan (9.2 percent), Germany (5.4 percent), and Australia (4.4 percent). Only then, with export to China being less than Australian, do the United States rank. Note—because it is interesting—that on the New Silk Road route the two neighboring countries, South Korea and Japan are absent, from which account for up to a fifth of Chinese export. To some extent, it is so also because they are highly developed and have their own advanced infrastructure.

Dependence on the Chinese economy is multi-threaded and goes far beyond direct export and import. In the subject literature, even a neologism has been coined *sinodependency index*, that is, an indicator reflecting the changes in the S&P 500 stock index,[7] which depends on the ranking of 135 companies included therein and earning revenues from operations in China (Economist 2012). The Chinese economy is growing, stock exchange quotations are rising—and vice versa. When in 2009–2012, marked by the global crisis, the sinodependency index increased by nearly 130 percent, and the S&P 500 index increased by just over 50 percent. In other words, if it had not been for the continuation of the Chinese boom, the economic situation and stock exchanges, which mirror it in many other countries, including the most developed ones, would have been much worse. Therefore, someone who wishes China ill means harm to themselves.

CONCLUSION

Advocating globalization while at the same time pointing to the imperative of its greater inclusion, recognizing the indispensability of reducing the scale of commercial and financial imbalance in the global economy, caring even more than some highly developed countries for ecological balance (although they contributed to its earlier disruption), China slowly takes the path of economic policy suggested by the new pragmatism (Kolodko 2014b, Bałtowski 2017, Galbraith 2018). Neoliberalism hardly exists there, corrupt capitalism is gradually decreasing (albeit too slowly), and the notions related to new pragmatism are multiplying (Hu 2018).

China can essentially help in shaping the desired face of the future, limiting the growing global threats and the risk of a great catastrophe reaching far beyond the economic sphere. Moreover, this threat is real if, on the one hand, it was possible to re-direct the economy onto the neoliberal tracks *business as usual* and on the other hand if it was impossible to control the escalation of new nationalism. However, one can hope that none of them will happen, and this is largely thanks to China.

NOTES

1. The population of the Middle East is estimated at around 450 million, if we include in this part of the world also African Egypt with 97 million inhabitants (geographically Asian Sinai has around 1.4 million inhabitants) and Cyprus with only 1.2 million people. Without these two countries, the Middle East—geographically located in Asia in its entirety, apart from the small, 23,764 square kilometers European fragment of Turkey—it is home to about 350 million people. This is the total number of the inhabitants of Saudi Arabia, Bahrain, Iraq, Iran, Israel, Yemen, Jordan, Qatar, Kuwait, Lebanon, Oman, Palestine, Syria, Turkey, and the United Arab Emirates.

2. The member countries of ASEAN, Association of Southeast Asian Nations are Brunei, Philippines, Indonesia, Cambodia, Laos, Malaysia, Myanmar, Singapore, Thailand, and Vietnam. This grouping is inhabited by about 650 million people (8.7 percent of all humankind) and produces around 10.5 global gross product (counting per purchasing power parity, PPP).

3. SAARC member countries, South Asian Association for Regional Cooperation *South Asian Association for Regional Cooperation*) contains: Afghanistan, Bangladesh, Bhutan, India, Nepal, Maldives, Pakistan, and Sri Lanka. These countries are inhabited by about one billion 770 million people (almost 24 percent of all humankind), who produce about 13.7 percent of the world's gross product (counting per PPP).

4. Other countries with a population exceeding 100 million are, in the order of population size, the United States (327 million), Brazil (208), Nigeria (191), Russia (143), Mexico (125), and Ethiopia (196). Soon, this group of non-Asian countries with similarly numerous population will be joined by Egypt.

5. Similar processes take place in other parts of the world, also in post-socialist Eastern European economies, the most developed of which can compete to an increasingly smaller extent with low wages. For example, in Poland in December 2017, the average gross monthly wage in the enterprise sector fluctuated around 1,450 dollars, calculated at the current exchange rate, which at that time was subject to strong appreciation. These data refer to companies employing more than 9 employees, so for the entire economy the appropriate amount may be even 700 dollars lower.

6. This is another paradox, but it is the pressure of the West, especially the so-called Big Three, that is, the European Commission, the European Central Bank and the International Monetary Fund, that Greece should improve its fiscal situation also by privatizing state property, prompted the government in Athens to sell the port of Piraeus. The investor turned out to be China COSCO Shipping Corporation.

7. S&P 500 is a stock exchange index managed by Standard &Poor's, the value of which is determined by the quotations on the New York Stock Exchange and NASDAQ 500, the largest from the point of view of capitalization of enterprises, mainly American ones.

Chapter 13

Recipe for a Crisis

In the day and age where it seemed to some people that neoliberalism, having led to a widespread financial and economic crisis, followed by the social and political one, had been consigned to where it belongs, that is to the trash bin of history, the same is rearing its ugly head again. It is no cause for celebration that in many places of the destabilized world, where neoliberalism used to be settled in nicely, it was supplanted these days by new nationalism and populism, more often right-wing than the left-wing one, oddly enough. You do not fight evil with evil, nonsense cannot be addressed with another nonsense. Therefore, it is hardly a cause for jubilation when neoliberalism gives way to new nationalism and one has to make an even greater effort to offer something new, something progressive and socially attractive to replace those two harmful economic and political systems and the defective economic policy followed by their proponents. Undoubtedly, the new pragmatism is such a proposal, but there is a long way before it prevails.

AT THE COST OF MANY FOR THE BENEFIT OF FEW

Currently, a decade after the outbreak of the devastating crisis in 2008–2009—first in the United States, then in the United Kingdom, which had financial ties with the latter, then a nearly global one—the professional community has no doubts that neoliberalism was its main underlying cause. It is an ideology, school of economics and, last but not least, an economic policy which cynically feed on such magnificent liberal ideas as freedom, free choice and democracy, as well as private property, entrepreneurship and competition, favoring enrichment of few at the expense of the majority. This goal is furthered by the kind of deregulation of the economy which puts the world of labor at a disadvantage to the world of capital, by the financialization of the economy, pushed ad absurdum at the turn of the twentieth and twenty-first century, and by manipulating the fiscal redistribution in a manner that favors the wealthier social strata. It was also furthered by the notorious tax reform in the United States under the presidency of Ronald Reagan, in 1986.

Suffice to point out that while in 1979, when he was running for the office (he was president in the years 1981–1989), the average hourly rate in the United States was $18.78 (at 2008 dollars), in 2008, at the time the crisis broke out, it amounted to less, $18.52! What happened to the fruits of the major increase in labor efficiency, what happened to the national income growth? Well, as a result of neoliberal practices, they went to a few at the expense of the majority. This is vividly demonstrated by other facts, for instance that between 1970 and 2010 the share of profits in GDP increased by nearly 10 percentage points, because the share of wages fell from over 53 percent to below 44 percent.

While over three decades, from 1979 to the precrisis 2007, net income (after taxes and budget transfers) of 1 percent of the richest Americans increased by ca. 280 percent, that of the poorest 20 percent of the society rose only by ca. 20 percent, that is, it didn't grow enough each year to be felt by the society. No wonder then those income inequalities kept increasing and now they are at the highest level among all rich capitalist states. The most commonly used measure in this respect is the Gini index, which theoretically ranges from zero (when everybody receives the same part of income) to one (when somebody takes over the entire income). Currently, in the United States, it stands at ca. 0.4. By comparison, in Poland, it is 0.3 and in the more egalitarian Denmark, it fluctuates around 0.25.

PEOPLE FIRST LOSE TEMPER, THEN TAKE TO THE STREETS

It is precisely the growing income inequalities and the widening areas of social exclusion that caused people to first lose temper and then take to the streets, also to the famous Wall Street, the occupied one. Things were aggravated by the irritating nonchalance of a section of political elites as well as of the media and "famous economists" furthering the agenda of those elites, who tried to put the blame for the glaring income and wealth inequalities, growing due to neoliberal practices, hence an intentional policy, on objective processes: on the current phase of technological revolution and globalization. This way a part of the anger was skillfully focused on aliens—on other countries and immigrants, on the Chinese and Mexicans, and elsewhere on Muslim or Central Eastern Europeans—and, as a result, on the irreversible globalization, and another part on one's own establishment, which was by no means entirely blameless. Moreover, it turned out it was grist to the mill that brings waves of new nationalism, xenophobia, protectionism and anti-globalization resentments. It would be worthwhile to draw the right conclusions from there but, sadly, it is not happening. At least not in (still) the strongest economy of the world, the originator of the last global crisis, United States.

Actually, in the year Donald Trump took power, a yet greater error was committed than the one "achieved" by Reagan. A yet greater one because this time a moth's flight toward a flame starts already after the great lesson of recent years' crisis and everybody should be wiser in the hindsight. So should neoliberals. Unfortunately, neoliberalism's signature greed coupled with populism's naivety—both characteristics uniquely combined by the current resident of the White House—create a mix that is so toxic for logical thinking that, while you can never step in the same river twice, it turns out that stepping into the same swamp is doable. That is exactly the path Americans are taking by pushing the tax law through their Congress. I call it pushing because by voting at night they defeat the democratic opposition by one vote; because they succeed in doing so by buying off their own senators, in return for evidently particularistic concessions; because at the House of Representatives it is necessary to redo the vote as racing against the pre-Christmas time produced faulty bills.

While Republicans are pushing the propaganda of success, and President Trump is shouting "Jobs, Jobs, Jobs!" from his Twitter account, writing that "this is truly a case where the results will speak for themselves, starting very soon," democrats unanimously protest against the tax changes passed, resorting to such drastic terms as "heist" or "cheat." Well, maybe not a robbery as everything was done within the law and without breaking the Constitution, but it does seem like a fraud.

WHAT'S THE POINT OF ALL THIS?

People can sense what is cooking because only 27 percent of Americans support the new law and as many as 52 percent are against the solutions being implemented. They can count themselves and they put more trust in pragmatic arguments of nonpartisan pundits than in biased pro-governmental experts and economists corrupted by the neoliberal lobby. While the latter is announcing a major economic growth acceleration due to decreased taxes for companies, CIT, independent centers—including the governmental ones, some of them being really outstanding—calculate that the additional GDP growth by 2027 will be the negligible 0.4–0.9 percent, or next to nothing. According to the Congressional Research Service analysis, a CIT reduction by 10 percentage points (the law cuts it by 14 points, from 35 to 21 percent) can increase the long-term growth rate by mere 0.15 percent. So what was the point of this battle?

What do you mean what the point was? To ensure that other changes jointly implemented under the trendy banner of tax cuts for companies, help enrich few at the expense of many. As a deputy prime minister and minister of finance of Poland (in 1994–1997 and again in 2002–2003), I myself used to cut taxes, including CIT, radically but sensibly: first down to 32 percent from 40 percent (bearing in mind that when I took office, the economy was after the infamous shock without therapy), and then from 28 percent down to the present 19 percent, but this was accompanied by other fiscal changes that promoted not only capital formation and investments but also concern for desirable income relations and human capital development. Growth picked up pace, income inequalities dropped, long-term public debt did not increase. This will not be the case of the United States, though the reduction of the very high CIT rate with the simultaneous elimination of the many tax reliefs that impair the system has its advantages. Growth will not significantly accelerate, unemployment rate will not fall, inequalities will grow and the debt will increase.

It is quite baffling how light-heartedly the authors and supporters of the tax reform are treating the unavoidable budget deficit growth and the consequently increasing public debt, which is already immense. With the exceptions of the apologists of the package, there is basically a general consensus that in the coming ten years the public debt will increase by as much as one and a half trillion US dollars. And this debt already exceeds 20 trillion US dollars, ca. 7 percent over the US GDP. It is clear that in such a situation the Fed will increase interest rates more aggressively, which will naturally weaken the propensity to invest, and slow down the growth.

NEOLIBERALISM 2.0

Democrats hope that the taxpayers (seen as electorate by the political class) who have been misled by the government propaganda will sniff out those neoliberal manipulations and already in the fall of 2018 their vote will strip the Republicans of the majority in the American Congress, both in the Senate and in the House of Representatives. Maybe so, though not necessarily, as the way the tax package is structured, lower taxes and reliefs will benefit, in the coming years, a great majority of taxpayers, including those from less wealthy and more populous strata. However, their reductions disappear in 2025 and then their moment will come to pay for the cuts for the rich, which are not time-limited. Let us add that this will happen already after next elections, presidential, parliamentary and local alike. In total, throughout the entire decade of 2018–2027, the subsequent higher taxes, those regulated in the years 2026–2027, will neutralize the benefits of the earlier period, from 2018 to 2025. After 2025, as many as 53 percent of taxpayers will pay more to the IRS, and these will be households from lower tax brackets.

Impartial analysts have calculated that the greatest beneficiaries of the reform will be the wealthiest, rich multinationals and property owners. Indeed, one must have quite a nerve and display a reprehensible short-term bias in their economic and political thinking to push, in the context of what happened over the last four decades, for tax solutions which will by no means cut taxes for the poorest 20 percent of the population, as it is estimated that by 2027 tax cuts will total $10, while for one per mille of the wealthiest, this benefit will amount to $278,000.

Hence, it turns out neoliberalism, apparently still undefeated despite the recent crisis, is condemning the American economy to another, yet a greater crisis. This is not only a private business of the United States as, though the country's relative role in the world economy will be gradually decreasing, it will still play, in several decades to come, a key part in world finance, and the US dollar will remain, in the foreseeable future, the main reserve currency. In addition, that is why also others will pay for this new episode of neoliberal excesses. It is worth remembering whom we will have to thank for that.

Chapter 14

How to Destroy a Country

The Economics and the Politics of the Greek Crisis

A FOUR-HUNDREDTH PART OF WORLD ECONOMY

Greece is a beautiful country that has contributed a lot to the history of our civilization, including the concepts of logic and democracy. Before our eyes a drama is unfolding there, whose essence is not easy to understand as there is no shortage of controversies. Greece is a small country. The population, out of which one-third lives in the capital city of Athens, is less than 11 million people; the same as London, or three-fourths of the nearby Istanbul. If the population in Greece is increasing, it is only due to the never-ending wave of refugees and migrants coming from Asia, Middle East, and Northern Africa as Greeks themselves are not growing in numbers from one year to another—the population growth is around zero. Few Greek children are born each year, and the population is aging. On average, people live to over eighty years old (women live about eighty-three years, and men about seventy-eight). We can attribute this to the Mediterranean climate rather than to the economy. Median age is about forty-four years old, one of the highest in Europe and worldwide. People retire at the age of about 61.9 (in France 59.7). While the number of old age pensioners that the system needs to support is increasing, the funding available is dwindling.

The result is that 40 percent of pensioners receive benefits below the minimum poverty level. So the proud Greeks who live in their homeland—not to mention the large Diaspora scattered all over the world—represent a tiny fraction in this global city, just 0.15 percent of the nearly 7.3 billion–strong world population. I say "in the city," as it is no longer a "village," because for several years now most of us, Earth inhabitants, have been living in cities. It's also the case in Greece, where urban population represents as much as 78 percent of the total number.

Greece is a small economy. In the first half of the decade beginning in 2010 there was a sharp decrease in production, by about 25 percent. Meanwhile in Poland, production increased by about 11 percent. As a result, in 2015, Greece became the first western country which Poland was able to surpass in terms of GDP per capita. In Greece, per capita GDP (PPP) amounted to 25,600 USD, while in Poland it was already 26,400 USD. While this is not much to celebrate in Poland, it is a definite concern in Greece. Currently, Greek GDP (PPP) amounts to only 0.25 percent of total world production and less than 1.5 percent of the gross product of the European Union, of which Greece has been a member since 1981.

While the Greek drama continues, James K. Galbraith has got involved in it as an author and adviser by publishing a book that is sure to stir a lively debate (Galbraith 2016b).

The initial K, which stands for Kenneth, James Galbraith's middle name, was passed down from his father, John Kenneth Galbraith (1908–2006), one of the greatest economists of the twentieth century. But James Galbraith does not live in the shadow of his father, the author of the fundamental masterpiece *The Affluent Society* (Galbraith 1958). With a certain distance, he considers himself an economic dissident, or with a sense of irony, a rebel, but he is a world-renowned economist, known and respected for his publications.[1]

In an earlier, provocatively titled book, *The End of Normal* (Galbraith 2014), Galbraith disposes of the useless orthodox economic thought, and explains the global economic crisis. In this book, he demonstrates that what we have been dealing with lately, especially in the last several or even twenty years, is not just another accident, or another turbulence in the capitalist market economy, but a systemic crisis of modern capitalism, specifically of its Anglo-American neoliberal version. Galbraith's argument leads to the conclusion that there's no going back to the "good old days," or, if you will, to "normally" functioning capitalism, that is to an unrealistic textbook vision of it.

The world has changed considerably in the last quarter of a century. Today, and especially tomorrow, what used to be beneficial in the past, has no use today. It is not possible to stop the course of history, let alone reverse it.

Galbraith's book includes a powerful charge of firsthand information and high-end interpretations. His information is firsthand because the author has participated in Greek events as a government adviser to the unorthodox finance minister Yanis Varoufakis,[2] with whom Galbraith had collaborated at the Lyndon B. Johnson School of Public Affairs at the University of Texas in Austin. And I say high-end because the author provides not only lots of proven facts, verified data, references to source documents, but also most often a correct theoretical interpretation of them. At the same time, he formulates harsh, sometimes even extreme political assessments, when he tries to argue that a series of measures imposed on Greece from the outside was and still is harmful not only because of the ignorance of those who devise them, but also because of the desire to dominate and push to peripheral positions, if not downright neo-colonize the country.

Galbraith says:

> This is economic policy as moral abomination. It is not designed to succeed as economics. It is failing because it is designed to fail. Europe's leaders know what they are doing. The policy is not intended to restore growth and prosperity; a policy whose clear effect over years and years is decline and destruction must have been actually intended to achieve that effect. (. . .) The only other possibility is that these leaders are incompetent beyond all reasonable imagining. (Galbraith 2016b, 33)

This is strong and even accusatory language. However, reading Galbraith's book is an eye-opening experience, with readers able to see the truth for themselves and to realize who is to blame, who should take responsibility and, consequently, to see the poor standard of the media reports and the bias of some "well-known economists" or newspaper, TV and online "experts" who speak on the Greek saga. Let's hope that Galbraith's voice will make it harder to dupe those who take an interest: there's no shortage of them and there will be surely more as subsequent phases of the drama unfold and come to their climax. How it will end remains an open question.

FROM SMALL FRICTIONS TO A GRAND CRISIS

It is amazing how a minor disturbance resulted in a crisis with global implications. In 2010, the Greek budget deficit was only 0.2 percent, one five-hundredth of GDP of the EU. Now it's a challenge its policies cannot cope with, even though there is a way out. Why pay more when it is possible to pay less? Why give into chaos when it's possible to steer the process? Why suffer defeat, when the case can be won?

Greece can either escape the mounting difficulties or allow them to crush it. To escape, it is necessary to reduce Greek debt by about half. Of course, provided that Greeks will also do their part by changing the economic structure and properly setting its institutions. This is only possible with a social market economy, not a neoliberal economy, because this would be a continuation of the past, of a moth's flight into the fire, and it is not possible to fly in that direction for too long.

Galbraith, sometimes strongly, maybe even too strongly, distances himself from free-market capitalism, which is devoid of institutions and policies promoting social cohesion, when he states:

> The point of life and work in Greece should be stability and fairness, not competition and enrichment. Those who wish to get very rich will go elsewhere, in any event. You can build a good society with the others. (Galbraith 2016b, 90)

The trick is to build an affluent society by properly associating concern for the economic efficiency with efforts to ensure social justice and competition with stability. It is possible.

All it takes to get crushed is to insist on the current policy of further belt-tightening, cutting budget expenditures, raising taxes and, of course, privatizing, or selling national assets en masse to foreign entities (and selling them for cheap as whoever sells quickly, sells cheaply). What awaits at the end of this path is not stability, growth, and a transition to the phase of sustainable socioeconomic development; what awaits us there is a crisis, even more serious than the one before, starting from Greece exiting the eurozone, the so-called Grexit, which would be (will be?) more expensive not only for Greeks, but also for their foreign partners, especially from the EU.

Allow me to digress here. Careful observers could see certain analogies between the present harsh stance against Greece and the attempts to impose a similar policy on Poland in the mid-1990s. Some external centers, ranging from the then orthodox International Monetary Fund, and our local home-grown neoliberals—as if not disgraced enough by the failure of their shock without therapy[3]—both called for similar moves. These would have by no means contributed to a more dynamic economy; instead, they would have certainly entailed even greater dependence on foreign capital. However, back then, it was possible to effectively resist such pressures by implementing a proper program of structural reforms and sustainable development—the "Strategy for Poland."

Joseph E. Stiglitz referred to this when he wrote:

> Poland's former deputy premier and finance minister, Grzegorz W. Kolodko, has argued that the success of his nation was due to its explicit rejection of the doctrine of Washington Consensus. The country did not do what the IMF recommended—it did not engage in rapid privatization, and it did not put reducing inflation to lower and lower levels over all other macroeconomic concerns. But it did emphasize some things to which the IMF had paid insufficient attention—such as the importance of democratic support for the reforms, which entailed trying to keep unemployment and adjusting pensions for inflation, and creating the institutional infrastructure required to make a market economy function. (Stiglitz 2002, 181)

Today I can add that surely the then Poland's political position and overall geopolitical environment of those times did not favor imposing something like what Varoufakis now describes as economic waterboarding. Poland took a dangerous turn, caused by the ideology and policy of the first phase of neoliberalism, but emerged unscathed. Will Greece?

Perhaps it is worth, in this context, highlighting one more similarity. The method often used when imposing absurd policies is to make irrational assumptions and to promote them publicly, of course making use of established "authorities" on economic matters and of "independent" media. And all this in order to give credibility to the incredible, bring the public around to the preposterous and gain approval for something that should be fundamentally rejected. Such absurd policy was shock without therapy in Poland in the early 1990s, needless cooling-off in late 1990s and the economy-stifling belt-tightening early in the second decade of the twenty-first century. Back in late 1989 in Poland, the GDP was expected to decline just for one year as a neoliberal economic policy based on wrong assumptions of the Washington Consensus[4] was pursued. However, Washington Consensus had been tailored to the Latin American realities and did not sufficiently account not only for cultural and social, but even for all economic circumstances of a deeply unbalanced real socialism economy. So GDP was supposed to go down by just 3.1 percent, causing an unemployment level of no more than 400,000 (later on, it was supposed to steadily decrease) and a single-digit inflation rate (on a monthly basis) within a quarter. The reality turned out to be dramatically worse. The recession that started in the second half of 1989 lasted for two and a half years more and the cumulated GDP drop reached, in real terms, as much as 18 percent. The unemployment level skyrocketed, eventually exceeding 3 million, and the single-digit inflation rate on a monthly basis became a fact only in late 1997 as a result of successful implementation of the "Strategy for Poland."[5]

It's similar in Greece. The so-called *troika*—the European Commission (EC), European Central Bank (ECB) and International Monetary Fund (IMF)—in fact blackmailed and forced Greece to officially accept the economically nonsensical program, which provided for a quick return to the path of economic growth, of course after a period of appropriate belt-tightening, and a short-term shallow decline in national income. In particular, the IMF in its memorandum in the beginning of the current decade, assumed there would be recession caused by a sharp fiscal adjustment, except that this was to last for a short time, amount to 5 percent and after two years, in 2013, the economy was supposed to be on a growth path. In reality, the recession lasted more than five years, and GDP fell by over 25 percent. There was no economic recovery and growth in production, which resulted in negative consequences for the employment and unemployment, for the budget, and in a drastic reduction in the scope and quality of public services, including education and health.

How could one propose, promote, enforce a "program" (while certainly not believing in it), which was supposed to lead, after years of sacrifices, to a situation where the public debt in 2020 would still be as high as 120 percent of GDP, or twice as high as the one permitted by the Maastricht fiscal criterion of monetary convergence? As a result of the awful policies imposed by the "troika," the production was declining and the debt increasing. These occurred despite budget cuts and tax increases. As a result, the relative public debt, calculated in relation to decreasing production, is growing, though its size is no longer increasing in absolute terms.

Interestingly, a quarter of a century earlier, when neoliberals in Poland pushed for authentic shock with illusory therapy, the IMF was trying to temper their aspirations. I witnessed this, when heading the Institute of Finance and taking part in many discussions. The then minister of finance was more papal than the pope of monetarism and neoliberalism, the IMF dominated by Americans, especially those coming from the so-called Chicago School of Economics. In the case of Greece, the fund initially held onto the old but no longer useful orthodoxy, and only recently, as of 2015 clearly changed the tone and sought to moderate the radical aspirations of the "dvoika," namely the EU and the ECB.

As for the dvoika, Galbraith approaches them with harsh and even sarcastic criticism when discussing meetings of finance ministers of nineteen countries belonging to the eurozone, the so-called Eurogroup. He writes:

> A dreary ritual known for wasting time and accomplishing little (Galbraith 2016b, 208) and in another place: The end of Eurogroup meetings and hosting of the Institutions at the Hilton will be a modest plus on the budget. (Galbraith 2016b, 86)

DON'T PLAY WITH FIRE

When I published an article entitled "Africanization of Greece" (Kolodko 2015a), Olivier Blanchard, the then-chief economist of the IMF, wrote that he did not agree with my characterization of the IMF or its leadership as dogmatic. Now I can agree that it is currently far from dogmatism which, unfortunately, dominates the thinking of some European politicians, starting from Germans. Blanchard added:

> *There was probably a small space for an agreement before the referendum (as argued in my blog* (Blanchard 2015), *and we, the Fund, were working on it). With the economic deterioration, and the bad blood between Tsipras and the Europeans, I am not sure the space is still there.*[6]

What next? Certainly we shouldn't play with fire, but we shouldn't sweep it under the carpet, either. Greek authorities are correct when they're not getting tricked into socially harmful and economically irrational (in the long run) excessive budget cuts and further tax increases, representing a high burden on the population, in order for the state to have funds for the endless repayment of foreign debt it has been forced to incur. Of course, one can agree to some reduction in spending, and accept raising some taxes, especially those increasing the burden for the wealthier strata of society. In Greece, there is no shortage of the poor, but there are also wealthy people or even lavishly wealthy ones.

Is what Syriza's government is/was doing an amateur approach and populism or is it a pragmatic and professional tactic[7]? On the one hand, James K. Galbraith, a strong supporter and advocate of Syriza, has no doubt about the responsible approach of the Greek leftist government. He points out that during negotiations with partners from the "troika" the government has been very careful, not to play games, not to present negotiating positions from which concessions are planned in advance, but simply to spell out in a transparent and honest way where the lines are that they will not cross (Galbraith 2016b, 108). On the other hand, Olivier Blanchard, "number 2" in the IMF, wrote to me that when it comes to the Syriza position, we never had a good sense of what it truly was.[8]

Elsewhere Galbraith notes:

> (. . .) a crisis brought on by the neoliberal financial policies of the early part of the 2000s, and then aggravated and prolonged by the austerity ideology that succeeded the crisis, and by the profoundly counterproductive policies with which Europe has reacted to the crisis. The possibility that an anti-austerity government might lead the beginning of a recovery from the austerity regime is, I think, a present reality and it is, of course, a nightmare in certain quarters. (Galbraith 2016b, 78)

Sound familiar? De'ja vu?

Yes, Poland was in a similar situation at the turn of 1993 and 1994, when following the "shock without therapy" fiasco, a left-centrist formation was democratically elected to power. There were the ominous forecasts of a "rolling destruction" (Leszek Balcerowicz, former finance minister in the "Wall Street Journal"), "300 percent inflation rate in half a year" (Jan Krzysztof Bielecki, former prime minister) and "national disaster" (Jan Winiecki, former Polish representative at the European Bank for Reconstruction and Development, EBRD. Much to their (and to some others') disappointment, it turned out that the years 1994–1997 saw a period of economic success, with a record GDP growth rate in thirty years, and huge institutional progress, resulting in Poland joining the Organization for Economic Co-operation and Development (OECD) two decades ago. The unemployment level decreased dramatically, by over one million people, and the inflation rate fell by about two-thirds. Yes, for some it was a real nightmare.

Back to Greece, it is already recording a primary budget surplus as in its budget it allocates less public money than it receives. In other words, if you leave out the costs of servicing public debt, the budget obtains more money than it is spending. We should acknowledge that nothing like that is happening in Italy or in France. But it is also necessary to note that the earlier demands of the "troika" for the surplus to reach 4.5 percent of GDP, were economically absurd and politically preposterous. The next proposal, this time by just the "dvoika" (the IMF did not make such radical demands), for the surplus to stand at 3.5 percent of GDP was also unacceptable. And even if the acceptance of it had been forced by political means, it would not have been possible economically.

It is also worth noting that the leftist government of Greece is a democratic one. People, who have been plunged into poverty for years, took to the streets, but still democracy has—so far—prevailed. And creditors have to reckon with it if they treat democracy seriously. What are the alternatives? A return to the "black colonels" dictatorship, in Europe, in the EU, in the second decade of the twenty-first century? One would have to be politically blind and economically ignorant to believe that a democratic majority in Greece will accept an extreme program of excessive sacrifices spanning over a decade, if not more. This is not only contrary to logic, it's also unethical.

Thanks to subsequent "assistance" maneuvers, a majority of Greek obligations was successfully shifted from private banks, which were co-responsible for the Greek crisis, to public organizations including the EU and IMF. Currently, around 80 percent of debt is owed to a special EU institution, the *European Stability Mechanism*, to the ECB, and to the IMF. The next years saw an expensive game of moving the growing debt from the private to the public sector, which was similar to the principle of privatizing profits and nationalizing losses, well "tested" during the 2008–2009 financial crisis. Those "saving" Greece were lending to it subsequent installments of funds so that it could pay off its private creditors, which it did. This was the main point of the crisis that has already lasted seven years, so lean for Greeks, but not for the overwhelming majority of their well-fed creditors.

3 × 25

While the Greek debt rose from little over 100 percent of GDP in 2010 to 180 percent of GDP in 2016, Greece was pushed by outside forces as well as by the next series of "assistance," into the syndrome of triple 25:

- Over 25 percent recession since 2010.
- Over 25 percent unemployment rate.
- 25 percent of the population living below the poverty level.

This is something unheard of for a developed country during times of peace. At the same time, rich banks, mainly German, French, Swiss, Austrian, and from Cyprus, are shunning responsibility, passing on the costs of their earlier reckless lending, to European taxpayers. Admittedly, some of these banks had to write off the unrecovered debt, but this cost them a lot less than the profit they made from this practice.

Who should now pay the costs of lack of prudence and unwise policies? Greeks, who already work (if they have a job at all) the longest in Europe (2,042 hours per year), about 6 percent more than Poles (1,923 hours), and 49 percent more than Germans (only 1,371 hours)? Out of the OECD countries, only South Koreans work more annually (2,134 hours). Of course it's easy to tell Greeks to get down to work, but one needs to also answer the question of where to find this work? Hopefully not one that involves building barricades.

Incidentally, these striking differences show how much both Greeks and Polish people still have to do to substantially lift up their economy and living standards. They cannot work longer hours, but perhaps, more efficiently. However, this does not necessarily require cuts in public spending, but rather a change in what the money is spent on. Expenditure could even go up, provided that at the same time corruption will decrease and additional expenses will go to improving the quality of human capital, especially to education, as well as to improving the infrastructure, without which private enterprise cannot develop faster. For those and other countries that are at a relatively lower level of development—which Poland (69.8 percent of the European Union's average of USD 37.800 at PPP) and Greece (67.7 percent) still are—all this, coupled with better management, higher labor discipline, and improvement in the quality of institutions[9] is a necessary condition for productivity to grow at faster rates and for the development gap to diminish.

The "troika"—the EC, the ECB, and the IMF—has a much greater share of responsibility for the crisis than Greece. Of course, the previous governments in Athens (and not the Syriza government that has only been in power since February 2015—and part of the Greek society share the blame; the original sin was committed by the Greeks. Living beyond their means for too long, which contributed to a widespread entitlement mentality, highly unionized economy with strong anarcho-syndicalist tendencies, tax evasion, inadequate fiscal system, corruption, overly soft financial policy—these were the original causes of the crisis. Other factors that contributed to the crisis spreading include some structural deficiencies of the Greek economy, such as production base being relatively weaker and less diversified compared to other countries with a similar national income, underdeveloped export sector (except for tourism), a deficit economy that is not open enough and greatly dependent on imports and foreign capital, and excessive defense expenditures.

The author of the *Poisoned Chalice* points to some of those flaws, but he seems to have slightly less to say when it comes to the original causes of the Greek syndrome, focusing on the subsequent stages of its escalation. While he is right to do so, it would have benefited the narrative as a whole if he had been blunt about the recklessness of the Greek and their governments in the 1990s and 2000s. They could have better prepared for joining the eurozone, which took place in 2001, but also they shouldn't have been accepted then as it was well known, at least among experts from Brussels and Frankfurt, that the data provided by the government in Athens about meeting Maastricht fiscal criteria, including the real budget deficit amount, were quite misrepresented. Well, ill-conceived political considerations, once more, took a priority over the economic ones. The architects of euroization were committed to including as many countries as possible in the single currency area, so for Greece they turned a blind eye to the structural and institutional weaknesses and to some statistics being manipulated, and they only opened it wide when it was too late.

Of course Galbraith is aware of the Greek weaknesses. He emphasizes that:

> it is true that the Greek government was always a weak borrower. It is true that the country has a large civil service, a patronage-based politics, aggressive unions, and dubious accounts. (Galbraith 2016b, 32)

Nevertheless, he clearly takes the side of Greece, directing his criticism toward the rich countries having a structural surplus of trade balance, especially the large Germany, but also the small Austria or Holland. To be able to place part of their competitive and high quality production and surplus capital abroad, they needed countries that served as outlets and places for some long-term direct investments and short-term speculative investments. But we shouldn't forget that, as the saying goes, it takes two to tango. And both Germany and Greece were all for it. One country's surplus becomes another country's deficit; the richer one's receivables become the poorer one's debt; the propensity to lend to someone stronger corresponds to the willingness to borrow from somebody weaker.

According to Galbraith:

> The flow of goods from Germany to its markets was matched by a flow of credit, either directly to state purchasers of arms and infrastructure, as in Greece, or indirectly via private financing of residential and commercial construction booms, as in Spain and Ireland. In all cases the unbalanced flow of

> goods matched the accumulation of debts; the Greek instance was merely the most extreme. The Greek story is properly a European story in which, as in all European stories, Germany takes the leading role. (Galbraith 2016b, 3)

In a nutshell, Greece, as well as the other countries that got into similar trouble, though to a lesser extent, would not have found themselves in such a deplorable situation, if it wasn't for their richer partners having their eyes set on their individual interests.

Let me add that similar conclusions can be drawn with respect to some crises that occurred across the Atlantic, starring the United States on the one hand, and some Latin American countries, on the other, especially Argentina over a decade or so. However, in this case, after the decline of the fixed exchange rate of peso (so-called currency board) in 2002, this country was able to resort to devaluing it against the dollar. This mitigated, at best, the consequences of the collapse as it didn't save Argentina, still grappling with its results to this date.[10] Meanwhile, Greece cannot do something like that as it is in the eurozone. It cannot devalue "its" euro against euro and so the only way to improve the economy's international competitiveness in this situation is the so-called internal devaluation, which boils down to reducing the costs of manufacturing, mainly the costs of salary and social benefits. Hence the pressure from foreign countries, having their vested interest, for reduction of salaries and social transfers that add to the costs of salaries.

It's not the time to blackmail Greeks and to excessively corner them. And that's what is actually happening. This is what the "troika" is doing, with Germany playing a special role in this practice. If this country as well as other creditors, understandably, wants to get their money back, it needs to finally realize that only part of it can be recovered as Greece is insolvent. And Germany is greatly to blame as it would impose on it—both directly and indirectly through the "troika" where it has a lot of clout together with France—a bad and harmful policy of "tightening the belt" beyond reasonable measure. And now Greeks are supposed to cut their pensions and keep lowering their standard of living, by increasing prices and taxes, to pay off an exorbitant debt?

Politicians are often slaves to their own words. First, the German–French duo referred to in the media as "Merkozy"—the German chancellor Angela Merkel and the president of France, Nicolas Sarkozy—unwisely maintained that the debt cannot be restructured at the expense of private creditors. A similar position was held, for some time, by Christine Lagarde, the head of IMF, former French minister of finance, which is of significance here. So who was supposed to pay for it? The working, and more and more often, nonworking people of Greece? Or maybe taxpayers from the countries to which Greece owed larger and larger sums? Politicians—mostly those from Berlin, Paris,

Brussels, and Frankfurt—have put themselves in a very awkward situation as their earlier imprudent statements meant to prove how hard and steadfast they are, now are holding them back. We will not cave in! Let Greeks pay what they owe! The thing is they are so burdened with debt also through the fault of those politicians, that they simply have no funds to fully pay it off.

Now we need to admit, openly communicating to our own societies that we have a moral duty and an economic necessity to bear part of the costs of relieving the Greek tensions. And those who could not be bothered by the ethical dimension of the matter should know that coming to terms with irrecoverability of part of the debt is cheaper than unrealistically insisting on its repayment, which leads to a yet more widespread crisis.

HOW TO REDUCE DEBT?

I have been advocating for reprofiling the Greek foreign debt for a long time now. My commentaries on this matter have been published by magazines that are opinion leaders in economic circles—*The Economist* (Kolodko 2011c) and *Financial Times* (Kolodko 2011b, 2012). Not only because of their merit, but also because they were written by Poland's former deputy prime minister and minister of finance, with proven experience in reducing irrecoverable debt.

Adjusting the level of debt to the possibility of servicing it in a long term must be, understandably, based on continuing a tough financial program and appropriate changes in the functioning of the economy. We, Polish people, happen to know a thing or two about that. In September 1994, acting in the capacity of Poland's deputy prime minister and minister of finance, I signed a memorandum of understanding on a conditional reduction of our debt by half, with creditors from private banks being members of the London Club. Earlier on, in 1991, similar agreements were reached with creditor-countries from the Paris Club. These were tough terms, and the progress in meeting them was implacably monitored by the IMF. If it weren't for those decisions and the resulting adjustment processes, we would have been doing much worse as there would have been no chance for normal trade relations with foreign countries, favorable access to global financial markets or for rapid inflow of foreign direct investment, all of which had a major impact on our growth dynamic.

Reasonable and progressive financial commentators might have concluded that it's worth using somebody else's arguments, thus expressing their support for my proposals, though they did not do it outright. Since it made sense back then in Poland—and it did!—and it was successful, maybe it'd be worth trying it now as well, even though it's different time and place. It would! I believe that writing off half of Greece's public debt is fully warranted. Then the debt would be brought down from the current over EUR 320 billion to 160 billion, or below 90 percent of GDP. It would still be 50 percent more than authorized under the relevant Maastricht criterion, but the debt of this size—comparable to debt of France or Germany—would be possible to pay. In the present amount it is not and will not be.

Since I wrote already five years ago in the "Financial Times," that "EBC must rescue Greece or pay more later," now when the "later" has already come but it's still not too late—I will add that I fully stand by this view. But now the price of rescue measures is much higher. One must pay for the lack of common sense and economic imagination, for short-sightedness and ostensible political correctness. It's a shame the payment comes also at the expense of others who have nothing to do with all this mess.

In a nutshell, Greece will not pay all of its current debt. There's no point in deluding ourselves and muddling through unrealistic solutions, the way it is being attempted with perseverance worthy of a better cause. Postponing a pragmatic settlement only increases the costs of crisis. We are facing a sharp alternative: either Greece will pay off the agreed substantial part of its external obligations in an organized manner, as suggested by common sense and realism, or much less and in a chaotic manner. Pushing further on Greeks to bleed so that creditors, who have already made a small fortune "helping" them in the past, could keep lining their pockets is an economic, social, and political nonsense, both from the perspective of Greek economy and from that of the European Union as a whole. Rational reprofiling of the Greek debt (I suggest talking of "reprofiling" as some won't even hear of "writing off" or "reducing" it) by lowering it to the threshold of recoverability must be undertaken or else not only Greece will enter a nightmarish phase of its crisis, but the crisis will also spill over the entire area of Europe, also outside the single currency area.

The risk is immense, much greater than the one assumed in many different scenarios of Grexit, which would mean the end of euro as we know it. This would be a strong blow to the entire European integration process. This process is not Europe's private matter as it has a direct and indirect impact on economic relations with many non-EU countries and regions and is being watched in other parts of the world—from MERCOSUR[11] in South America and NAFTA[12] in North America to ECOWAS[13] and SADC[14] in Africa to ASEAN[15] and SAARC[16] in Asia. And, naturally, by China. If the European integration process collapses, then integration processes in other parts of the world will hang in balance. And there is no better way to adapt to the challenges of irreversible Globalization than through the processes of regional supranational integration, as then it will be easier to coordinate global policy on a worldwide level, which is necessary to keep a global balance, not only the economic one, in a longer term.

In economics and economic policy, one needs both knowledge and imagination to go beyond preconceived notions that are incompatible with the fast, sometimes quite dramatically, changing reality. In politics, which is defined as the ability to leverage opportunities that come our way, imagination is even more needed. What if someone plants some kind of a Trojan horse on us? Not only don't we know what the weather, prices, exchange rates, supply, demand will be like but, most of all, there's no knowing what "they" will do. They—meaning the coalition and the opposition, friends and foes, our country and world at large, the poor and the rich, and, of course, the notorious markets. Curiously enough, sometimes politicians themselves don't know what their next move will be, as politics is more like no-holds-barred wrestling than chess. There is no way to plan everything, but we can try to foresee, though it's not easy. At times, however, as it is the case of the Greek drama, this is extremely difficult.

WHAT A BEAUTIFUL CATASTROPHE!

Successive scenes of this saga parade before our eyes like pages of an economic and political thriller. No writer could invent what is going on these days. Neither Homer, nor Sophocles, well, maybe only Nikos Kazantzakis, the author of the immortal "Zorba the Greek." Interestingly enough, Zorba's first name was the same as that of prime minister of Greece in the years 2015–2019, Alexis, and his adventure ends up in a big fat catastrophe. When all he has built with a newly met friend goes tumbling down, he asks him, laughing, if he's ever seen such a beautiful catastrophe?! He hasn't because there has never been one like that. Nor one like what "troika" is concocting these days for Greece during this one of a kind Troj(ik)an war, but this catastrophe, if it happens, will not be beautiful and there will be nothing to laugh about or dance around.

But there is also an episode in this story where an old French woman who ended up in Crete, is dying and her female neighbors won't even wait; they steal her furniture, carpets and sheets while she's still on her deathbed. A bit like rich creditors, who wanted Greece, pushed to the brink of death, to surrender to them its family silver in the form of attractive assets worth no less than EUR 50 bln. Prime Minister Tsipras did not agree to this dictate of western creditors. Assets in more or less that amount are to be ring-fenced and, though subject to foreign control, three-fourths of them are to be used in Greece: half to recapitalize the devastated Greek banks, and one-fourth for investments. The last fourth would go to repay part of foreign liabilities.

The author of our thriller would have to be very imaginative to predict that at the next turning point of the negotiations/confrontation with troika (there have been more of those moments and there is more than one ahead of us), left-wing government prime minister will announce a national referendum. Its outcome was easy to foresee, even though Greeks were blackmailed that if they voted for "no," they would have to leave the eurozone or maybe even the EU. They voted for "no" and, for the time being, they are not leaving. The referendum question was worded in an extremely cunning way as there were many ways to interpret the negative response: I am against, nay, for. However, Greeks are not the only ones against (sacrifices) and for (euro). Also an overwhelming majority of Germans are in favor of Greece staying in the eurozone, but only half of them in favor of granting "financial assistance" to it, although the former is impossible without the latter.

After the referendum, which was meant to strengthen Prime Minister Tsipras's bargaining position in his efforts to reject the austerity package pushed on Greece, he presented to the troika their own package as his proposal, albeit slightly softened. This way he got his compatriots angry while getting his partners cornered: you must accept what you basically suggested yourselves. And so it happened. However, the troika, at the bidding of Germany and the Netherlands and some small states with conservative governments—Slovakia, Estonia, Finland, Latvia, Lithuania, Malta and Luxembourg—this time demanded that to lend credence to this offer, top-level political guarantees are necessary. This was about immediate (which is very difficult, considering the legislative complexities) adoption of laws amending regulations on the fiscal system and tax rates (especially raising VAT and CIT, job market deregulation, greater pension system discipline and extended retirement age) as suggested in the Brussels package.

Prime Minister Tsipras said the day after the Brussels summit—another one touted as a "breakthrough"—that he did not believe in the labored deal but he had accepted it. He referred to proposals contained there as "irrational," but he was willing to implement them to "avoid a disaster for the country, the collapse of the banks." But how do you implement an irrational agreement? Another paradox was that any implementation of those changes (and, mind you, apart from the parliament, there is also the constitutional tribunal that has already questioned decisions to trim certain social transfers and benefits awarded in the past) requires support from part of the opposition for the Syriza government as many of its deputies are also "for" and surely "against." Zorba is scratching his head.

Prime Minister Tsipras succeeded at what economists did not quite manage, though they used rational arguments based on correct economic theory. He is slowly convincing some of his largest creditors, especially France and Germany, to accept the indispensability of cutting not budget expenditure but foreign debt. Earlier on, French president Francois Hollande and Italian prime minister Mateo Renzi were open to talks on reducing the Greek debt, which is a sign of their economic pragmatism and class as politicians, considering that Greece owes them over EUR 42 bln and over EUR 37 bln respectively (ca. EUR 57 bln to Germany). After all, it is more difficult to take this bitter pill when you have your own problems with lingering budget deficit and a major public debt, which stands at ca. 95 percent GDP in France and exceeds 120 percent GDP in Italy. There's no need to point out that in both these cases it greatly exceeds the limit allowed under the Maastricht treaty.

Ostensibly it should be easier for everybody to follow this path, though still an uphill one, as the IMF surprised all the other players in the summer of 2015 by fiercely criticizing the bailout deal offered to Greece by the eurozone. IMF believes that Greece's public debt is currently "highly unsustainable" and urged a debt relief "well beyond what has been under consideration to date."

How to get out of this dead-end? Different proposals are being put forward. Well, I suggest making two shelves. The shorter one is already there. It's the ring-fenced Greek assets worth EUR 50 bln, aimed to restore the financial liquidity and capacity for output growth. What we need to put on the longer shelf is part of the debt, 150 billion euro, and these liabilities should be frozen for twenty-five years at their face value, that is with no interest charged, and then the whole amount is written off. Of course, provided that Greece solves the part of the task that is allocated to it, proving to itself and others that it is capable of strengthening its market economy institutions and of streamlining its fiscal and other policy. I believe it is capable.

Hence, we are in for next riddle: How will Germany and those marching alongside it justify their consent to reducing the Greek debt? Well, this is what they should do if they want to recover more money than they would in the alternative situation of a chaotic Grexit. The cue on how to get out of the pickle politically in this wandering world came from Barack Obama on the day the deal was struck on solving the conflict situation around Iran's nuclear program. US president said that the compromise reached—as this must be a compromise—is not built on trust but on verification. The same can be said, a year before the parliamentary election, by German chancellor and bureaucrats from Brussels to Greece, but for their own benefit. It's no longer about getting out of this mess without losing face but mostly without losing common sense.

How can one destroy such a country? Why insist on a policy that is harmful? To the society, to economy, to the state, and to the European integration. For money? What money? Holding on to orthodoxy and dogmatism will no longer bring any financial benefits to the rich co-perpetrators of the Greek drama, and will only make them incur even greater costs. For prestige? What prestige? After all, they no longer stand a chance of going down in history as good guys. To get out of this with no extra losses, it's necessary to escape forward, or reach out for unconventional solutions.

It would be good to be clear about who is responsible for this whole economic and political mess but there won't be a consensus on that. Decisions are taken in such procedures and modes that it's easier to articulate mutually exclusive accusations than to determine who authored specific solutions. Sometimes reasoned objections, some other times tendentious allegations are directed toward huge structures such as "troika" or Greece, toward organizations such as the EU or the IMF, toward specific politicians such as the Greek prime minister or the German chancellor, minister of finance having his office in Athens or his partner (or opponent?) in Berlin.

DIVERGENT POINTS OF VIEW

In the book *Welcome to the Poisoned Chalice: The Destruction of Greece and the Future of Europe* James K. Galbraith staunchly rejects the view that the Greek crisis is a clinical example of the irresponsibility of both the government and the governed, and tries to argue that the foreign environment of Greeks, the one involved for years in "overcoming the crisis," is much more at fault for the current situation than Greeks themselves. Hardly anyone is as well versed as himself in its realities and multiple aspects. This can be clearly seen in his book, which also includes his technical memos and economic policy recommendations made on the spot. There are fragments that read like a live report, a riveting reportage from a unique journey to Athens, Brussels, Paris, Berlin, London. At times we can also see documents addressed to the Greek minister of finance, some other times to its American counterpart, which were drafted as strictly confidential. Now they are becoming public domain and they are available also to us to read and review.

Let's be aware, however, that opinions are greatly divided even among luminaries of economics and political science. This is how Francis Fukuyama reacted to my opinion published in the summer 2015 (Kolodko 2015b):

> I broadly agree with your piece. There's no conceivable scenario under which Greece can pay its debt, so I don't understand why debt forgiveness isn't on the table.[17]

My line of thought is essentially shared also by the chief economist of the World Bank and its senior vice president for Development Economics, Kaushik Basu:

> The stereotyping of Greeks that has gone on for so long (as you point out) and with so little validity that a lot of damage has been done and it will take a lot of effort to undo this (if at all).[18]

One of the leading Chinese economists, Gang Fan, director of China's National Economic Research Institute, NERI, commented on my statement in more radical terms:

> Yes, we are expecting you speak out. Some people in US mess up the "facts" and their "wishes," and in their "analyses," they pick up facts to fit their wishes. And no one makes apology for their wrong predictions.[19]

Different opinions are expressed by Nobel Prize winners in economics. Robert J. Aumann of the Hebrew University of Jerusalem's Federmann Center for the Study of Rationality reacted to my essay with those words:

> I am not really familiar with the facts. Very superficially, it seems that they cannot pay their debts, i.e., are bankrupt. Indeed, it appears from their electing Tsipras (. . .) that they don't want to pay their debts, are in some sense repudiating them. There is not very much you can do about that, except being more careful about lending them money in the future.[20]

Edmund S. Phelps, director of the Center on Capitalism and Society at the Columbia University, wrote:

> I must say I thought (. . .) that you were insufficiently critical of Greece's stance.[21]

James K. Galbraith is much less skeptical about Greece and its faults than I, so he certainly risks criticism from more than one of his eminent American colleagues.

While the many controversies around the Greek syndrome are understandable, opinions on responsibility can be extreme both among experts and among public at large. Some, in Greece, behave reprehensibly by painting Hitler's moustache on posters of Angela Merkel visiting Athens, others, in Germany, yield to xenophobia and, demanding "Germany for Germans," hypocritically claim they only subsidize others, while refusing to remember they once earned much more on economic expansion, not always a responsible one, also in Greece. This can bring to mind the times of the Council for Mutual Economic Assistance, Comecon, which was dissolved a quarter century ago when the real socialism collapsed. While in Moscow you can still find economists that are deeply convinced Moscow was the one subsidizing Polish economy for years, in Warsaw an irrefutable belief is cherished that Poland subsidized the Soviet Union through various trade and investment channels. Similar views are held in Bratislava and Prague, in Budapest and Sofia. This is often the case of "mutual" assistance and "multilateral" benefits.

As for experts and "experts" on Greece, it's pretty baffling how easy it is to spread all kinds of negative stereotypes. Of course, as always in such situations, some media play their shameful role here. When they deserve it, Galbraith spares no bitter words and "good" wishes to them:

> (. . .) the role of the "Guardian" and the "Financial Times" as the mouthpieces of the Brussels apparat, throughout the Greek drama, is one for which I cordially hope their editors fry in hell. (Galbraith 2016b, 161).

I am convinced that journalists and commentators of some Polish newspapers will also join them there.

Perhaps there's a proverbial light in the tunnel. Agencies report on a preliminary agreement on reducing part of the Greek debt in exchange for the extraordinary adjustment effort made by Greece. BBC informs:

> The head of the Eurogroup of finance ministers, Jeroen Dijsselbloem, has said he hopes a deal with Greece on reforms and debt relief can be agreed later this month. (. . .) Greek MPs passed controversial new pension and tax reforms (. . .). The IMF believes Greece needs debt relief and says it will not sign off on a review of Greek reforms unless such relief is granted. (. . .) German Finance Minister Wolfgang Schouble also said he was "confident" that a solution would be reached (. . .). (BBC 2016)

On the one hand, it's amazing that this time IMF is on the offensive and demands debt reduction. It's as if the pope suddenly demanded sexual freedom. It was easier for the Fund to do this about-face as the costs of such unavoidable procedure are mostly incurred by the "dvoika," that is, European structures. We need to help Germans reach this conclusion, too, as they have as much to say as to lose in this matter. After all, the losses have already been incurred, in major part. Now it only has to be politically admitted (which is not easy) and properly entered in the books (which is less difficult).

On the other hand, it's astonishing that the mighty of the world as well as analysts, economists, and financial commentators rubbing elbows with them took so much time to reach a conclusion which was obvious already several years ago. Some might say "better late than never," but others will ask why it happens at such a great expense? Also at the expense of those who will now bear the burden of debt reduction. But now the debt is much higher. It is, to a significant extent, no longer an obligation to western banks and their shareholders (and the political beneficiaries of their sponsorship), but an obligation to public organizations represented by "troika" or, ultimately, to us, European Union's taxpayers. Still, there's no doubt:

it's better to pay the costs of gradually getting out of the Greek syndrome this way as otherwise we'd have to pay the consequences of a much more costly chaos.

TROJ(IK)AN WAR

At the same time, I am aware that giving help to Greece in the form of a conditional write-off of part of its debt involves a risk of the demonstration effect. Others may demand similar solutions—countries that are structurally weak, struggling with deficit and excessive public debt, mostly Portugal and Spain. That's why when dragging Greece from the economic mire in which it has found itself, EU must have in place a tough and effective EU policy toward other countries, so that with reasonable support they can themselves handle the crisis processes that plague them. It should be, however, emphasized that the risk of demonstration effect is much greater in the event of Greece's bankruptcy and leaving the eurozone. This cannot be done calmly, according to a plan, without the crisis spilling over to other weak countries. If Greece can't cope, soon Portugal and Spain, perhaps also Cyprus and Ireland and later even Italy can be in a similar situation.

I believe that not only economists will be fascinated to read the last part of Galbraith's book, "Appendix: A Summary of Plan X" (Galbraith 2016b, 189–98), discussing the potential turn of events and the various challenges that would (will?) have to be faced in the event of Grexit. It reads like expertly written economic *science fiction*, like a *counterfactual history*, or, colloquially speaking, *what if* novel? It is all the more intriguing that it may turn out that what is *what if*? now, a very professional one, may still become very useful advice for policy, not only the economic one.

Considering the subtitle of the book—"The Destruction of Greece and the Future of Europe"—according to Galbraith, the coming years look bleak for our continent. Especially that it has been swept by more crises than the still unsolved and even escalating Greek syndrome. Let me re-iterate: things happen the way they do because a lot happens at the same time. Refugee crisis, the confusion over Brexit (Kolodko 2016a), devolutionary tendencies within the European Union and conflicts near its borders, in Ukraine and Turkey, are just the most important ones among other crises which put the one in Greece in a more complex political context.

The situation is still as difficult as unpredictable, but it's possible to find a way out as long as political common sense and true European solidarity prevail, and the economic policy follows the theoretical premises of the New Pragmatism. The coming years will show if that will happen. It may, it should, it doesn't have to.[22]

NOTES

1. See his last book on income and property inequalities (Galbraith 2016a).

2. He is the author of several interesting books, also on the European and world economic crisis. See: *inter alia*, Yanis Varoufakis, *And the Weak Suffer What They Must? Europe's Crisis and America's Economic Future*, London: Bodley Head, 2016 and *The Global Minotaur: America, Europe and the Future of the World Economy*, London: Zed Books, 2015. Is it not interesting that while an American professor is writing a book about the Greek crisis and its implications for the future of Europe, a Greek professor writes about the European crisis and its consequences for America?

3. We were writing about it, along with my coauthor, as these processes were occurring. See: Kolodko and Rutkowski, 1991.

4. To understand what the author thinks of the term, see: John Williamson, 2005.

5. More on the assumption called shock therapy and its failure, and the successful implementation of the "Strategy for Poland" see: Kolodko and Nuti, 1997.

6. Personal correspondence.

7. I make this distinction between two different tenses as, depending on when you read these words, Syriza is either still in power or has already moved to the opposition.

8. Personal correspondence.

9. More about the importance of institutions, in behavioral rather than organizational terms, see: North, 2002.

10. For more about the origin, course and consequences of the Argentine crisis of the early twenty-first century see: Edward Epstein and David Pion-Berlin, 2008.

11. MERCOSUR, *Mercado Común del Sur* or Common Market of the South, is a regional integration agreement, whose full members are Argentina, Brazil, Paraguay, Uruguay, and Venezuela and associate countries are Bolivia, Chile, Peru, Ecuador, and Colombia.

12. NAFTA, *North American Free Trade Agreement*, whose members are the United States, Canada and Mexico.

13. ECOWAS, *Economic Community of West African States*, has fifteen members: Benin, Burkina Faso, Gambia, Ghana, Guinea, Guinea-Bissau, Liberia, Mali, Niger, Nigeria, Cape Verde, Senegal, Sierra Leone, Togo, and Ivory Coast.

14. SADC, *Southern African Development Community* is a loose integration grouping consisting of fifteen countries: Angola, Botswana, Democratic Republic of the Congo, Lesotho, Madagascar, Malawi, Mauritius, Mozambique, Namibia, South Africa, Seychelles, Swaziland, Tanzania, Zambia, and Zimbabwe.

15. ASEAN is *Association of South-East Asian Nations*, whose members are Brunei, the Philippines, Indonesia, Cambodia, Laos, Malaysia, Myanmar (Burma), Singapore, Thailand, and Vietnam.

16. SAARC, *South Asian Association for Regional Cooperation*, is made up of Afghanistan, Bangladesh, Bhutan, India, Maldives, Nepal, Pakistan, and Sri Lanka.

17. Personal correspondence.

18. Personal correspondence.

19. Personal correspondence.
20. Personal correspondence.
21. Personal correspondence.
22. Published in: *Rivista di Politica Economica* (2016), April–June: 37–61.

Chapter 15

Economics and Politics of the Currency Convergence

The Case of Poland

Political decisions regarding the economic sphere always require a compromise as they are enmeshed in conflicting interests. It seldom happens that a given envisaged theoretical solution has virtually only pros and totally no cons. If that were the case, economists would be unnecessary as there would be no matter subject to comparative analyses, or their task would be as easy as it seemingly is to assess which of the good and defect-free scenarios is better.

Reality, however, is far more complicated, to such an extent, at times, that no wonder even the most professional circles, rational in their assessments, are unable to reach a consensus. This is all the more obvious if a problem is complex, multilayered, likely to generate conflict, if it goes beyond one country's borders and the time horizon typical of politics, and, most of all, when benefits and losses intersect. Estimating their balance is difficult and risky as it must rely not only on correct economic models but also on making various assumptions, which are controversial by their nature.

This is exactly the situation of the common multistate currency areas. Some of them have been successfully functioning for years. Curiously enough, this happens in poor, sometimes very poor countries, as is the case of CAF (XOF) franc used by fourteen African states, or of the East Caribbean dollar (XCD) bringing together six countries and two dependent territories (Kolodko 2011a). However, the most important common currency area is that of the euro (EUR), which has been circulated for fifteen years now in—currently—nineteen EU member states and in eleven countries and territories which do not belong to the EU. Moreover, currencies of some other states are more or less strictly linked to euro. While other common currency zones are faring quite well, serious problems are mounting in the eurozone. It's not surprising then that some—recently more often due to the world financial crisis—are predicting the collapse of the common European currency (Brown 2012) or calling for its controlled elimination and for returning to national currencies.

Certainly, the eurozone reality is far from what is theoretically assumed for the so called optimum currency area (Mundell 1961) and it's been a known fact for a while that macroeconomic tensions as well as structural and institutional weaknesses at the time euro came to being where greater than it was presented (Mundell 2000, 2003; McKinnon, 2002). Neither is the situation as good as others claim: "The idea that the euro has 'failed' is dangerously naive. The euro is doing exactly what its progenitor (. . .) predicted and planned for it to do" (Palast 2012).

In the opinions and projections I express, I am far from the nationalist megalomania, such as nurturing a pipedream of Poland becoming a "great power" (Friedman 2009) or even a "European economic power." We are in for nothing of that sort and while such illusions provoke more amusement than anger, we need to be aware of how great Poland's contemporary significance is in geopolitics, especially on the continental scale. Undoubtedly, it is greater in the context of politics than economy, but the intersection of those two elements is truly stronger than ever before. In this very context, it is worthwhile and necessary to look at the challenges facing Poland in relation to euro. Other post-socialist countries also have similar dilemmas, and as the EU expands, there will be more of these,[1] but here let me focus on threats and opportunities shaping up for Poland in this area. Of course, the future of its economy will depend on many other factors and the potential euroization, that is, putting the euro into circulation, is not the most important matter, but definitely one deserving special attention. The reason is measures aimed to improve the economic structure, the institutional reinforcement, the macroeconomic stability and the pro-growth economic policy may bring even better effects, if they are coupled with being part of the common euro currency zone.

GLOBAL TURBULENCES AND EUROPEAN DRIFT

Everybody knows that: things happen the way they do because a lot happens at the same time. The build-up of crisis phenomena and processes in the global economy and its various regions is already so significant that, while not long ago it was the ambition of nearly every luminary of social sciences, especially of the economic ones, to write a text about Globalization and European integration, now the pendulum is swinging back and we're in for a crop of publications about the move away from Globalization, isolationism and nationalisms, protectionism, and, as regards our continent, about the prospect of the breakup of the European Union. Neither the Globalization reversing not the Union's breakup is by any means inevitable, but both are possible, which has its obvious implications. Hence a few fundamental questions should be asked in science, and a few assumptions made in politics. The nightmare is that, again, theory is failing to provide, on time, hints for practice and it becomes increasingly risky, or even fatally wrong.[2]

Firstly, it should be determined whether Globalization is indeed in reverse or even has ceased, or it is and will be continued (Kolodko 2011a, 2014b). There is no absolute certainty, but I believe that despite the growing protectionist tendencies and various nationalisms, sometimes referred to as the economic patriotism, it is an irreversible process. This is due to the nature of the contemporary and future technological progress, and, most of all, due to the supranational networking of economies and of the system of powerful interests of transnational corporations. If so, we may turn our back at the world, but instead, we should integrate with it, in a smart manner, that is by maximizing, in economic terms, our own benefits and minimizing the inevitable attendant costs. This is true of large and smaller countries alike, especially the latter ones as they should develop the most in the open economy. Curiously enough, and also surprisingly to many, currently China is becoming the champion of opening and free trade and the advocate for Globalization, while the United States, under the new administration, may take the opposite positions.

Secondly, being situated where Poland is—at the heart of Europe—one needs to strengthen the scientific case for the far-reaching European integration and adopt an assumption in the development strategy and policy that it is not only desirable but actually unavoidable to continue this process. Moreover, for medium-sized and small countries, the participation in a regional integration, especially one having such an advanced form as the European Union, is the best way to adapt to the challenges, that is to threats and opportunities involved in the inevitable Globalization. Specific conclusions follow from these observations for non-European countries that are enmeshed in their attempts at regional integration.

FROM DESTRUCTION TO CONSTRUCTION

Of course, if somebody claims that, in the light of the growing xenophobia and parochialism—from the United States to France, from Venezuela to Nigeria, from the United Kingdom to Turkey—there will come a turning point after which Globalization will collapse; if somebody believes that, as a result of the drift of the last several years, EU is in the state of inevitable decomposition, then he or she is asking quite different questions to those we are dealing with here. What I am striving to answer is how to escape forward, how to couple economic and political dilemmas to move from the threat of destruction to the opportunity of constructing something better.

Poland has virtually nothing to offer to the world and cannot directly support Globalization—as we produce just under 0.9 percent of the global output, and represent just 0.5 percent of the world's population; and yet, at the European level, maybe ironically, we have never had a greater chance to make a creative contribution.

If our *raison d'etat* is to care for a dynamic and triply sustainable (in economic, social, and environmental terms) development amidst peaceful coexistence with our surroundings, then Poland should join the eurozone. It's not about us having the right and duty to do so under the treaty of accession, supported by a national referendum, but about this being profitable to us, to the society and economy. I hasten to add that, on balance, since, as nearly always, we need an objective profit and loss account here. And, of course, not unconditionally.

Economists have their idiosyncrasy of attaching too much weight to economic issues. Well, this is our domain, while, in reality, economic interests are all too often sacrificed at the altar of politics; all too often, the noneconomic lack of common sense prevails over economic pragmatism. This is why such pragmatism should be sought all the more. However, let us start from politics.

If Poland's government, having a definite support of the president and a majority in both houses of parliament, should announce, in concert with the National Bank of Poland, its readiness to start efforts to adopt euro, this would change not only the European politics. In a situation where a structural and institutional crisis of the EU is underway, where the scenario of the "Europe of two speeds"[3] can be more and more clearly seen on the horizon, where new nationalism rather than new pragmatism (Kolodko 2014b; Bałtowski 2017) seems to be taking the upper hand (Economist 2016), strengthening one of the main links of the process that is the European common currency project, would be of fundamental importance to the economic integration with all of its political and cultural consequences. And not only to ours, the European one, as the EU is being watched with attention worldwide—from MERCOSUR in South America to ASEAN in South East Asia, from SADC in the south of Africa to ECOWAS in its West, from NAFTA to SAARC in South Asia. If the integration in Europe is successful, it will also gain momentum in other parts of the world, and the regional integration processes are a great way to adapt to the challenges of globalization.

Poland joining the eurozone would have a special meaning in the light of the United Kingdom exiting the EU. As part of the eurozone, Poland would immediately cease to be a peripheral country and become an important element of the core of this formation, on par with Spain having a similar population potential, and the Netherlands, which has fewer inhabitants but is clearly richer.[4] Things could be that way, especially that the position of Italy, unable to cope with its secular stagnation, is relatively weakening. The courageous accession of the tiny Lithuania to the common currency area two years ago did not change the continental geopolitics, whereas our accession to it (which would be possible in 2020 at the earliest) would be of major significance.

Since we're talking about politics, it's clear that we need to take the opportunity to give up on the illusory attempts to replace the Weimar triangle with the Vishegrad square and let go of the pipedreams of a Poland-led intermarium. Poland is not supposed to lead but it should not be on the margin, either. Poland accepting euro and euro accepting Poland can only help it because with our potential we don't mean much in the world, but we do in Europe. Being part of the eurozone, we would mean even more in the EU, while the Union, in turn, would mean more in the global economic and political game. This may be once again a case where quantity translates into quality.

BENEFITS AND COSTS

Political arguments will surely prevail, but, truly, what should be more important is the economic ones. I would not advocate a decision on such an important issue as replacing the existing national currency with common European money, if I had any doubts as to the profitability of this venture. But I would not force such a solution, either, without first garnering support for it among a greater part of the society, which today is against it. The society, however, can be convinced with rational arguments proving it would be beneficial to them. There already was such a time more or less ten years ago, when a great majority of Poles were in favor of the euro, but the politicians did not follow the vox populi then. Now they should not go against it, but instead garner relevant support as a result of a matter of fact and fair debate.

Here, I leave aside the imperative to make a relevant amendment to the Constitution, because if the Law and Justice government, in the current political set-up, put forward this proposal, it would easily have the necessary qualified quorum, as it would get support also from some MPs from the opposition benches. This is especially true of those who constantly declare their support for free market economy and European integration.

The greatest benefit would be the elimination of the currency risk in the area where turnover is settled in euro (and in currencies quite rigidly linked to it), and this accounts for ca. 70 percent of our exports and imports. Many entrepreneurs are disoriented as to the profitability of various ventures as they do not know what their costs and revenue will be in international relations, and thus they have no guarantee as to their potential transactions. This uncertainty spreads to the sphere of investment, because as there's no telling what will be profitable to manufacture, the profitability of investment projects is also unknown. The exchange rate unpredictability is one of the underlying causes of the relatively low capacity utilization, followed by a weak dynamics of investment or, at times, its absolute level even diminishing. Since this is obviously harmful to the economic growth, the introduction of the euro would eliminate this factor.

At the end of the day, the prices of goods and services that we buy on the market include transaction costs resulting from converting zlotys into euro and back in exports, imports and foreign travel. On that account, as it can be estimated, we pay, first as manufacturers, and then as consumers, over a dozen billion zlotys more. This is roughly what we spend on the 2–3 percentage points of the higher VAT. Latvians and Slovenians are spared this cost (and, at the same time, easy gain for financial intermediaries, banks and currency exchange bureaus, from which we should expect resistance to the introduction of the euro).

All this, by contributing to Polish companies' greater international competitiveness on the microeconomic scale and better stability on the macro scale, would drive the economic growth, and, consequently a more palpable improvement of the population's standards of living. I believe that being part of the eurozone, in the next decade, we could achieve a roughly 0.5 percent higher yearly GDP growth. This is a lot as, in terms of compound interest, this would give as much as 15 percent more in just one generation.

There is no validity to counterarguments put forward by the opponents of the euro, who claim that once we convert our earnings to it—with the average gross salary amounting to EUR 1,200 in 2020—they will drop in real terms; by no means. Not in principle as all prices will be converted as per the same rate, including rents and also taxes. So the purchasing power of earnings—salary, pension, scholarship, social allowances, profits—will be the same before and after the convergence. Yes, there will be cases of prices being rounded up, but, on the one hand, the scale of this phenomenon will be blocked by the strong consumers' position and by the competition on the market, and, on the other hand, prices will be rounded down sometimes, too. Surely, this will not represent an inflationary impulse as inflation is a process of the overall price level growing, and in this cases we would, at most, deal with a short-term friction.

It's also hard to defend the argument that by having our own currency we can be shielded from the impact of external shocks. Sometimes we can, and sometimes the exchange rate fluctuations do more harm than good. Before the weakening of the Polish zloty helped Poland after the shock wave of the global economic crisis in the years 2008–2009, the overvaluation of our currency—and let me remind you that at its peak it was exchanged at ca. 3.20 per euro—had carried with it a series of bankruptcies, even those of well-governed companies. It contributed to a near-demise of the export-oriented shipbuilding industry, and it was hardly the only casualty of the practice of yielding to the dogma that a free and fully floating exchange rate system is perfect. Then, the undervalued exchange rate of PLN 4.90 for 1 euro was temporarily helpful, but earlier on the exorbitant rate of PLN 3.20 was doing permanent damage, eliminating from the market a number of well-governed companies with skilled and disciplined staff.[5] And I suppose it goes without saying that if the euro had been in circulation in Poland for years, like in Slovenia, where it was introduced in 2007, there would have been no foreign currency-indexed mortgage crisis, or the problem of the Swiss franc debtors.

A LESSER BURDEN OF DEBT

A major benefit of the euroization of the Polish economy would be the palpable reduction of public debt and costs of its servicing. Poland's reserve assets amounts to nearly EUR 110 billion,[6] or roughly one fourth of our national income calculated in GDP terms. It's a lot and it's very ineffective as, on balance, this costs us ca. 2 percent of the GDP, which stems from the variation between the percentage rate of reserves and that of the public debt. In other words, on the one hand, Poland has large funds invested in very low-interest foreign securities, mainly secure and stable bonds to finance budget deficits of reliable governments from the United States and Canada to Germany and France, to Australia and New Zealand; on the other hand, the government issues its own bonds and sells them abroad at a much higher interest rate. It's as if we were borrowing our own money from somebody, but at a higher interest rate than the one this person pays us for lending it to them.

On our way to the euro, we need to rationally use these reserves, and there is no better way than to earmark their significant part—maybe up to 75 percent—to repay some of the foreign debt. This would mean reducing the public debt by 17 percentage points, to ca. 35 percent of the GDP. Then we would find ourselves in the better league of countries, as the rating of the Polish economy would go up, both the official one expressed by credit rating agencies and the real one, expressed by financial markets.

I realize that it won't be easy to redeem our debt in foreign currencies, as the profitability of our bonds is very attractive to their holders. If we succeeded for less than the equivalent of 75 percent of reserves, even half of it would be of great significance. The same amount could go to a special sovereign welfare fund, out of care for the next generation, and the rest—to pay the contribution to the European Central Bank's capital and to the minimum reserves.

This would be a qualitative change leading to Poland's better international financial position and, while we're at it, to a drop in interest rates. Meanwhile, the budget would carry year to year a quantitatively lesser burden of the public debt.[7] I hasten to add that this idea will face the most fierce attack—and, of course, not a direct one but one using other arguments—from the advocates of the international financial world, for whom it is as advantageous as it is costly for Polish taxpayers, to maintain such huge foreign currency reserves, on the one hand, and quite a big foreign debt, on the other; roughly a third of the debt is obligations to foreign partners.

CONVERGENCE EXCHANGE RATE OF PARAMOUNT IMPORTANCE

Assuming that all this time we'll comply with Maastricht currency convergence criteria—the way we finally do, and which is under threat if the current government's policy is continued (Assessment 2016)—what matters most is the exchange rate at which the euro should be introduced. It is fortunate that zloty happens to be weaker now; it is estimated to be undervalued by 10–15 percent. This is a good starting point for negotiating the convergence exchange rate, which should stand between 3.80 and 4.00 zlotys per euro. It's very important as an undervalued exchange rate drives imported inflation while overvalued zloty is harmful to exports by Polish companies, and, after all, we should pursue the strategy of export-driven growth. In other words, export should grow faster than import, and both these categories should grow faster than the GDP. To make it happen, export must be cost-effective but import cannot be too expensive, either. Hence the trick is to find an economically balanced exchange rate and to negotiate it politically first as the reference exchange rate and then as the one used for the final convergence.

It's worth pointing out that wit Poland accepting the euro and the euro accepting Poland, we would see the trend reverse. Indeed, while pessimist opinions seem to be predominant, also in some professional circles, the strengthening of the common currency area by the largest of the eleven post-socialist transformation economies could contribute some optimist notes. While refraining from overestimating the expectations and from giving them more importance than to hard material facts, this is indeed important.

So is it worth going toward the euro? Do chances of success, the arguments for, and the economics and politics of the whole endeavor speak in favor of it? Can we solve the Grexit problem, as there must be a clarity on this matter before we commit (Galbraith 2016b, Kolodko 2016b)? Yes, though we must be aware of the attendant risk and of the huge area of uncertainty. Nevertheless, it's easier to get away scot-free from the current crisis with Poland in the euro and the euro in Poland, and it may be beneficial to Poland, too.[8]

NOTES

1. For more on some specific factors inherent in the accession of this group of economies to the eurozone, see Nuti (2006).
2. This observation is true of many countries, presently including the still most important economy of the United States, due to the threats involved in what will certainly go down in history as "Trumponomics." If only some of the new US president Donald Trump's announcements as regards the unconventional economic policy are implemented—especially the protectionist practices, violating the free trade treaties and going back on the previous arrangements on climate policy to prevent global warming—in the long run it will harm not only the United States, but also the entire global economy.
3. Actually it would be more appropriate to talk of "Europe of three" or even "four speeds," as we have not only nineteen EU member states which belong to the eurozone and nine member states outside it, but also fifteen more states which, while being European, are not part of the EU—from the very rich Iceland, Norway, and Switzerland to the very poor Albania, Bosnia and Herzegovina and Moldova.
4. While Poland has a population of 38.5 million, and a GDP at purchasing power parity (PPP) of ca. USD 1.05 trillion, the Netherlands is inhabited by ca. 17 million people and has a GDP of USD 866 billion, and Spain—by 48.5 million people with a GDP of USD 1.69 trillion. Per capita income in those three countries stands, respectively, at USD 27,700, 50,800, and 36,500 (PPP).
5. The fluctuations from PLN 3.20 to 4.90 per euro represent a huge spread. They made themselves felt, though with a much smaller amplitude, also at the turn of 2016/2017, in connection with the turbulence around the internal noneconomic policy in Poland and the surprising outcome of the US election, among other things.
6. Up to 39 percent of Polish currency reserves are stored in US dollar, up to 29 percent in euro. The remaining part of the portfolio is invested in other currencies plus a relatively small portion in gold.
7. In 2017, the budgetary cost of servicing the public debt in its foreign part amounts to over PLN 10 billion (cost of servicing the domestic debt is slightly over 20 billion). It has increased by 2.7 percent compared to 2016.
8. Published in: Kolodko (2017b).

Chapter 16

Determinants and Implications of the Eurozone Enlargement

The issue of the euro is not just an internal affair of the Euroland or, more broadly speaking, of the European Union as a whole, but also an international or even a global problem, because it's the currency in which ca. 20 percent of all foreign exchange reserves are held. Globally, it's the second reserve currency after the US dollar (ca. 63.5 percent). According to IMF's data, total reserves amount to ca. USD 11.3 trillion,[1] of which we know the currency composition for the equivalent of 9.65 trillion. These are the so-called allocated reserves. The rest, 1.65 trillion, are unallocated reserves. Slightly over 4.5 percent of the former are denominated in the Japanese yens, 4.5 percent in British pound sterling, 2 percent in Canadian dollars, 1.1 percent in Chinese renminbi, RMB and only 0.16 percent in Swiss franc. The remaining 2.4 percent are reserves in other currencies, for example, Australian, New Zealand, Singaporean and Hong Kong dollars, Korean won, South African rand and Saudi riyal.

It's understandable that in the foreseeable future, despite all the trouble it got itself into, (Prasad 2014), USD will keep playing the leading role in global economic relations, not only as reserve money but also as the principal means of payment in international transactions and the major measure of value of goods on the global market. However, with time it will have to give some ground to other currencies, including Chinese renminbi. As regards the euro, though only one-fifth of those reserves are kept in it, surely its fate will have a more-than-proportionate impact on the global economy's stability. And that's despite the euro's share of all countries' aggregate reserves declining by over seven percentage points since 2009.[2]

This downward trend can be expected to reverse, though it depends on a number of varied factors, especially those related to economy but also to politics. In many respects, the situation in both those spheres is volatile and difficult to predict. It is beyond any doubt, however, that both the overall condition of the EU's single currency area and the euro's international status as one of the world's reserve currencies, will be significantly affected by the changes in the methods of eurozone regulation and supervision as well as by the enlarging area of its circulation. This process also has its complex political, social, economic, and technical determinants. The most difficult problems, hence the most important ones, are those involved in fiscal determinants of convergence with the eurozone of the economies that are now outside the single currency area.

CURRENCY CONVERGENCE CRITERIA

The euro is in circulation in nineteen out of twenty-eight EU member states. In eleven of them—in Austria, Belgium, Finland, France, Germany, Ireland, Italy, Luxemburg, the Netherlands, Portugal, Spain—it has been so since the clearing system was established in 1999 and the euro was put in circulation in 2002, and since 2003—with huge problems until today (Galbraith 2016b, Kolodko 2016b)—in Greece. Then, in 2008, the area was joined by two Mediterranean countries, Cyprus and Malta, and five post-socialist countries, in the following order: Slovenia in 2007, Slovakia in 2009, Estonia in 2011, Latvia in 2014 and Lithuania in 2015. Euro is also in circulation, pursuant to the agreements signed, in four tiny European states: in Andorra, Monaco, San Marino and Vatican, and de facto also in Liechtenstein, the fifth one from this category, where it functions side by side with the official Swiss franc, and based on its unilateral introduction, in Montenegro and Kosovo.

Out of nine EU member states that are still outside the euro area, only two of them, Denmark and the United Kingdom, pursuant to the Maastricht treaty opt-out clause (1993), are not obliged to join the monetary union. All the other countries, including Sweden, a EU member state since 1995, and five post-socialist countries—Bulgaria, Czech Republic, Hungary, Poland and Romania—have the right and duty to join the European monetary union pursuant to their membership treaties. So far they have neither exercised that right nor complied with the duty, mostly because they did not meet the required convergence criteria.

In line with the treaty, one can expect all of them—of course except the United Kingdom which is leaving the EU—to join the eurozone, though there's no telling when that will happen and in what order. One can also conjecture that with the further enlargement of the monetary union and the resulting accession of subsequent post-socialist economies—Bulgaria and Romania most probably being the first ones—and especially if the problems besetting the Euroland are effectively solved, also Denmark will adjust its strategy and may give up on its own currency.

The economic integration processes as part of the European Union are regulated by a legal framework, whose main element is the *Treaty on the Functioning of the European Union* (TFEU).[3] In accordance with the treaty provisions, EU member states pursue their own economic policy, but, at the same time, some coordination measures are undertaken at the supranational level. TFEU lays down the basic policy-making methods and principles for the single economic policy (Postula 2015). These issues are dealt with in chapter 1 "Economic Policy" of Title VIII "Economic and monetary policy." The key provisions of this chapter are provided in Article 121, which speaks of multilateral surveillance and coordination of economic policies, and Article 126 about avoiding excessive budget deficit. It stipulates the form of corrective actions against countries which have too high public debt or excessive public finance sector deficit. In accordance with Article 140 of TFEU, the European Commission and the European Central Bank are obliged to make reports, every two years, on the progress made by the member states not meeting the requirements to adopt the euro in fulfilling their obligations regarding the achievements of economic and monetary union. These are so-called member states with a derogation (Article 139 of TFEU).

The monetary convergence is contingent on meeting five nominal financial criteria.

1. The inflation criterion provides that the rate of inflation may not be more than 1.5 percentage points higher than the arithmetical average for three EU member states with the lowest rate of inflation.
2. The interest rate criterion requires the long-term interest rate to be no more than 2 percentage points higher than the arithmetical average for three EU member states with the most stable prices.
3. The budget deficit criterion does not authorize deficit to be higher than 3 percent of GDP.
4. Public debt criterion sets the limit of the government debt at 60 percent of GDP.
5. Exchange rate criterion allows the maximum +/- 15 percent fluctuation margin around the central rate.

Although the common European currency exists already for almost twenty years, it is no surprise that the controversies about this bold project remain. The furthest going skepticism dares to refer to this endeavor—or the a particular issue, as the upper limit of acceptable fiscal deficit not exciding a threshold of 3 percent of country's GDP—as something nonsensical (de Grauve 2010; Pasinetti 1998; Stiglitz 2018). Yet far from perfect, the supporting of economic and political integration by applying the common currency does make sense.

An economy aspiring to join the eurozone should have a floating exchange rate mechanism in place and for two years leading up to the conversion, it should be a member of the European exchange rate mechanism, ERM-2. In this period, the exchange rate of the domestic currency against the euro may, generally speaking, can deviate from the central parity negotiated between the candidate state, the European Central Bank and the European Commission *in minus* or *in plus* by 15 percent.[4] In practice, when enforcing the exchange rate stability criterion, a more narrow and asymmetric margin from +15 percent to -2.25 percent is in effect. However, it is not always the case. In particular, two departures from that rule have been applied in current practices: pegged exchange rate or revaluation.

With respect to the Baltic states—Estonia, Latvia and then Lithuania—the use of a pegged exchange rate or currency board arrangement was accepted instead of a two-year participation in ERM-2 with a floating but stable exchange rate. For Lithuania, a country which was the last of the current member states to join the eurozone, a wide range of +/- 15 percent deviations was formally applicable throughout the entire period of participation in ERM-2, for ten years, from mid-2004 until entering the eurozone in 2015. Without major tensions, Lithuania maintained, in the two-year reference period, a pegged exchange rate against the euro as used previously as part of the currency board arrangement and it was at this exchange rate, 3.4528 lits per 1 euro, that the national currency was finally converted to the euro.

In the reference period, devaluation is prohibited, but revaluation is acceptable. That was the case of first Greece and then Slovakia. It was similar with Ireland, which has been a member of the eurozone since its creation. Over there, with work productivity growing faster than elsewhere, Irish pound followed a strengthening trend. This type of appreciation pressure, contrary to short-term currency strengthening due to speculation, promotes economic equilibrium and is considered "healthy." The Irish pound in the period leading up to the conversion to the euro stood, on average, 4.6 percent higher than the central rate, with the maximum deviation approaching 11 percent (Schadler 2005).[5]

To join the European monetary union, one must meet all the criteria in a durable and sustainable manner. They are of importance to the functioning of the single monetary area as they concern achieving and maintaining a high level of price stability, stable exchange rate, convergence of long-term interest rates and a stable overall situation of public finance. There is also a sixth criterion, which requires national legislation on monetary and fiscal matters to be compatible with the EC law.

More detailed treaty provisions as regards the coordination of economic policies of the EU members states were formulated in the *Stability and Growth Pact* (SGP) passed in 1997, composed of a relevant resolution[6] and two regulations of the European Council,[7] pursuant to which EU member states are obliged to have sound public finance and meet both fiscal criteria. From the perspective of budgetary policy, of key importance is the fiscal criterion referred to as the avoidance of excessive deficit. SGP, expanding on the treaty provisions regarding the avoidance of excessive deficit, introduced the duty to prepare a medium-term convergence plan and stability plan indicating the medium-term budgetary target.[8] Every year, in April, eurozone member states submit with the European Commission and the EC their stability programs, and nonmember states, their convergence programs. These programs must contain relevant information on the state's medium-term budgetary target and explanation of the intended way to achieve it (Postula 2012). Moreover, the states must present an analysis and evaluation of the results of economic changes affecting the state's fiscal position.

EXCESSIVE DEFICIT PROCEDURE

The implementation of both stability and convergence programs is monitored by the European Commission. Based on its recommendations, the EC launches the excessive deficit procedure, EDP, if the criteria are not met. The procedure imposes on the state a duty to present the planned corrective actions to improve the condition of public finance. If none are implemented or those in place are inadequate, various kinds of sanctions may be imposed. These refer to a greater extent to eurozone member states, but there are also possibilities to apply them to EU member states that are still outside the single currency area.

The insufficient effectiveness of SGP made it necessary to significantly modify it (Schick 2010; Schaechter, Kinda, Budina and Weber 2012). The so-called six-pack was used to that end,[9] which was aimed to ensure more effective budgetary control and public debt control. The legislative changes to the principles of fiscal policy that were introduced as part of it (Marneffe, Van Aarle, Van Der Wielen and Vereeck 2011) were confirmed and specified in the Treaty on Stability, Coordination and Governance in the Economic and Monetary Union (known as the fiscal compact). In particular:

- The existing fiscal criterion regarding the deficit limit and public debt limit was developed (3 percent of GDP and 60 percent of GDP respectively).
- A duty was introduced to reduce public debt at an average rate of one twentieth per year of its excess over the limit.
- Structural deficit should be reduced by 0.5 percent of GDP until the medium-term budgetary target is achieved.
- Costs of pension reforms can be deducted from the deficit.

Moreover, it was recommended that a fiscal rule should be introduced in respective member states' national law, enforcing sustainability of the structural balance of the general government sector (achievement of the medium-term budget target).

Without getting into a detailed discussion, one can formulate a view that most member states did not have an economic policy in place that would take full account of the idea of SGP, so no wonder its goals were not achieved, either. As a result, the condition of public finance in most European Union member states was deemed insufficiently stable.

Irrespective of any regulatory specifications introduced at the EU level as part of the modified SGP, the principal parameters subject to fiscal evaluation are still the public sector deficit and debt. In the years 2005 to 2016, the ratio of general government deficit to GDP stood at levels that made it necessary to initiate excessive deficit procedure for most countries.

In the last two years, 2016–2017, the fiscal situation was relatively good. Following the favorable economic situation in 2016, public finance was balanced in two countries and in as many as nine there was a budgetary surplus. It was similar in 2017. Currently, the excessive deficit procedure is imposed on three member states: on the United Kingdom since 2008 and on France and Spain since 2009. Only in two countries, Estonia and Sweden, it has never been applied to date and in all the others it was periodically imposed by the European Commission and lifted upon implementing relevant corrective actions.

After many years of financing budget deficits, noncompliance with the second fiscal criterion has been frequent. In non-eurozone economies it has been the case also due to the decline in the value of national currency in the countries where the public debt consisted partly of debt in a foreign exchange that was gaining strength at the time. In the period 2005–2016, out of twenty-eight EU member states eleven complied with this criterion. It must be emphasized that as many as eight of those countries are post-socialist economies: Estonia, Latvia, Lithuania and Slovakia, eurozone member states, and Bulgaria, Czech Republic, Poland and Romania, which are still outside the eurozone. In 2016 in as many as seventeen countries public debt (calculated according to ESA, *General Government Gross Debt*) stood above 60 percent of GDP. Record-breakers in this respect are Greece and Italy, where this index exceeds the acceptable limit respectively three times and more than twice. In 2017, the situation was similar, though the two countries got closer to the debt limit, recording a slight budget deficit. In Finland, with 2016 public debt amounting to 63.1 percent of GDP, the deficit stood at 1.7, while the Netherlands, with the debt of 61.8 percent, recorded a surplus of 0.4 percent of GDP. Against this backdrop, one can conclude that in 2018 the country may successfully go below the Maastricht threshold.

It's worth emphasizing that in some economies, for example, Greece and Italy, the fiscal criterion relating to the acceptable debt was not met already at the time the euro came into being. Such tolerance for noncompliance with its own intentionally hard rules right from the inception of the single currency is one of the original causes of the difficulties faced by the eurozone at a later time. This makes itself felt now, as well, and will represent a major burden also in the future. One can double the public debt very fast while it's very hard and time-consuming to halve it.

FISCAL CRITERIA AND THE POLISH QUESTION

For Poland in the years 2004–2017, the public sector debt did not exceed the reference value of 60 percent of GDP. The inflation criterion, that is, keeping the rate of inflation under control at a level no more than 1.5 percentage points higher than the average for three EU member states with the most stable prices, was complied with by Poland in periods of several and over a dozen months ever since it became a member of the EU and is complied with now. Equally irregular was the country's compliance with the interest rate criterion and currently this criterion is also met. When assessing the stability of prices and interest rates it's worth noticing the variability of the reference value, namely lack of specifically defined level of inflation. Meanwhile, with respect to the second fiscal criterion regarding the budgetary balance, situation was worse. Except for 2007, until 2014 the public sector deficit exceeded 3 percent of GDP, hence corrective actions in the form of excessive deficit procedure, EDP, were implemented twice. The first decision to apply it was made in 2004, though the European Council formally adopted it in 2005 (2005/183/EC), when Polish authorities were required to take the necessary corrective actions to reduce the deficit by 2007.

It's interesting that on July 8, 2008, the European Council abrogated the decision taken three years earlier on the existence of an excessive deficit in Poland (2008/622/EC), even though it quickly turned out that, in the end, the budget deficit to GDP stood at 3.6 percent that year. On the one hand, the evaluators were impressed by the exceptionally low deficit in the previous year, as in 2007 it stood at only 1.9 percent of GDP, on the other hand 2008 marked the beginning of the global economic crisis, which resulted, also in Poland, in a higher-than-average dynamics of expenditure at the end of the year. Let us add that there is no quarterly reporting of the sector deficit as per ESA (*European System of National and Regional Accounts*), so the data on the condition of public finance is always available with a certain delay.

In 2009, the deficit was growing fast until it doubled, which stemmed mostly from reduced revenues, with greater part of the deficit generated outside the state budget, in the insurance subsector and by local authorities (local governments). Consequently, in the middle of the year, the Council adopted decision 2009/589/EC, where it declared again the existence of an excessive deficit and required its reduction until 2012.

In mid-2013, the EC concluded that Poland had taken effective actions but after adopting the original recommendation, adverse economic events took place, which had serious negative impact on public finance. These events were related to subsequent waves of global economic crisis reaching also Poland, which could not be without consequences for budgetary revenues and expenditures.

In the convergence program submitted by the government on April 30, 2015, it was assumed the target deficit values would amount to 2.7 percent of GDP in 2015 and to 2.3 in 2016. Meanwhile, the European Commission's spring 2015 forecast provided for a deficit of 2.8 percent of GDP in 2015 and 2.6 in 2016. Based on those data, in July 2015 the European Council adopted decision to abrogate a decision on the existence of excessive deficit.

The size and structure of the excessive general government deficit recorded in Poland were quite varied. On the one hand, in the years 2004 to 2008, the economic upturn was not sufficiently leveraged to limit the deficit, on the other hand there were structural reasons for it becoming excessive. In the period under discussion, one can observe diverse ways the budget policy addressed the changing external and internal circumstances. The main measures in the area of structural challenges involved the commitment and use of ever increasing EU funds and a systematic though dynamic enough tax streamlining process. In 2009, social security premium reductions came into force, decreasing the size of the tax wedge and thus the cost of labor. Next, in 2012, a long-term process of extending and equalizing the retirement age was started, which was unfortunately reversed in 2017. Fiscal consolidation has been in place since 2011, involving an increase of some tax rates (VAT, excise duty, personal income tax freeze), as well as limiting part of the pension rate allotted to Open Pension Funds, OFE. Measures intended to streamline public expenditures have also been relatively effective. The changes in the public sector operating system (the new public finance law of 2009) have contributed to an improved quality of public finance.

The convergence program update sent by the Polish government to the European Commission in April 2017, provided for further reduction of the public sector deficit and of the public debt to GDP ratio.

In accordance with the government's assumptions, the public sector deficit should be reduced to 1.2 percent of GDP in 2020. This is to be possible due to the systematic decline in the share of expenditures and taxes in GDP.

According to the government's assumptions, the result of local government sector should be balanced as well.

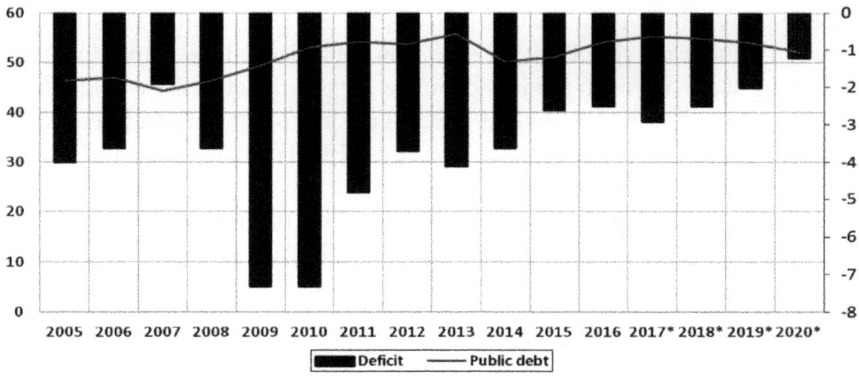

Figure 16.1 Budget Deficit and Public Debt in Poland in 2005–2020 (in percent of GDP), *Forecast. *Source*: Eurostat data and Convergence Program 2017 Update.

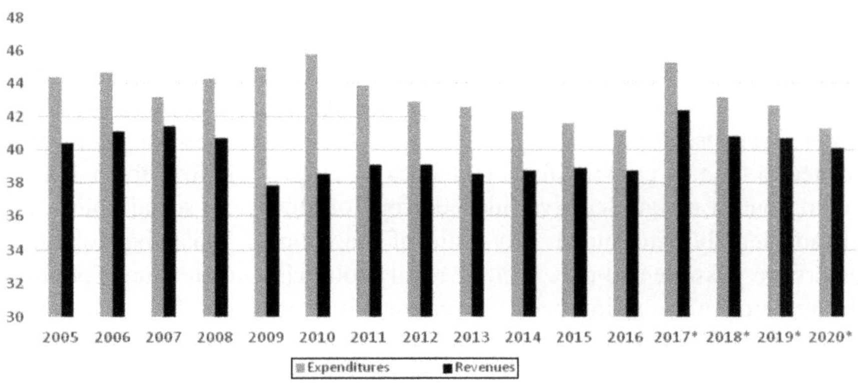

Figure 16.2 Revenues and Expenditures of the Public Finance Sector in Poland in 2005–2020 (in percent of GDP), *Forecast. *Source*: Eurostat data and Convergence Program 2017 Update.

If we were to trust those assumptions to come true, Poland would undoubtedly not be in danger of having the excessive deficit procedure imposed on it again, on the contrary: Poland could be an example for others to follow as a country with one of the lowest public sector deficits not only among EU member states. However, we should ask ourselves how feasible the scenario presented in the convergence program update is.

FORECASTS, WARNINGS, AND PROPOSALS

The Polish government, when forecasting in the "Convergence Program 2017 Update" the macroeconomic developments until 2020, assumed that the economy would grow twice as fast as the EU as a whole. Thus the gap between Poland and rich Western European countries will be narrowing, with a growing share of Polish production in the gross product of the whole grouping. Currently, it stands at only 2.9 percent at zloty to euro market rate, while it is 5.3 percent at purchasing power parity, PPP. The latter measure is more adequate and better reflects the actual situation.

GDP in 2017 grew faster than announced by the government and then expected by various organizations monitoring Polish economy: as much as ca. 4.3 percent compared to just 3.6 percent growth provided for in the 2018 draft budget. Nevertheless, the forecast for the gross product dynamics in the years 2018 to 2020 was maintained. According to the "Convergence Program 2017 Update," it should amount to 3.8, 3.9, and 3.9 percent in the subsequent years, while according to the 2018 budget, 3.8 percent is expected in each of these years (and 3.6 percent in 2021).

The weakening of the production dynamics, though a minor one, implies a more modest tax base broadening than in 2017. Of course, ceteris paribus, so here we should leave aside the changes in the efficiency of the collection of receivables as well as any changes in the amount of taxes and other forms of fiscal revenues. In this context, one needs to emphasize the risk of tensions related to the fast-growing fixed budget expenditures. Many of them, mainly arising out of a significantly widened scope of the state's social policy, are already legally determined as a result of the adopted legislative solutions, others are possible and may become reality following unambiguous political declarations of the ruling party, government and president. This is, unfortunately, the case of the announcement on the yearly successive increase of defense spending from the current 2 percent of GDP to 2.5 percent in 2030. The question is how realistic the governmental and nongovernmental budget deficit forecasts will prove in the end.

It's interesting that the European Commission expected a much lower deficit in 2017 than the Polish government did, only 1.7 versus 2.9 percent. Consequently, it is more optimistic as to the developments in 2018–2019, for

Table 16.1 Forecasts for GDP Growth in Poland in 2017–2020 (in percent)

Specification	*2017*	*2018*	*2019*	*2020*
European Commission	4.2	3.8	3.4	
OECD	4.3	3.5	3.2	
IMF	3.8	3.5	3.0	2.8
World Bank (*General Government Structural Balance*)	4.5	4.0	3.5	3.1
Commerzbank	4.5	3.8	3.2	
Fitch	4.4	3.6	3.2	
Convergence Program 2017 Update	3.6	3.8	3.9	3.9

Source: Own compilation based on data provided by particular entities.

Table 16.2 Forecasts of the Public Finance Sector Balance in Poland in 2017–2020 (in percent of GDP)

Specification	*2017*	*2018*	*2019*	*2020*
European Commission	–1.7	–1.7	–1.9	
OECD	–2.3	–2.3	–2.3	
World Bank (*General Government Structural Balance*)	–3.0	–3.1	–3.1	–2.6
S&P	–1.7	–2.0	–2.5	–2.5
Convergence Program 2017 Update	–2.9	–2.5	–2.0	–1.2

Source: Own compilation based on data provided by particular entities.

which it also assumes lower deficits than those expected by the government: 1.7 and 1.9 percent respectively versus 2.5 and 2.0 percent.

Meanwhile, there is an optimistic concurrence of opinion between the government and international organizations as to the relative size of public debt in the coming years.[10] Better yet: international organizations and rating agencies are even more optimistic than Polish authorities because while the latter forecast public debt to GDP ratio in 2020 at 54 percent, Standard & Poor's, for example, sees it nearly four percentage points lower, at only 50.3 percent of GDP.

There is much greater disparity of opinion among experts, whether theoreticians of finance and economics from Poland and abroad or economic policy practitioners. We asked them for relevant forecasts, and the group of distinguished thirty respondents included former prime ministers, deputy prime ministers for economic affairs, ministers and deputy ministers of finance and economy, members of the Monetary Policy Council, current members of the European Parliament as well as members of public finance and budget committees at both houses of Polish parliament (Sejm and Senate), presidents of large commercial banks and experts of the World Bank and International Monetary Fund; many of whom are professors.

Low values of standard deviations compared to the means suggest that the spread of experts' responses around the mean is rather small. This suggests

Table 16.3 Forecasts of Public Debt in Poland in 2017–2020 (in percent of GDP)

Specification	*2017*	*2018*	*2019*	*2020*
European Commission	53.2	53.0	53.0	
OECD	53.9	53.9	53.7	
IMF	54.2	53.8	53.5	52.9
S&P	49.5	48.7	50.3	50.3
Convergence Program 2017 Update	53.1	54.2	54.6	54.0

Source: Own compilation.

Table 16.4 Experts' Test: Forecasts of GDP Growth, Fiscal Deficit, and Public Debt in Poland in 2017–2020

Specification	*GDP growth (in percent)*				*Budget Deficit (in percent of GDP)*				*Public Debt (in percent of GDP)*			
Year	2017*	2018	2019	2020	2017*	2018	2019	2020	2017*	2018	2019	2020
Minimum	3.6	3.5	1.7	2.0	1.5	2.0	1.5	1.0	50.5	52.0	51.5	51.0
Average	4.0	3.9	3.5	3.2	2.5	2.7	2.8	2.8	54.3	54.4	54.6	54.7
Maximum	4.5	5.0	4.6	4.3	3.3	3.5	4.5	5.0	56.0	57.0	57.5	59.3
Standard deviation	0.30	0.38	0.47	0.54	0.47	0.37	0.59	0.89	1.23	1.14	1.43	2.06
Variance	0.09	0.14	0.22	0.30	0.22	0.14	0.35	0.79	1.52	1.31	2.04	4.25

* Expected implementation.
Source: Own calculations.

that our panel of thirty specialists was pretty consistent in their responses. One can notice that standard deviations have a tendency to increase across the years which would suggest that our experts are less certain as to their predictions when time horizon increases.

Extreme opinions as to the economic growth rate in the four-year period under discussion are 5.0 percent in 2018 and 2.0 percent two years later. Meanwhile, for one time sequence they are highest in 2020, amounting to 4.3 and 2.0 percent. As for the public debt to GDP ratio, extreme opinions refer to 2020, where the forecast levels range from 50.5 to 59.3 percent. In the entire time interval analyzed, nobody assumes exceeding the threshold of 60 percent of GDP.

As regards budget deficit, nobody predicts a surplus, which is understandable in Poland's realities, with forecasts ranging between 1.0 percent and as much as 5.0 percent of GDP in 2020. For 2018, three people expect the 3 percent limit to be exceeded, with three others thinking it might amount to exactly 3.0 percent of GDP. For 2019, there are ten and four people respectively who believe so, and for 2020, eleven and three. In other words, only 10 percent of respondents from this select group expect the 3 percent deficit to be exceeded already in 2018, one-third of them in 2019 and 36.7 percent in 2020. To emphasize the significance of these figures, we can reverse the presentation of results and stress that up to two-thirds of experienced specialists and responsible economic policy-makers do not expect the budgetary Maastricht convergence criterion to be exceeded and hence do not expect the return of the excessive deficit procedure, at least until 2021.

It's more than interesting; it's quite fascinating that there should be such differences among eminent economists and experienced economic policy practitioners of the highest level. A four-point discrepancy in the budget deficit estimate does not stem from applying fundamentally different prediction models, but from making quite different assumptions as to the scale of fiscalism and efficiency of the state collecting its receivables, on the one hand, and as to the dynamics of budgetary expenditures, on the other hand. As a matter of fact, in the forecast optimistically anticipating a deficit of only 1 percent of GDP (that is, even more optimistically than the government) for 2020, its author assumes that the economy will grow by 3.5 percent in every year of the period 2018–2020. Meanwhile, the skeptic expecting the deficit to be five times higher at the end of that period, as high as 5.0 percent of GDP, sees the production growth rate slowing down over that time from 3.9 percent to 2.2 percent. In total, with respect to real economy, this makes a 2.3 p.p. difference, over the whole four-year period, between those two forecasts (aggregate GDP growth by 15.2 percent and by 12.9 percent of GDP respectively), but also these are two qualitatively different perspectives on the fiscal consequences of the course of events.

Looking into the future in a responsible manner, one needs to be mindful not only of the danger of the debt growing higher than expected by the government due to fiscal deficit being much larger than forecast, but also due to zloty weakening. External debt accounts for one-third of Poland's public debt, hence its nominal value in national currency depends on the foreign exchange rate. When developing forecasts for the years 2018 to 2021 and planning the 2018 budget, the government assumed that the average annual euro to zloty exchange rate would be stable and in each of those four years it would remain at the level from late 2017, that is, 4.25. It surely won't happen, even though it's impossible to predict its development in this time horizon. Since there is a free-floating currency regime, the exchange rate fluctuates according to the surges of the financial market. Interestingly enough, just in the first half of 2018 is oscillated between 4 and 4.30 zlotys for euro.

The Poland's government, however, is very optimistic about the matter. After a sound economic growth in 2017, as well as the improvement of the state of public finances, the convergence program update adopted at the end of April 2018 has been marked by a highly optimistic picture of the coming years, assuming further systematic decrease in the budget deficit (2.1, 1.5, 1.1, 0.7 percent of GDP in years 2018, 2019, 2020, 2021 respectively) as well as public debt (50.4, 50.4, 48.7, 46.0 percent of GDP in years 2018, 2019, 2020, 2021 respectively).

Reducing the deficit to just 0.7 percent of GDP in 2021 would be a significant achievement of macroeconomic policy and a reflection of further stabilization of public finances; however, achieving this goal seems unlikely, given the proliferation of new, additional budget transfers due to vast social policy expansion.

Against this backdrop, the budget policy should be very prudent in the coming years. As a top priority, one should show self-restraint in earmarking further expenditures as in the long term they should grow more slowly than revenues and both categories more slowly than the national income in order to gradually reduce the scale of fiscal redistribution. It is doubtful whether the scale of budgetary imbalance can be controlled and the deficit held in check solely through increasing the discipline of collecting budgetary receivables. It can't be ruled out that with the growth of additional expenditures that have already been determined in political and legislative terms, it will be necessary to increase taxes.

However, the government may opt for another path. Since it decided, alas, not to introduce the euro in Poland for the time being, it can be tempted, even though it is obliged to maintain the budget deficit to GDP ratio as set out in the SGP, to exceed the 3 percent threshold again. Especially that in that situation—of course assuming the deficits will not be too high—it could be quite confident it won't hit the public debt barrier of 60 percent of GDP. Now, let's remember that it's not only one of the nominal Maastricht convergence criteria, but there has also been, for twenty years, a relevant provision on that matter in the Constitution of the Republic of Poland. Its Article 216.5 stipulates that "it shall be neither permissible to contract loans nor provide guarantees and financial sureties which would engender a national public debt exceeding three-fifths of the value of the annual gross domestic product." This principle means in practice that if the 60 percent threshold is exceeded—for example, as a result of external debt growing due to weak zloty—the budget for the next year must be balanced. So far, luckily, this mechanism has not been activated and it would be good if it continued to function only as a warning and preventive instrument.

In other words, considering all real and financial as well as social determinants, politicians may decide that in the event of acute budget tensions accumulating, and in view of the inability to cut spending as an adjustment measure, combined with the natural unwillingness to increase taxes, a deficit exceeding 3 percent of GDP is a reasonable choice. Then the excessive deficit procedure would be back, and experience shows (or some say so) that you can live with it, whether inside or outside the euro area. However, it's better to maintain the structural deficit, apart from the cyclical fluctuations, at the lowest possible level to control the state's borrowing needs, and decrease, in the long term, the public debt, the burden of which is carried by the society—consumers and producers alike, both households and entrepreneurs.

Sadly, an additional factor has emerged for Poland, unprecedented in the history of the EU. The European Commission triggered procedure under Article 7.1 of the EU Treaty in connection with Poland's alleged breach of the rule of law. According to the Commission, Poland, though now it meets the nominal convergence criteria, does not meet the criteria of membership in the EU as such, as it is in breach not only of some principles and values underlying the integration grouping, but also of its own law, including the constitution. This complicates the situation despite the country's relatively good economic position. This way a sort of seventh convergence criterion has appeared, but in essence the matter boils down to what's required in criterion sixth, or the compatibility of national legislation with EU regulations codified in the *acquis communautaire*. It needs to be sorted out.

CONCLUSIONS

It is beyond any doubt that the euro single currency area does not represent an optimal currency area the way this issue is presented in the economy theory (McKinnon 2002). It is all the more interesting to note that the coauthor of this concept (Mundell 1961) supported this project at the time it was, not without difficulties, coming into existence (Mundell 2000). A lot of misunderstandings in the assessment of the euro area functioning, and of the sense of the whole single currency project as a factor that cements the integration process stem from confusing the causes of disturbances and crisis phenomena with their manifestations and consequences (Tanzi 2013; Hall 2014). Obviously, there are some feedbacks but, after all, the euro was not the original cause of the financial frictions; the cause was that disturbances in real economy and in public finance spilled over into the monetary sphere. It was especially the insufficient supervision over the banking sector and capital market that had a negative impact on the condition of the euro (Sandbu 2015).

There are both voices predicting the demise of the euro (Brown 2012) or, in the extreme version, advocating its deliberate abolition (Kawalec and Pytlarczyk 2013), and academic papers (Pisani-Ferry 2011) and professional opinions (EU 2017) pointing out directions for its improvement and ways to strengthen it. Other authors, bearing in mind the euro's imperfection, and also the immense costs of its potential abolition, though not ruling it out, are considering a fundamental institutional reform of the eurozone (Moździerz 2015; Dallago 2016). We adopt a pragmatic economic approach, which is taking account not only of the theoretical arguments showing the systemic defects and structural weaknesses of the eurozone, but most of all, of the practical realities.

We are in the ex post phase; the euro has already been born, though it was conceived not without many sins, and is alive; it has already come of age. Therefore, today the right question is: is it more costly to keep and adequately reform the eurozone or to dismantle it? Let us emphasize that such dismantling could be a controlled process only in a theoretical digressions or in a computerized model; in practice it would quickly prove to be sheer chaos with disastrous consequences. Therefore when contemplating, in comprehensive terms, the costs and benefits of the euro's continued existence and reforms *versus* withdrawing from it and its abolition, it's easy to see a clear advantage of the former solution. And that's why—rather than for political reasons and due to the power of inertia—the euro shall overcome. There is no absolute certainty about it but there is very high likelihood: close to one.

The continuation of the euro project, obviously with its relevant modifications, has its implications and involves specific challenges. Of crucial importance here is the issue of enlarging the euro area by accepting new states meeting all the required currency convergence criteria. What speaks in favor of joining the eurozone is mostly economic reasons but the political ones should not be disregarded, either, in a situation where nationalist resentments and protectionist tendencies are gaining ground (Economist 2016). There is a ground—and the imperative—for both, parallel deepening the integration of the current, through strengthening the relevant institutions and policies, and enlarging it by including the new members.

Replacing national currency with the euro—assuming that the conversion is carried out at the adequate dynamic equilibrium exchange rate—strengthens the economy's competitiveness, eliminates the exchange risk and reduces transaction costs. At the same time, money becomes relatively cheaper due to Euroland's lower interest rates than those in EU member states maintaining their own currencies. Importantly, when joining the eurozone, a country's foreign currency reserves are liquidated, and only part of them is transferred to the European Central Bank's common foreign exchange pool. The freed-up funds can be used to pay off some of the foreign debt and to invest in infrastructure (Kolodko 2017b).

In this context, it is to be expected that in the 5–10 year horizon the eurozone may include all of the twenty-seven EU member states. Of course, assuming that the Greek syndrome will be solved and Grexit will not happen nor will any other country leave the euro area. It's very unlikely, but not completely impossible. Meanwhile, it is not out of the question that in the second half of 2020s the EU population will grow to include new member states from the Balkan region: Albania, Bosnia–Herzegovina, Macedonia, and Serbia. There is also a possibility that Montenegro will become the twenty-eighth EU member state (as counted already after the Brexit), automatically enlarging the Euroland area, as the euro is already in circulation there, and, interestingly enough, this may happen earlier than Poland joining the eurozone, considering the government's clear and repeatedly expressed position on that matter.[11] It would be all the weirder considering Poland has for many years been treated—and rightly so—first as the leader among post-socialist economies undergoing market reforms (Kolodko 2000a), and then as a country whose post-socialist transformation has been the most significant success (Piatkowski 2018).

It must be emphasized that the requirement of achieving a similar level of economic development, as formulated by some authors and politicians, is too far-fetched; there is no such imperative. Furthermore, the adoption of the euro by subsequent post-socialist countries, with their GDP per capita (according to PPP) now fluctuating around 50–90 percent of the average value for the EU as a whole, will speed up the process of bridging the income gap.[12] Hence those thinking that catching up with the more developed economies should come before the currency convergence are mistaken because the currency convergence itself can become an additional instrument of the real convergence, so badly needed by Europe in its integration efforts.[13]

NOTES

1. As of the end of the third quarter of 2017 (exclusive of monetary gold).

2. In 2009, euro represented 27.7 percent of global reserves, and USD 62.0 percent (IMF 2014, Appendix I, International Reserves, p. 2).

3. The consolidated version of the *Treaty on the Functioning of the European Union*, Official Journal of the European Union, C 83/01 of 30.03.2010.

4. When the Treaty of Maastricht was being adopted, this range was only +/- 2.25 percent. In 1993, it was widened to +/- 15 percent.

5. Poland has had a floating exchange rate mechanism in place since 2000, but is not part of ERM-2.

6. Resolution of the European Council (EU) of June 17, 1997 on the Growth and Stability Pact, Official Journal C 236 of 2.8.1997, p. 1.

7. Council Regulation (EC) no. 1466/97/EC of July 7, 1997 on the strengthening of the surveillance of budgetary positions and the surveillance and coordination of economic policies, Official Journal L 209 of 2.8.1997, p. 1 and Council Regulation (EC) no. 1467/97 of July 7, 1997 on speeding up and clarifying the implementation of the excessive deficit procedure, Official Journal L 209 of 2.8.1997, p. 6.

8. Declaration of December 16, 1996 and EC Regulations of June 16, 1997.

9. The adopted legislative acts came into effect on December 13, 2011. These were four joint regulations of the European Parliament and of the Council, one Council regulation and one Council directive, that is, a nonlegislative act:

- Regulation (EU) of the European Parliament and of the Council No. 1173/2011 of November 16, 2011 on the effective enforcement of budgetary surveillance in the euro area,
- Regulation (EU) of the European Parliament and of the Council No. 1174/2011 of November 16, 2011 on enforcement measures to correct excessive macroeconomic imbalances in the euro area,
- Regulation (EU) of the European Parliament and of the Council No. 1175/2011 of November 16, 2011 amending Council Regulation (EC) No. 1466/97 on the strengthening of the surveillance of budgetary positions and the surveillance and coordination of economic policies,
- Regulation (EU) of the European Parliament and of the Council No. 1176/2011 of November 16, 2011 on the prevention and correction of macroeconomic imbalances,
- Council Regulation (EU) No. 1177/2011 of November 8, 2011 amending Regulation (EC) No 1467/97 on speeding up and clarifying the implementation of the excessive deficit procedure,
- Council Directive 2011/85/EU of November 8, 2011 on requirements for budgetary frameworks of the member states.

10. We are passing over some economists' scare-mongering comments and alarmist warnings (publicized by some media) about the allegedly inevitable and fast approaching collapse of public finance, which, in the coming years, is sure to lead to

exceeding the public debt limit of 60 percent of GDP. Such doom saying is far from being professional as it is politically and ideologically rather than factually motivated.

11. Prime Minister Mateusz Morawiecki in early 2018, when asked about the possibility of Poland joining the eurozone, replied: "We have a long way before we achieve a more real convergence with the hard core of the eurozone (. . .). As for Poland's adoption of the euro, there is no change of our approach, our rhetoric in this respect; this is not a topic today that we take into consideration" (Obserwator Finansowy 2018).

12. Compared to the average GDP per capita of the EU as a whole, calculated at PPP in eleven post-socialist member states, it stands, on average, at 68 percent, from 49 percent in Romania to 88 percent in Czech Republic. Outside the EU, in the poorest Balkan country, Albania, it is only 29 percent.

13. Published in Kolodko and Postula (2018).

Conclusion

The unique interface between megatrends shaping the reality in all of its aspects—technological, economic, cultural, social, political, and environmental alike—inspires the assertions, increasingly common both in daily speech and in academic papers, that a time of epoch-making transformations is upon us. Our world is at the crossroads and we are facing the question of how to intellectually grasp the deeply and fast-changing realities. It is not the first time the "world is at the crossroads." Even in our lifetime, this has happened already a couple of times, though faced with the choice of paths to go forward, we have never dealt with changes of such magnitude. Neither is it the first time that we can hear that "the world as we know it is coming to an end." Some people believe it has already ended. By no means, though contemporarily it is more complicated than ever before. Hence, we need to try and understand the new quality in which the elements of continuity intermingle with the elements of change. This sui generis dialectic between the continued existence of the old and the emergence of the new is intellectually fascinating as it offers a wealth of input for research in social sciences—from economics and sociology through psychology and political science to law and philosophy. No wonder then that the luminaries of social sciences, especially economists, increasingly talk of the imperative of a new paradigm—a new theoretical interpretation of the reality around us.

Having come to yet another crossroads, one cannot be standing astride for too long, hesitating about which way to go. It is certainly a fact that there is nowhere to go back to, but it is not clear which course to set going forward. Generally speaking, it should be set by the imperative of integrated development, which is balanced in three dimensions: economic, social, and environmental. At such a level of generalization, consensus is easy, but it becomes more and more difficult as more concrete and operational aspects are discussed. When looking for a new economic paradigm, one needs to adopt a couple of fundamental prerequisites.

First, the goals of economic development need to be thoroughly reflected on and redefined. At the microeconomic level, profit maximization remains a natural goal, though it should take account of the needs of all other stakeholders: employees and consumers, suppliers and buyers, tax system and the natural environment, government and the local community. Accordingly, economy must be properly regulated; the free-market capitalism is a utopia. Corporate social responsibility, CSR, cannot be left to the potential good intentions of capital owners and to marketing statements of managers, but, instead, it must be secured with relevant state-imposed laws, which will enforce desirable behaviors.

Secondly, on the macroeconomic scale, the goal of maximizing the gross domestic product, GDP, should be abandoned. The goal now should be an optimized satisfaction of the population's needs by improving its prosperity (there are a number of creative proposals for alternative metrics), and the principal way to achieve that is by ensuring the right synergies between market spontaneity and vitality, and the regulatory and strategic state policy.

Thirdly, good economics, rather than being a single discipline, must increasingly become an interdisciplinary knowledge and science. A lot of what economics needs to be concerned with happens at the intersection with other spheres: technology, culture, society, government, security and environment—domains studied by the allied social sciences.

Fourthly, though the historical moment is exceptional, we are experiencing no Copernican turn, not even a Keynesian one, which rings more familiar to us economists.

Indeed, the moribund liberal capitalism, which led to the Great Crisis of 1929–1933, paved the way for the intellectual revolution in economics brought about by John Maynard Keynes and his theory. The outstanding Polish economist, Michal Kalecki, also had his original contribution. The magnitude of the Keynesian revolution lies in that it demonstrated not only the actual causes of and the mechanisms governing the business cycle and periodic crises but also ways to prevent them, or at least mitigate their severity. Meanwhile, contemporarily, as neoliberalism, having led to a Yet Greater Crisis, as I call it, is on the brink of collapse, the era of heterodoxy has come—that of coexistence of different schools of economic thought, where no trend will rule supreme or even clearly prevail over others.

The turn of the third decade of the twenty-first century is a period of hard times. Such episodes in history usher in creative innovations in the economic thought but all kinds of irrational ideas also abound. Adding to this is the coronavirus pandemic, whose wide-reaching consequences are leaving a mark on the economy, aggravating social and income inequalities in many countries, though, in parallel, reducing the same between wealthy and less developed countries. Globalization is (temporarily) weakening, digitalization (permanently) is strengthening, and production and supply chains are being (continuously) restructured. On the microeconomic scale, as business is increasingly moving online, companies are under a growing influence of firms that are especially advanced when it comes to intellectual property and have huge data sets at their disposal. On the global scale, China is emerging from the pandemic relatively stronger than the United States, as it has managed to avoid recession and is quickly returning to the path of above-average economic growth. While in the autumn of 2020 President Xi Jinping is outlining the path of development for the coming five years, emphasizing the importance of expansion of high-tech sectors and reducing the dependence on the external world, the cardinal errors in President Donald Trump's economic policy, especially resorting to protectionism and unilateralism, are casting a shadow over the United States.

In such hard times, all sorts of idées fixes come to life. What may prove particularly risky is the coupling of the MMT, the so-called Modern Monetary Theory, MMT, with the concept of the Universal Basic Income, UBI. The former allows for a far-reaching monetary expansion, which could allegedly finance all sorts of expenditure without any trouble. The latter calls for publicly funded income for all citizens, regardless of their circumstances, in the amount close to the social minimum level. The two theories seem to beautifully converge: UBI requires additional public spending from the national budget in the order of at least a dozen percent of GDP, while MMT is willing to provide the necessary funds scot-free. Well, not quite.

Prosperity is still determined by the value of goods manufactured and services provided—which, in turn, depends on labor productivity and capital efficiency—rather than on the quantity of the money issued ("printed"). The requirement for maintaining stability and liquidity and preventing speculation warrants central banks' unorthodox intervention in money markets. Another reasonable solution is periodical increase in the fiscal deficit to finance extraordinary expenditure at the time of crisis, and, consequently, growth in the public debt, which is easier to service at all-time low interest rates. However, these will go up with time. This is one more reason why we should not be tempted by the illusory concepts such as MMT or UBI. What is needed is a correct economic theory to serve as a foundation of the policy of optimized money circulation, which, in turn, is a contributing factor for economic dynamics and equilibrium.

It should be reiterated that a comprehensive economics has two facets: descriptive and normative. The first one is a theory of the functioning of economy, which analyses economic mechanisms, explaining the essence of cause-and-effect relationships and feedbacks. The second one is a theory of economic policy, which formulates the lines of action and identifies the instruments with which to change the social and economic reality for the better. Undoubtedly, the problem is how do we determine what it means and who should decide what is better? Moreover, this is where these two facets of economics meet, as well as the confluence of theory and practice, and of science and policy occur. One must recognize those three interfaces and their implications.

It happens to politicians to say they know what to do and how in the economy, but they do not know how to win the election afterwards (or, to keep the people humbly disciplined under authoritarian rule, where democracy falls short). Well, often they do not know. In an era of so much talk of knowledge-based economy, one needs to increasingly strive for knowledge-based policy. Unfortunately, the latter is all too often based on ignorance or at unsystematized crumbs of knowledge at most.

Meanwhile, it happens to theoretical economists to think they understand the nature of policy-making (which should be understood as solving contentious issues and taking responsibility for one's decisions), while in fact they have a dim idea of it. This makes an integrated approach to economics, that is, its descriptive and normative treatment, even more desirable. Otherwise, political decisions can prove off the mark, in the same way this can happen in medicine if a cure is unrelated from diagnosis. There is no need to go as far as to have presidents, prime ministers, ministers or chairpersons of central banks complete MBA in economics, as their role is to change reality rather than explain it, but certainly high ethical and professional competence must be required from them as well as the ability to surround themselves with expert advisors.

In the long run, broadly defined economic policy is successful only when current decisions overlap with the pursuit of long-term goals and when, rather than feeding on illusions that politicians sadly tend to succumb to, it is oriented toward a coherent, far-reaching vision. Such a vision should be the driving principle of the long-term development strategy and of a policy based on knowledge rather than dictated by emotions. To make it happen, high-class leadership is required, particularly in such challenging times. In an era of irreversible globalization, the leadership should be also characterized by the ability for supranational policy coordination. Unfortunately, this is clearly lacking.

Nevertheless, we should retain a certain degree of optimism as human genius and the great achievements of the contemporary civilization in the field of science, technology and culture make a whole lot of our problems solvable. In theory. The trouble is that the economic theory can explain to us quite satisfactorily what and why is happening this way rather than another, whereas policy-making is often incapable of applying the findings of science in practice. The crux of the matter is the transition from the theoretical economics to practical policy-making (and to company management at the microlevel), from the science that explains to a practice that decides. It is vital to combine those perspectives, to ensure an interface of sorts. Of course, whoever wishes to practice purely descriptive economics, they are free to do so. In the same way as medical scholars may limit their research to aspects such as analysis and diagnostics. The social meaning of their efforts is such that they are accompanied by others—a physician who knows how to care for health and an economist who suggests how to improve the economy. Meanwhile, things are bad if policy-making is influenced by economists who believe they know how to improve the economy, though they cannot correctly interpret its course.

There is not and will not be "new Keynes" then as in those hard times this is neither possible nor necessary. What is desired instead is a multi-aspect and unorthodox economic thought which can be useful to economic policy and management in countries as diverse as the United States and China, Canada and Bangladesh, Poland and Egypt, France and Mozambique, Japan and Brazil. There is no need for two hundred economic theories for two hundred national economies, but one, "the only correct" theory cannot be imposed on everybody. The theory of everything does not exist, so it is illusory to search for it; let us leave it to alchemists. Meanwhile, it is useful to construct practically oriented theories, always bearing in mind that economics and policy-making are contextual. What can work in one time and place may bring simply harmful results elsewhere.

With such an approach in mind, it is worth indicating some inspiring trends in the modern economic thought, which adequately address developmental challenges. Those deserving mention include the "mass flourishing" concept of Edmund S. Phelps (Phelps 2013; Phelps, Bojilov, Hoon, and Zoega 2020), which highlights the meaning of innovation, "new structural economics" of Justin Yifu Lin (2012b), "economics for the common good" of Jean Tirole (2017), and "progressive capitalism" of Joseph E. Stiglitz (2019). It is also in this area that one should place new pragmatism—a proposal to integrate the descriptive and normative economics that cares for the economy of moderation and its balanced and sustainable development.

Bibliography

Acemoglu, D., and Robinson, J.A. 2012. *Why Nations Fail. The Origins of Power, Prosperity, and Poverty*. New York: Crown Business.

Arthur, W.B. 2015. *Complexity of the Economy*. Oxford and New York: Oxford University Press.

Ashworth, J. 2020. *Quantitative Easing*. Newcastle upon Tyne: Agenda Publishing.

Assessment. 2016. *Assessment of the 2016 Convergence Programme for Poland.* May 26. Brussels: European Commission, Directorate General Economic and Financial Affairs.

Anderson, J.L. 2017. "Accelerating Revolution." *The New Yorker*, 12(8): 42–53.

Bałtowski, M. 2017. "Evolution of economics and the new pragmatism of Grzegorz W. Kolodko." TIGER Working Papers. No. 136. Warsaw: Kozminski University.

Baun, Michael J. 2019. *An Imperfect Union: The Maastricht Treaty and the New Politics of European Integration.* New York: Routledge.

BBC. 2016. "BBC News. Greece hopeful of deal on next bailout loan tranche." Accessed May 9, 2016. https://www.bbc.com/news/world-europe-36250497.

BBC. 2020a. "BBC News. Coronavirus: Worst economic crisis since 1930s depression, IMF says." Accessed April 9, 2020. https://www.bbc.com/news/business-52236936.

BBC. 2020b. "BBC News. Latest news in Europe." Accessed April 17, 2020. https://www.bbc.com/news/live/world-52305053.

BBC. 2020c. "BBC News. Calls for debt relief for world's poorest nations." Accessed April 7, 2020. https://www.bbc.com/news/business-52178968.

BBC. 2020d. "BBC News. Coronavirus: 'Millions will be left in poverty,' World Bank warns." Accessed March 31, 2020. https://www.bbc.com/news/business-52103666.

BBC. 2020e. "BBC News. Coronavirus: Marathon talks over EU virus rescue package stall." Accessed April 8, 2020. https://www.bbc.com/news/world-europe-52211650.

BBC. 2020f. "BBC News. Coronavirus: EU could fail over outbreak, warns Italy's Giuseppe Conte." Accessed April 9, 2020. https://www.bbc.com/news/world-europe-52224838.

BBC. 2020g. "BBC News. Coronavirus: WHO chief urges end to 'politicization' of virus." Accessed April 9, 2020. https://www.bbc.com/news/world-52224183.

Bell, D.A. 2015. *The China Model: Political Meritocracy and the Limits of Democracy*. Princeton, NJ: Princeton University Press.

Berg, A.G. and Ostry, J.D. 2011. "Inequality and Unsustainable Growth: Two Sides of the Same Coin?" IMF Staff Discussion Note SDN/11/08, April 8, 2011. Washington, DC: International Monetary Fund.

Berger, R., Chong, J.Ch., and Herstein, R. 2013. "China's Social Market Economy: The Leverage of Economic Growth." *International Journal of Asian Business and Information Management*, 4(1): 21–30.

Berthold, R. 2017. "About the 19th National Congress of the CPC." *China Today*, November: 30–31.

Blanchard, O. 2015. "Greece: Past Critiques and the Path Forward." iMF Direct. The International Monetary Fund's global economy forum, July 9, 2015. https://blogs.imf.org/2015/07/09/greece-past-critiques-and-the-path-forward/.

Block, F. 1994. "The Roles of the State in the Economy." In *The Handbook of Economic Sociology*, eds. N.J. Smelser and R. Swedberg, 691–710. Princeton, NJ: Princeton University Press.

Bok, D. 2010. *The Politics of Happiness: What Government can Learn from the New Research on Well Being*. Princeton, NJ: Princeton University Press.

Bremmer, I. 2010. *The End of the Free Market. Who Wins the War Between States and Corporations?* New York: Portfolio.

Brzezinski, Z. 2007. *Second Chance: Three Presidents and the Crisis of American Superpower*. New York: Basic Books.

Brown, B. 2012. *Euro Crash: The Exit Route from Monetary Failure in Europe*. Houndmills, Basingstoke and Hampshire: Palgrave Macmillan.

Brown, K. 2019. *What Does China Want? China's World*. London, New York: I.B. Tauris.

CB. 2020. "The Conference Board, April. The Conference Board Total Economy Database." Accessed May 11, 2020. https://www.conference-board.org/data/economydatabase/index.cfm?id=27762.

Charlesworth, H.K. 2003. *The Economics of Repressed Inflation*. Abigdon, Oxon: Routledge.

Cheremukhin, A., Golosov, M., Guriev, S., and Tsyvinski, A. 2015. *The Economy of People's Republic of China from 1953*. NBER Working Paper, No. 21397, July.

China Daily. 2017a. "China's private sector regains strength on optimistic economic outlook." *China Daily*, August 2, 2017.

China Daily. 2017b. "Xi Jinping and His Era." *China Daily*, November 18–19, 2017.

Chłoń-Domińczak A. and Strzałecki, P. 2013. "The minimum pension as an instrument of poverty protection in the defined contribution pension system—An example of Poland." *Journal of Pension Economics and Finance*, 13(3): 326–350.

Cieślik, J. 2016. *Entrepreneurship in Emerging Economies: Enhancing its Contribution to Socio-Economic Development.* Houndmills, Basingstoke, Hampshire: Palgrave Macmillan.

CNBC. 2020. "CNBC Politics. 'A bill has to come due for China': White House advisor Navarro threatens coronavirus retaliation." *CNBC*, May 11, 2020. Accessed May 12, 2020. https://www.cnbc.com/2020/05/11/coronavirus-trump-advisor-navarro-threatens-retaliation-against-china.html.

Csaba, L. 1996. "The political economy of the reform strategy: China and eastern Europe compared." *Communist Economies and Economic Transformations*, 8(1): 53–65.

Csaba, L. 2009. *Crisis in Economics?* Budapest: Akadémiai Kiadó.

Dallago, B. 2016. *One Currency, Two Europes: Towards a Dual Eurozone.* Singapore: World Scientific Publishing.

De Grauwe, P. 2010. "Crisis in the Eurozone and How to Deal with It." CEPS Policy Brief, No. 204.

Deneen, P.J. 2018. *Why Liberalism Failed.* New Haven and London: Yale University Press.

Diamond, J. 2019. *Upheaval. Turning Points for Nations in Crisis.* New York, Boston, London: Little Brown.

EBRD. 2004. *Transition Report: Infrastructure.* London: EBRD.

EBRD. 2019. *Transition Report: Better Governance, Better Economies.* London: EBRD.

Economist. 2012. "Teenage angst." *The Economist*, August 25, 2012.

Economist. 2016. "Trump's World. The new nationalism." *The Economist*, November 19, 2016.

Economist. 2018. "China moves into Latin America." *The Economist*, February 3, 2018.

Economist. 2019. "I'm from a company, and I'm here to help." *The Economist*, August 24, 2019.

Economist. 2020a. "Everything's under control. The state in the time of covid-19." *The Economist*, March 26, 2020.

Economist. 2020b. "Has Covid-19 killed globalisation?." *The Economist*, May 16, 2020.

Economist. 2020c. "There is less trust between Washington and Beijing than at any point since 1979." *The Economist*, May 9, 2020.

Economist. 2020d. "The pandemic is driving America and China further apart." *The Economist*, May 9, 2020.

Economy, Elizabeth C. 2018. *The Third World Revolution: Xi Jinping and the New Chinese State.* Oxford, New York: Oxford University Press.

Emerging Europe. 2017. "Poland to switch from emerging to developed market." *Emerging Europe*, October 16, 2017.

Epstein, E. and Pion-Berlin, D., eds. 2008. *Broken Promises? The Argentine Crisis and Argentine Democracy.* New York, Toronto: Lexington Books.

EU. 2017. "Reflection paper on the deepening of the economic and monetary union, May 31." Brussels: European Commission.

EU. 2020. "European Economic Forecast." Institutional Paper 125, May 2020, Brussels: European Commission.

Financial Times. 2017. "Xi Jinping signals departure from low-profile policy." *Financial Times*, October 20, 2017.

Financial Times. 2020. "FT Interview: Emmanuel Macron says it is time to think the unthinkable." *Financial Times*, April 16, 2020.

Fischer, S. 1999. "A View from the IMF." In *Economic Policy and Equity*, eds. V. Tanzi, K. Chu and S. Gupta, 13–18. Washington, DC: International Monetary Fund.

Fisher, I. 1973. "I Discovered the Phillips Curve: A Statistical Relation between Unemployment and Price Changes." *Journal of Political Economy*, 81(2): 496–502.

Forbes. 2020. "The World's Most Valuable Brands. Forbes 2019 Ranking." Accessed May 10, 2020. https://www.forbes.com/powerful-brands/list/#tab:rank.

Fortune Global 500 (subsequent years). CNN Money. http://fortune.com/global500.

Foster, J.B. and McCheseny, R.W. 2014. *The Endless Crisis. How Monopoly-Finance Capital Produces Stagnation and Upheaval from the USA to China*. New York: Monthly Review Press.

Friedman, G. 2009. *The Next 100 Years: A Forecast for the 21st Century*. New York: Doubleday.

Frydman, R. and Phelps, E.S. 2020. "Beating the Coronavirus Is the Best Stimulus. Directing businesses to fight the pandemic would help workers more than an infrastructure splurge." *The Wall Street Journal*, April 7, 2020.

Fukuyama, F. 1989. "The End of History." *The National Interest*, Summer, 1–18.

Fukuyama, F. 2020. "What Kind of Regime Does China Have?" *The American Interest*, May 18, 2020.

Galbraith, J.K. 1958. *The Affluent Society*. New York: Houghton Mifflin Company.

Galbraith, J.K. 2014. *The End of Normal: The Great Crisis and the Future of Growth*. New York: Simon and Schuster.

Galbraith, J.K. 2016a. *Inequality: What Everyone Needs to Know*. Oxford, New York: Oxford University Press.

Galbraith, J.K. 2016b. *Welcome to the Poisoned Chalice: The Destruction of Greece and the Future of Europe*. New Haven, London: Yale University Press.

Galbraith, J.K. 2018. "Backwater Economics and New Pragmatism: Institutions and Evolution in the Search for a Sustainable Economics." TIGER Working Paper Series, No. 138. Warsaw: Kozminski University.

Garrett, G. 1998. *Partisan Politics in the Global Economy*. New York: Cambridge University Press.

Garrett, G. 2001. "Globalization and Government Spending around the World." *Studies in Comparative International Development*, 35(4): 3–29.

Haberler, G. 1977. *Stagflation: An Analysis of Its Causes and Cures*. Washington, DC: American Enterprise Institute for Public Policy Research.

Hall, P.A. 2014. "Varieties of Capitalism and the Euro Crisis." *Journal of West European Politics*, 37(6): 1223–1243.

Halper, S. 2010. *The Beijing Consensus: How China's Authoritarian Model Will Dominate the Twenty-First Century*. New York: Basic Books.

Harvey, D. 2005. *A Brief History of Neoliberalism*. Oxford and New York: Oxford University Press.

Heilbroner, R. and Milberg, W. 1995. *The Crisis of Vision in Modern Economic Thought*. New York: Cambridge University Press.

Hu, B. 2018. "The Belt and Road Initiative and the Transformation of Globalization." Distinguished Lectures Series, No. 26. Warsaw: Kozminski University.

Huang, Y. 2017. *Cracking the China Conundrum: Why Conventional Economic Wisdom Is Wrong*. New York: Oxford University Press.

Huxley, A. 1952. *The Devils of Loudon*. London: Chatto and Windus.

ILO. 2020. "ILO Monitor 2nd edition: COVID-19 and the world of work Updated estimates and analysis. April 7." Accessed April 8, 2020. https://www.ilo.org/wcmsp5/groups/public/---dgreports/---dcomm/documents/briefingnote/wcms_740877.pdf.

IMF. 2014. *IMF Annual Report*. Washington, DC: International Monetary Fund.

Jackson, T. 2011. *Prosperity without Growth*. Economics for a Finite Planet. London: Earthscan.

Jacques, M. 2009. *When China Rules the World: The End of the Western World and the Birth of a New Global Order*. New York: Penguin Books.

Jones, G. 2020. *10% Less Democracy: Why You Should Trust Elites A Little More and the Masses A Little Less*. Stanford: Stanford University Press.

Kawalec, S. and Pytlarczyk, E. 2013. "Controlled Dismantlement of the Eurozone: A Strategy to Save the European Union and the Single European Market." *German Economic Review*, 14(1): 31–49.

Kissinger, H. 2011. *On China*. New York: Penguin Press.

Kissinger, H. 2014. *World Order*. New York: Penguin Press.

Klein, M. and Pettis, M. 2020. *Trade Wars Are Class Wars: How Rising Inequality Distorts the Global Economy and Threatens International Peace*. New Haven: Yale University Press.

Kolodko, G.W. 1986. "The Repressed Inflation and Inflationary Overhang under Socialism." Bureau of Economic and Business Research, Faculty Working Paper No. 1228. Urbana-Champaign: University of Illinois.

Kolodko, G.W. 1989. *Reform, Stabilization Policies and Economic Adjustment in Poland*. Helsinki: UNU–WIDER.

Kolodko, G.W. 1999. "Equity Issues in Policymaking in Transition Economies." In *Economic Policy and Equity*, eds. V. Tanzi, K. Chu and S. Gupta, 150–188. Washington, DC: International Monetary Fund.

Kolodko, G.W. 2000a. *From Shock to Therapy: The Political Economy of Postsocialist Transformation*. New York: Oxford University Press.

Kolodko, G.W. 2000b. *Post-Communist Transition: The Thorny Road*. Rochester, NY and Woodbridge, Suffolk, UK: University of Rochester Press.

Kolodko G.W. 2002. *Globalization and Catching-up In Transition Economies*. Rochester, NY and Woodbridge, Suffolk, UK: University of Rochester Press.

Kolodko, G.W. 2004. "Institutions, Policies and Growth." *Rivista di Politica Economica*, May–June: 45–79.

Kołodko, G.W. 2008. *Wędrujący świat*. Warszawa: Prószyński i S–ka.

Kolodko, G.W. 2009. "A two-thirds of success. Poland's post-communist transformation 1989–2009." *Communist and Post-Communist Studies*, 42(3): 325–351.

Kołodko, G.W. 2010. *Świat na wyciągnięcie myśli.* Warszawa: Prószyński i S–ka.

Kolodko, G.W. 2011a. *Truth, Errors and Lies. Politics and Economics in a Volatile World.* New York: Columbia University Press.

Kolodko, G.W. 2011b. "Private sector role essential in Greek drama." *Financial Times*, June 22.

Kolodko, G.W. 2011c. "Poland's lesson for Greece." *The Economist*, May 12.

Kolodko, G.W. 2012. "ECB must rescue Greece—or pay more later." *Financial Times*, February 22.

Kolodko, G.W. 2014a. *Whither the World: The Political Economy of the Future.* Houndmills, Basingstoke, Hampshire: Palgrave Macmillan.

Kolodko, G.W. 2014b. "The New Pragmatism, or economics and policy for the future." *Acta Oeconomica*, 64(2): 139–160.

Kolodko, G.W. 2015a. "Africanization of Greece." *Roubini EconoMonitor*, July 6.

Kolodko, G.W. 2015b. "Greece: Don't play with fire, but don't sweep it under the carpet." *Roubini EconoMonitor*, June 12.

Kolodko, G.W. 2016a. "Brexitology." *Roubini EconoMonitor*, July 6.

Kolodko, G.W. 2016b. "How to Destroy a Country, The Economics and the Politics of the Greek Crisis." *Rivista di Politica Economica* (2): 37–61.

Kolodko, G.W. 2017a. "Will China Save the World." *Roubini EconoMonitor*, May 24.

Kolodko, G.W. 2017b. "Economics and Politics of the Currency Convergence: The Case of Poland." *Communist and Post-Communist Studies*, 50(3): 183–194.

Kolodko, G.W. 2018. "Socialism, Capitalism, or Chinism?" *Communist and Post-Communist Studies*, 51(4): 285–298.

Kolodko, G.W. 2019. "Economy and Security, or Cold War Two." In *Global Development: Challenges of Predictability and Manageability.* The 19th International Likhachov Scientific Conference, May 22–24, 2019, 100–105. St. Petersburg: St. Petersburg University of the Humanities and Social Sciences.

Kolodko, G.W. 2020a. "Economics and Politics of Post-Communist Transition to Market and Democracy: The Lessons from Polish Experience." *Post-Communist Economies*, 31(3): 285–305.

Kolodko, G.W. 2020b. *China and the Future of Globalization: The Political Economy of China's Rise.* London, New York: I.B. Tauris Bloomsbury.

Kolodko, G.W. 2020c. "After the Calamity: Economics and Politics of the Post-Pandemic World." *Polish Sociological Review* (2): 137–155.

Kolodko, G.W. and McMahon W.W. 1987. "Stagflation and Shortageflation: A Comparative Approach." *Kyklos*, 40(2): 176–197.

Kolodko, G.W. and Nuti, D.M. 1997. "The Polish Alternative. Old Myths, Hard Facts and New Strategies in the Successful Transformation of the Polish Economy." *Research for Action*, No. 33. Helsinki: UNU–WIDER.

Kolodko G.W. and Postula M. 2018. "Determinants and Implications of the Eurozone Enlargement." *Acta Oeconomica*, 68(4): 477–498.

Kolodko G.W. and Rutkowski M. 1991. "The Problem of Transition from a Socialist to a Free Market Economy: The Case of Poland." *The Journal of Social, Political and Economic Studies*, 16(2): 159–179.

Kornai, J. 1971. *Anti-Equilibrium. On Economic System Theory and the Task of Research*. Amsterdam: North Holland.

Kornai, J. 1980. *Economics of Shortage*. Amsterdam: North Holland.

Kornai, J. 1986. "The Soft Budget Constraints." *Kyklos*, 39(1): 3–30.

Kornai, J. 1990. *The Road to a Free Economy. Shifting from a Socialist System. The Example of Hungary*. New York: W.W. Norton and Company

Kornai, J. 1992. *The Socialist System: The Political Economy of Communism*. New Jersey: Princeton University Press.

Kornai, J. 2008. *From Socialism to Capitalism*. Budapest: Central European University Press.

Kornai, J. 2014. *Dynamism, Rivalry, and the Surplus Economy. Two Essays on the Nature of Capitalism*. Oxford: Oxford University Press.

Kozminski A.K., Noga A., Piotrowska K., and Zagorski K. 2020. *The Balanced Development Index for Europe's OECD Countries, 1999–2017*. Cham, Switzerland: Springer Briefs in Economics.

Kraemer, K.L., Linden, G., and Dedrick, J. 2011. "Capturing Value in Global Networks: Apple's iPad and iPhone." PCIC Working Paper, July. Irvine: Personal Computing Industry Center, University of California.

Krastev, I. and Holmes, S. 2019. *The Light That Failed: Why the West Is Losing the Fight for Democracy*. New York, London: Pegasus Books.

Krugman, P. 2020. *Arguing with Zombies: Economics, Politics, and the Fight for a Better Future*. New York: W.W. Norton and Company.

Lankov, A. 2013. *The Real North Korea: Life and Politics in the Failed Stalinist Utopia*. New York: Oxford University Press.

Lardy, N.R. 2014. *Markets Over Mao: The Rise of Private Business in China*. Washington, DC: Peterson Institute of International Economies.

Lardy, N.R. 2019. *The State Strikes Back: The End of Economic Reform in China?* Washington, DC: Peterson Institute of International Economics.

Lee, K.F. 2018. *AI Superpowers: China, Silicon Valley, and the New World Order*. Boston, MA: Houghton Mifflin Harcourt.

Legrain, P. 2010. *Aftershock: Reshaping the World Economy After the Crisis*. London: Little Brown.

Lin, J.Y. 2004. "Lessons of China's Transition from a Planned to a Market Economy." Distinguished Lectures Series, No. 16. Warsaw: Kozminski University.

Lin, J.Y. 2012a. *Demystifying the Chinese Economy*. Cambridge: Cambridge University Press.

Lin, J.Y. 2012b. *New Structural Economics: A Framework for Rethinking Development and Policy*. Washington, DC: The World Bank.

Lin, J.Y. 2013. *Against the Consensus. Reflections on the Great Recession*. New York: Cambridge University Press.

Macrotrends. 2020. "Macrotrends—The Premier Research Platform for Long Term Investors." Accessed May 14, 2020. https://www.macrotrends.net.

Maçães, B. 2018. *Belt and Road: A Chinese World Order*. London: Hurts.

Mansbridge, J.J. and Martin, C.J., eds. 2015. *Political Negotiation: A Handbook*. Washington, DC: Brookings.

Mao, Z. 1974. *Chairman Mao Zedong's Theory on the Division of the Three World and the Strategy of Forming an Alliance Against an opponent*. The Ministry of Foreign Affairs of the Republic of China.

Marneffe, W., Van Aarle, B., Van Der Wielen, W., and Vereeck, L. 2011. "The impact of fiscal rules on public finances in the euro area." *CESifo DICE Report*, 9(3): 18–26.

Marx, K. and Engels, F. 2011. *The Communist Manifesto*. London: Verso.

McKinnon, R. 2002. "Mundell, the Euro and Optimal Currency Areas." In *Money, Markets, and Mobility: Celebrating the Ideas of Robert A. Mundell Nobel Laureate in Economic Sciences*, ed. Thomas E. Courchene, 41–58. Montreal & Kingston, London, Ithaca: McGill–Queen's University Press.

McLean, B. and Nocera, J. 2010. *All The Devils Are Here: The Hidden History of the Financial Crisis*. New York: Portfolio.

Medvedev, D., Piatkowski, M., and Yusuf, S. 2020. *Promoting Innovation in China: Lessons from International Good Practice*. Washington, DC: The World Bank Group.

Milanovic, B. 2011. *The Haves and the Have-Nots: A Brief and Idiosyncratic History of Global Inequality*. New York: Basic Books.

Milanovic, B. 2016. *Global Inequality for the Age of Globalization*. Cambridge, MA, London, UK: The Belknap Press of Harvard University Press.

Milanovic, B. 2019. *Capitalism, Alone: The Future of the System That Rules the World*. Cambridge, MA, London, UK: The Belknap Press of Harvard University Press.

Moody, A. 2017. "Prescient author now rules the roost." *China Daily*, November 17.

Morris, I. 2010. *Why the West Rules—for Now: The Patterns of History and What They Reveal about the Future*. London: Profile Books.

Możdzierz, A. 2015. "Strengthening the Post-crisis Fiscal Rules—the Case of Spain, Slovakia and Sweden." *Equilibrium. Quarterly Journal of Economics and Economic Policy*, 10(2): 31–52.

Mundell, R.A. 1961. "Theory of Optimum Currency Areas." *The American Economic Review*, 51(4): 657–665.

Mundell, R.A. 2000. "The International Financial Architecture, The Euro Zone and its Enlargement in Eastern Europe." Distinguished Lectures Series. No. 1, Warsaw: Leon Kozminski Academy of Entrepreneurship and Management (WSPiZ).

Mundell, R.A. 2003. "The International Monetary System and the Case for a World Currency." Distinguished Lectures Series, No. 12. Warsaw: Leon Koźmiński Academy of Entrepreneurship and Management (WSPiZ).

North, D.C. 2002. "Understanding Economic Change and Economic Growth." Distinguished Lectures Series, No. 7, Warsaw: Leon Kozminski Academy of Entrepreneurship and Management (WSPiZ).

Nuti, D.M. 1986. "Hidden and Repressed Inflation in Soviet-Type Economies: Definitions, Measurements and Stabilization." *Contributions to Political Economy*, 5: 37–82.

Nuti, D.M. 2006. "Alternative Fiscal Rules for the New Member States." In *Euro Area Enlargement*, CESifo, Munich, November 24.

Nuti, D.M. 2018a. "Kornai: Shortage versus Surplus Economies." *Acta Oeconomica*, 68(1): 85–98.

Nuti, D.M. 2018b. *The Rise and Fall of Socialism*. Berlin: DOC–RI.

Obbema, F. 2015. *China and the West: Hope and Fear in the Age of Asia*. London, New York: I.B. Tauris.

OECD. 2005. *OECD Economic Surveys: China*. Paris: Organization for Economic Co-operation and Development.

OECD. 2013. *How's Life? 2013: Measuring Well-Being*. OECD Better Life Initiative. Paris: OECD Publishing.

Ormerod, P. 1997. *The Death of Economics*. New York: John Wiley.

Oxfam. 2020. "Oxfam International. Half a billion people could be pushed into poverty by coronavirus." Accessed April 9, 2020. https://www.oxfam.org/en/press-releases/half-billion-people-could-be-pushed-poverty-coronavirus-warns-oxfam.

Palast, G. 2012. "Robert Mundell, evil genius of the euro." *The Guardian*, June 26.

Pasinetti, L.L. 1998. "The myth (or folly) of the 3% deficit/GDP Maastricht 'parameter.'" *Cambridge Journal of Economics*, 22: 103–116.

Pei, M. 2016. *China's Crony Capitalism: The Dynamics of Regime Decay*. Cambridge: Harvard University Press.

Phelps, E.S. 2013. *Mass Flourishing: How Grassroots Innovation Created Jobs, Challenge, and Change*. New York: Princeton University Press.

Phelps, E.S., Bojilov, R., Hoon, H.T., and Zoega, G. 2020. *Dynamism: The Values That Drive Innovation, Job Satisfaction, and Economic Growth*. Cambridge, MA and London: Harvard University Press.

Piatkowski, M. 2018. *Europe's Growth Champion: Insights from the Economic Rise of Poland*. Oxford, New York: Oxford University Press.

Pieterse, J.N. 2019. *Globalization and Culture*. London: Rowman & Littlefield.

Pisani-Ferry, J. 2011. *The Euro Crisis and Its Aftermath*. New York: Oxford University Press.

Postula, M. 2012. "Possibilities for optimal fiscal policy-making in the European Union." *Research in World Economy*, 3(2): 42–60.

Postula, M. 2015. "Impact of the Council directive on requirements for budgetary frameworks of the member states on the polish public finance system, management and business administration." *Central Europe*, 1(23): 95–111.

Posner, R.A. 2009. *A Failure of Capitalism: The Crisis of '08 and the Descent into Depression*. Cambridge, MA and London, UK: Harvard University Press.

Prasad, E.S. 2014. *The Dollar Trap: How the U.S. Dollar Tightened Its Grip on Global Finance*. Princeton, NJ: Princeton University Press.

QS. 2020. "QS Top Universities. QS. World University Ranking: Who Rules?." Accessed May 14, 2020. https://www.topuniversities.com/university-rankings/world-university-rankings/2020.

Randers, J. 2012. *2052: A Global Forecast for the Next Forty Years*. White River Junction, VT: Chelsea Green Publishing.

Reykowski, J. 2020. *Disenchantment with Democracy: A Psychological Perspective*. New York: Oxford University Press.

Reymont, W. 1927. *The Promised Land*. New York: A.A. Knopf.

Ringen, S. 2016. *The Perfect Dictatorship: China in the 21st Century*. Hong Kong: Hong Kong University Press.

Rodrik, D. 2011. *The Globalization Paradox: Democracy and the Future of the World Economy*. New York, London: W.W. Norton & Company.

Rodrik, D. 2015. *Economics Rules: Why Economics Works, When It Fails, and How To Tell The Difference*. Oxford: Oxford University Press.

Roubini, N. and Mihm, S. 2010. *Crisis Economics: A Crash Course in the Future of Finance*. New York: The Penguin Press.

Sandbu, M. 2015. *Europe's Orphan. The Future of the Euro and the Politics of Debt*. Princeton, NJ: Princeton University Press.

Schadler, S.M. 2005. "Euro Adoption in Central and Eastern Europe: Opportunities and Challenges." *Seminar Volumes*, April 18. Washington, DC: International Monetary Fund.

Schaechter, A., Kinda T., Budina, N., and Weber, A. 2012. *Fiscal Rules in Response to the Crisis—Toward the 'Next-Generation' Rules. A New Dataset*. IMF Working Paper WP/12/187. Washington, DC: International Monetary Fund.

Schick, A. 2010. "Post-Crisis Fiscal Rules: Stabilising Public Finance while Responding to Economic Aftershocks." *OECD Journal on Budgeting*, 2: 1–18.

Seck, D. 2020. *Financing Africa's Development: Paths to Sustainable Economic Growth*. Cham, Switzerland: Springer.

Sedlacek, T. 2011. *Economics of Good and Evil: The Quest For Economic Meaning From Gilgamesh To Wall Street*. Oxford, New York: Oxford University Press.

Shambaugh, D. 2016. *China's Future*. Cambridge: Polity Press.

Sławiński, A. 2010. "Lessons from the Euro Zone Experiences for the CEE Entrants." *Argumenta Oeconomica*, 1(24): 49–64.

Stiglitz, J.E. 2002. *Globalization and its Discontents*. New York: W. W. Norton & Company.

Stiglitz, J.E. 2007. *Making Globalization Work*. New York: W.W. Norton & Company.

Stiglitz, J.E. 2018. *The Euro: How a Common Currency Threatens the Future of Europe*. New York: W. W. Norton & Company.

Stiglitz, J.E. 2019. *People, Power, and Profits: Progressive Capitalism for an Age of Discontent*. New York, London: W.W. Norton & Company.

Stiglitz, J.E., Fitoussi, J-P., and Durand, M. 2018. *Beyond GDP: Measuring What Counts for Economic and Social Performance*. Paris: OECD.

Strategia. 2017. *Strategia na rzecz odpowiedzialnego rozwoju do roku 2020*. Warszawa: Council of Ministers.

Sun, F. and Zhang, W. 2020. *Why Communist China isn't Collapsing: The CCP's Battle for Survival and State–Society Dynamics in the Post-Reform Era*. Lanham, Boulder, New York, London: Lexington Books.

Suskind, R. 2011. *Confidence Men: Wall Street, Washington, and the Education of a President*. New York: Harper.

Tanzi, V., Chu, K., and Gupta, S., eds. 1999. *Economic Policy and Equity*. Washington, DC: International Monetary Fund.

Tanzi, V. 2013. *Dollar, Euros and Debt: How We Got Into the Fiscal Crisis and How We Get Out of It*. Basingstoke, UK: Palgrave Macmillan.

Tinbergen, J. 1956. *Economic Policy: Principles and Design*. Amsterdam: North Holland Publishing Company.

Tirole, J. 2017. *Economics of the Common Good*. Princeton, NJ: Princeton University Press.

Tomkiewicz, J. 2016. "Tax System in Poland—Progressive or Regressive?" *Journal of Management and Business Administration. Central Europe*, 24(2): 107–122.

Trade Map. 2020. "Trade Map. Trade statistics for international business development." Accessed May 10, 2020. www.trademap.org.

Uhlig, H. 1986. *Die Seidenstrasse. Antike Weltkultur zwischen China und Rom*. Bergisch Gladbach: Lübbe.

UN. 2019. *World Population Prospects 2019*. New York: United Nations, Department of Economic and Social Affairs, Populations Dynamics.

UNDP. 2019. *Human Development Report: Beyond Income, Beyond Averages, Beyond Today: Inequalities in Human Development in the 21st Century*. New York: United Nations Development Programme.

Varoufakis, Y. 2015. *Global Minotaur: America, Europe and the Future of the Global Economy*. London: Zed Books.

Varoufakis, Y. 2016. *And the Weak Suffer What They Must? Europe's Crisis and America's Economic Future*. London: Nation Books.

Vogel, E. 2013. *Deng Xiaoping and the Transformation of China*. Cambridge: Harvard University Press.

Walicki, A. 1995. *Marxism and the Leap to the Kingdom of Freedom: The Rise and Fall of the Communist Utopia*. Stanford: Stanford University Press.

Wallace-Wells, D. 2019. *The Uninhabitable Earth: Life After Warming*. New York: Tim Duggan Book.

Washington Post. 2020. "U.S. officials crafting retaliatory actions against China over coronavirus as President Trump fumes." *Washington Post*, April 30.

WEF. 2019. *The Global Competitiveness Report 2019*. Geneva: World Economic Forum.

WEO. 2019. *World Economic Outlook, October 2019*. Washington, DC: International Monetary Fund.

WEO. 2020a. *World Economic Outlook, April 2020: The Great Lockdown*. Washington, DC: International Monetary Fund.

WEO. 2020b. *World Economic Outlook, October 2020: A Long and Difficult Ascent*. Washington, DC: International Monetary Fund.

Wheen, F. 2004. *How Mumbo Jumbo Conquered the World: A Short History of Modern Delusions*. New York: Public Affairs.

Wilkinson, R. and Pickett, K. 2010. *The Spirit Level: Why Greater Equality Makes Societies Stronger*. New York: Bloomsbury Press.

Williamson, J. 2005. "Differing Interpretations of the Washington Consensus." Distinguished Lectures Series, No. 17. Warsaw: Leon Kozminski Academy of Entrepreneurship and Management (WSPiZ).

Wolf, M. 2014. *The Shifts and the Shocks*. London: Allen Lane.

World Bank. 1993. *The East Asian Miracle: Economic Growth and Public Policy*. Oxford and New York: Oxford University Press.

World Bank. 2020a. *Heavily Indebted Poor Countries (HIPIC)*. Washington, DC: The World Bank.

World Bank. 2020b. *The World Bank in China*. Washington, DC: The World Bank.

Xi, J. 2014. *The Governance of China*. Beijing: ICP Intercultural Press.

Xi, J. 2017. "China's socialist democracy the most effective." Xinhua reports on President Xi's report at the 19th Party Congress this morning, Xinhua, October 18.

Xinzhen, L. 2017. "Setting the Course," *China Today*, November: 22–25.

Zelizer, V.A. 2011. *Economic Lives: How Culture Shapes the Economy*. Princeton and Oxford: Princeton University Press.

Zhang, H. 2017. "The 19th CPC National Congress Draws Blueprint for National Development." *China Today*, November: 18–21.

Index of Names

Index of Subjects

About the Author

Professor Grzegorz W. Kolodko is an academic, public intellectual and politician, a key architect of Polish economic reforms, and author of New Pragmatism—original paradigmatic and heterodox theory of economics and economic policy addressing the civilizational challenges and transformation of economic systems. He is the world's most quoted Polish economist.

Kolodko is member of the European Academy of Arts, Sciences, and Humanities, Doctor *Honoris Causa* and Honorary professor of a dozen foreign universities. He is the author of numerous books and research papers published in twenty-five languages, including international best seller *Truth, Errors, and Lies: Politics and Economics in a Volatile World*, nominated for the William Harrington Award "for an outstanding book that demonstrates how scholarship can be used in the struggle for a better world," and *China and the Future of Globalization. Political Economy of China's Rise*, a *Financial Times* Summer 2020 book.

He was a participant in the historical Polish "Round Table," which led to the first post-communist government in Central and Eastern Europe. While deputy prime minister and minister of finance (1994–1997) he led Poland to the OECD. Holding the same positions in 2002–2003 he played important role in Poland's integration with the EU.

He is also founder and director of TIGER—Transformation, Integration, and Globalization Economic Research at Kozminski University in Warsaw.

A marathon runner, photographer, and globetrotter, Kolodko has explored 170 countries and visited Antarctica as well.